MORE PRAISE FOR

THE PENSION PUZZLE

"Cohen and FitzGerald have done the impossible—they've made pension plans understandable. The financial planning puzzle no longer has a missing piece. Excellent and thorough!"
> —*David Chilton,* Author of The Wealthy Barber

"This book is the key that Canadians have been waiting for to unlock the pension puzzle. Reading it should leave you with a better understanding of what you need to do to build on the basic social security levels to achieve lifetime self-sufficiency. It should be required reading for everyone in, or about to enter, the workplace."
> —*Glorianne Stromberg, Investor Advocate and Former Ontario Securities Commissioner*

"Clear answers to the two most important retirement questions: How much money will you need, and where will it come from? Before you invest in an RRSP, read this book."
> —*Rob Carrick,* The Globe and Mail, *and Author of* E-Investing *and* The Online Investor's Companion

"It has always been difficult to find any book on pensions that is comprehensive and yet understandable to the average Canadian. This excellent book provides clear, readable definitions and descriptions of complex pension terms and issues, provides tips and worksheets to help the reader apply the information, and wraps the whole book in an historical context that is both honest and fascinating. It is an easy read, almost like talking to a very knowledgeable friend. It is a self-help book of the highest order."
> —*Gretchen van Riesen, Senior Director, Pension and Benefits Policy, HR, CIBC*

"Cohen and FitzGerald cut through the sometimes tedious pension lexicon and provide an easy-to-read, yet comprehensive analysis and commentary on Canada's multi-layered pension system."
> —*Jim Rogers, Chair, The Rogers Group Financial Advisors Ltd., and Past Chair, Canadian Association of Insurance and Financial Advisors*

THE

PENSION

PUZZLE

Your Complete Guide

to Government Benefits,

RRSPs and Employer Plans

BRUCE COHEN & BRIAN FITZGERALD

JOHN WILEY & SONS

John Wiley & Sons Canada Limited
22 Worcester Road
Etobicoke, Ontario
M9W 1L1

National Library of Canada Cataloguing in Publication Data

Cohen, Bruce, 1949-
        The pension puzzle : your complete guide to government benefits, RRSPs, and employer plans

Includes index.
ISBN 0-471-64642-3

        1. Pensions—Canada. 2. Old age pensions—Canada.
3. Registered Retirement Savings Plans. 4. Retirement income—Canada—Planning. I. FitzGerald, Brian, 1941- II. Title.

HD7129.C63 2002   332.024'01   C2002-903307-9

Production Credits
Cover and interior design: Interrobang Graphic Design Inc.
Printer: Tri-Graphic Printing

Printed in Canada
10 9 8 7 6 5 4 3 2 1

Preface   xi

PART ONE   The Pieces of the Puzzle   1

Chapter 1   How Much, How Long?   3
   Income Replacement Ratio   4
   Life Expectancy   6
   Relating Concepts to Cash   7
   Worksheet 1: How Much Do You Need for Retirement?   8
   Worksheet 2: Where Does Your Money Go?   9

Chapter 2   Are You on a Tricycle or a Bicycle?   11
   The Government Wheel   12
   The Employer Wheel   14
   The Personal Wheel   14
   Worksheet 3: Where Will You Get Your Retirement Money?   16

Chapter 3   Government Benefits: Cash for Life   17
   Why Does OAS Exist?   19
   How Does OAS Work?   19
   How Much Can You Expect?   21
   What About the Clawback?   21
   Worksheet 4: How Deep Does the Clawback Bite?   21
   Can OAS Be Received Outside Canada?   22
   Can You Count on Getting OAS?   22
   Worksheet 5: What Can You Expect from OAS?   23
   Low-Income Supplements   24
      Guaranteed Income Supplement   24

Spouse's Allowance 25
Survivor's Allowance 25
How Do These Supplements Work? 25
How Much Can You Expect? 27
Provincial Low-Income Supplements 28
Worksheet 6: The Price of Pessimism: OAS 29

Chapter 4   CPP: Pension Plan or Pyramid Scheme? 31
Calculating Your C/QPP Pension 34
Worksheet 7: Your C/QPP Contributory Period So Far 34
But You Don't Have to Wait Until 65 to Start Your Pension 36
Worksheet 8: What Can You Expect So Far from C/QPP? 37
Splitting Your Pension—Voluntarily or Otherwise 38
   If Your Marriage Splits Up, Your C/QPP Credits May Split Up Too 38
   If You're Still Together at Retirement Time, 39
      There's a Way to Potentially Save Tax
But None of this Matters if CPP Goes Broke, Right? 39
Worksheet 9: The Price of Pessimism: C/QPP 45

Chapter 5   The Tax Shelter Umbrella 47
Are RRSP Limits Too High? 47
Pension Adjustment (PA) 50
   The Factor of 9 51
Pension Adjustment Reversal (PAR) 53
Past Service Pension Adjustment (PSPA) 54
Is Your 18% Umbrella Big Enough? 55
   So, Is the System Fair? 57

Chapter 6   Employer Plans: Overlooked Value 59
Defined Benefit Registered Pension Plans (DB RPPs) 60
   Final Average Earnings Plans 62
   Career Average Earnings Plans 62
   Flat Benefit Plans—Multi-Employer Plans 63
   Flexible Pensions 64
Money Purchase Plans 64
   Defined Contribution Registered Pension Plans (DC RPPs) 65
   Group RRSPs (G-RRSPs) 66
   Personal RRSPs 67
   Deferred Profit Sharing Plans (DPSPs) 69
Which Plan is Best? 70
   Which Plan is Easiest to Understand? 71

Which Plan Offers the Greatest Security? 71
Which Plan is Best for Mobile Workers Who Change Employers? 72
Which Plan Offers the Best Deal for Retirees? 72
Which Plan is Best for Your Spouse? 72
Hybrid and Combination Plans 73
Worksheet 10: Pension Plan Shopping List 74

Chapter 7 Your Own Plan: RRSPs, RRIFs and Annuities 77
Tips for RRSPs 78
Tips for Both RRSPs and RRIFs 85
Tips for RRIFs and Annuities 87

Chapter 8 Will It Be STEW for You? 91
Not Cast in Stone 92
Reasonable Returns 92
Fudge It 94
Worksheet 11: What Should You be Saving for Retirement? 95

PART TWO The Real Nitty Gritty 107

Chapter 9 Who Makes the Rules? 109
Where Do You Find the Rules? 110
Annual Pension Statement 111

Chapter 10 When Can You Join the Plan—and Who Pays How Much? 119
Full-Time versus Part-Time 119
Mandatory versus Optional Plans 120
Should You Join the Plan if It's Optional? 120
Who Pays? 121
Defined Contribution Plans 121
Defined Benefit Plans 122
Past Service Contributions 123

Chapter 11 What Happens to the Money? 125
The F-Word: Fiduciary 125
Pension Fund Audit 128
How Do You Know You'll Get the Pension Promised? 128
Who Owns the Surplus? 128
Partial Plan Wind-Ups 130

Chapter 12   When Can you Retire?   **131**
The Early Retirement "Penalty"   131
  Past Service Pension Credits   133
Phased Retirement   133

Chapter 13   What Do You get in Retirement?   **135**
Defined Contribution Plan   135
  Purchasing a Life Annuity   135
  Lump Sum Transfer to Another Registered Vehicle   137
Defined Benefit Plan   137
  Final Average Plan   138
  Career Average Plan   138
  Flat Benefit Plan   138
  Reciprocal Agreements   139
  Integration With C/QPP   139
  Bridge Benefits   140
  Approved Downsizings   141
  Pregnancy and Parental Leave   141
  Flexible Pension Plans   142
Hybrid and Combination Plans   142

Chapter 14   What If You're Highly Paid?   **143**
Supplementary Employee Retirement Plan (SERP)   143
  Documentation   144
  Pension Due   144
  Vesting   145
  Funding   145
  How Strong Are the Ties That Bind?   146
Secular Trust   147
Individual Pension Plan (IPP)   147

Chapter 15   What Happens If You Change Jobs?   **151**
Vesting   151
Locking-In   152
  Option #1: Stay Put   152
  Option #2: Transfer the Money to Your New Employer's Pension Plan   153
  Option #3: Transfer the Money to an Insurance Company to Buy   153
    an Annuity
  Option #4: Transfer the Money to a Special RRSP or RRIF   154
Is There Any Way Just to Take the Money and Run?   154
Job Transfers Out of Canada   156

Chapter 16   LIRAs, LIFs and LRIFs   159
Why Were L-Plans Created?   159
Which L-Plan Rules Apply?   162
Can You Consolidate L-Plans?   163
Be Careful About Fees   163
What About Early Access?   164

Chapter 17   What About Death and Disability?   165
Beneficiary Designations   165
Beneficiaries and the Tax Man   166
Pre-Retirement Death   166
Death During Retirement   167
Joint and Survivor Pensions   167
Guaranteed Payments   168
Cash Refund Plans   170
What About Pre-Retirement Disability?   170

Chapter 18   What Happens If Your Marriage Ends?   171

Chapter 19   Can Your Employer Change the Plan?   173
Conversions   173
Winding Up   174
What if Your Employer Is Sold?   175
What if Your Employer Fails?   175

Appendix A Canada's International Benefits Agreements   177
Appendix B Highlights: Minimum Pension Standards   179
Appendix C Who's a Spouse for Pension Purposes?   191
Appendix D Retirement-Related Links   193
Appendix E The Actuarial Report: Keeping a DB Plan Healthy 197

Glossary   203

Index   207

Oh, no; not another guide to retirement planning! Aren't the bookstore shelves filled already?

Yes, it is very easy to find books that explain the RRSP rules or how to select a mutual fund. But those books consciously or subconsciously focus on just one dimension of Canada's retirement funding system: RRSPs. They typically dismiss or gloss over government programs—even though 95% of retirees collect those benefits. And those books say little or nothing about employer-sponsored programs, even though more than 40% of the Canadian workforce belongs to pension plans—a number that would climb substantially if there were solid membership statistics for Group RRSPs.

Newspaper Q&A columns, radio talk shows and Internet chat groups show growing interest in—and confusion about—pensions. That's only natural as the majority of baby boomers move through their 40s and 50s. Canada's retirement savings system is remarkably flexible, but complex. Defined benefit plans—covering more than four million people—are particularly hard to grasp. Many employees unnecessarily crimp their lifestyle spending because they do not understand the level of retirement security their pension plans guarantee. Conversely, many others might pay more attention to their own RRSPs if they understood the weaknesses in their employer-sponsored plans.

Also, early retirement incentives and corporate mergers are increasingly forcing people to make decisions that can substantially affect their quality of life in retirement. But, unfortunately, many financial advisors are not well versed in this area, so it can be difficult to get knowledgeable and objective guidance.

We hope this book fills the gap by explaining how the retirement funding system works in general and how employer-sponsored plans work in particular.

The idea for this book was based on our own experiences. Just before retiring from a major pension consulting firm, Brian conducted retirement planning seminars for employees of his firm's corporate clients. He searched for a book he could give out that explained the concepts in straightforward language. There wasn't one. Meanwhile, Bruce, a semi-retired personal finance writer, found he was getting more and more questions from friends about their pension plans and how the various aspects of their savings were supposed to fit together.

While we wrote the book, many others made it possible. Our first word of thanks goes to Marney Elsey and Stuart Hobson. Their assistance was invaluable because they are not financial experts. They are pension plan members who volunteered to serve as test readers. If you understand the stuff in this book, they deserve a lot of the credit.

Next in line for thanks are the financial professionals—and we stress the word professional—who graciously gave of their time in providing information and serving as test readers. They are Mario Galizia, Ross Gascho, Janice Jung, Bruce Macnaughton, Ian Markham, Maria di Paolo, Jim Rogers, Charlene Shaw, Glorianne Stromberg and Lyle Teichman. Sue Pitts and her team in the Old Age Security program were a great help, as were Nancy Lawand and her crew of Canada Pension Plan officials. Towers Perrin generously allowed us to use their reference library, where Karen Shirley gave advice and directed us toward much valuable material.

The task of gathering historical information was made much easier by those who have gone before us. We relied heavily on several books that are now out of print: *Your Pension* by Patrick Longhurst and Rosemary Earle, *Economic Security in an Aging Population* by Robert Brown, and *Fiscal History of Canada* by J. Harvey Perry. *The Watson Wyatt Special Memorandum* newsletters and the current edition of the *Mercer Handbook of Canadian Pension & Benefit Plans* were also quite helpful.

Special thanks go to Karen Milner, Elizabeth McCurdy and Abigail Brown at John Wiley & Sons Canada Limited. We've been overwhelmed by their enthusiasm and efficiency. They kept telling us, "You're writing the book that *I* need." We hope so.

Last, but not least, we thank our families and friends for their encouragement as well as their patience and understanding in letting us spend time at the keyboard instead of with them.

We've enjoyed writing this book. We hope you enjoy reading it and find it useful.

The Pieces of the Puzzle

Planning your retirement is much like solving a puzzle. There are many pieces and as you fit them together, the view becomes more clear. This book is aimed at helping you fit those pieces together. It's divided into two parts.

Part One deals with the fundamentals of retirement funding and how Canada's retirement savings system works. It's aimed at helping you figure out where you stand in that system. We've included worksheets to help you understand the information and apply it to your situation. If you have access to the Internet, you might find the worksheets easier to use if you download them from www.wiley.com/canada/pensionpuzzle. The worksheets are optional. If you wish, you can read the whole book without once putting pencil to paper.

Please note that we've used approximate figures for government benefits which change yearly and even quarterly. Internet users can find the actual figures for the current year at www.wiley.com/canada/pensionpuzzle. The planning exercises we've laid out have you exhausting your retirement money over a timeframe *you* choose—for example, 30 years. We've provided some life expectancy data that might help you select this timeframe, but actuarial tables really only work for large groups, not for individuals. Be conservative—assume that you will live a long time.

Part Two is for those whose employers sponsor Registered Pension Plans. It's effectively an owner's manual. We explain all of the key rules so you can better understand your pension plan and the degree to which it meets your needs.

Warning: This book provides a generalized and simplified explanation of a highly complex and legalistic system. It is based on legislation and regulations that were in effect or proposed at the time of writing in mid-2001. These rules change over time due to government decisions and court rulings. Please verify the information by consulting your pension plan materials, employer or the appropriate government agency. We also encourage you to consult a professional advisor for detailed guidance based on your particular circumstances.

CHAPTER ONE

How Much, How Long?

Marge often wonders how much she should be socking away each year for retirement. She has an RRSP, but never contributes the full amount she's allowed. That makes her feel guilty, especially during January and February when there's RRSP advertising everywhere she turns. She hopes she'll be able to retire comfortably, but doesn't really have a clue about how much money that requires.

Many, many people are like Marge. Are you among them?

In setting RRSP and pension limits, the federal government reckoned that you should be setting aside up to 18% of your pre-tax employment income. But, as you'll see later in this book, that rests on a range of assumptions that may not apply to your situation.

In any event, we suggest working backwards. Before you worry about what to save, see how much you'll need as a retiree. Then consider how much government programs and your employer's retirement plan will provide. With long service and a generous employer-sponsored plan, you may not have to do any saving beyond the pension contributions you're already required to make. On the other hand, you might find that you'll largely be on your own.

So, how much money do you need to retire? That's one of the most common questions financial advisors get. Unfortunately, there's no magic number. It depends on your current and desired lifestyle, family commitments, the age when you'd like to stop working full-time, whether you'd like to work part-time in retirement, your health and your life span.

That's a lot to consider, but there's a shortcut based on two concepts: your income replacement ratio and your life expectancy. The first concept establishes the income you need to be able to stop work without a major sacrifice in lifestyle. The second establishes how long that income must run. They're key factors in determining how much you should be saving now.

INCOME REPLACEMENT RATIO

"Where do you see yourself five years from now?" Ever had a job interviewer hit you with that question? How did you feel? If you loved answering it, all you have to do is precisely envisage your life as a retiree, price it out in today's dollars and adjust for inflation.

Then there are the rest of us. We know, as John Lennon remarked, that "life is what happens while you're busy making plans." So we don't make plans, or at least detailed ones. But we do worry, at least from time to time. Is there a fairly simple method we can use to be reasonably confident we'll be relatively comfortable in retirement?

Yes. It's called the income replacement ratio, and it's the approach used by most financial planners. It rests on the notion that, despite dreams of jetting around the world, retirees tend to maintain the values, habits and leisure activities they developed while working. Simply target the percentage of pre-retirement income you'll need to maintain your standard of living. If you're in your late 40s or 50s, you likely have a decent idea of what your income will be just before you take the gold watch. Those younger can only make their best guess and periodically revise that assumption.

Most retirement planners assume a 70–80% replacement ratio will do the job. Indeed, public service pension plans—which tend to be better than most—typically pay 70% pensions to those who retire after 35 years of service. (That includes benefits from the Canada or Quebec Pension Plan.) So, if you make $50,000 a year as a 59-year-old employee, you should theoretically be comfortable on $35,000 a year as a 60-year-old retiree.

Yes, that is a $15,000 pay cut, but it's not as big as it seems; employees face costs that retirees don't. Consider Linda, a British Columbia resident who was worried as her income fell from $50,000 to $35,000 when she retired in 2000. Linda previously had Canada Pension Plan and Employment Insurance payments deducted from her pay along with 1.5% for union dues. Pension and RRSP contributions took another 10%. She averaged $100 a month for commuting, plus $300 a month for office clothes, lunches, snacks and related expenses.

Linda, the Retiree, No Longer Faces These Expenses		
Income tax on $15,000 of salary	$5,559	
Canada Pension Plan	1,019	*
Employment Insurance	717	*
Union dues	470	*
Pension/RRSP	3,130	*
Commuting	1,200	
Office clothes, lunches, etc.	3,600	
Total work-related expenses	**$15,695**	

*Cost after subtracting value of tax credit or deduction

These costs—plus income tax—actually totalled more than her $15,000 retirement reduction. Are we suggesting that Linda will stop driving her car, wearing clothes or eating? No. But she'll have much more ability to manage those costs. Like Linda, you might be able to free up a fair chunk of cash as a retiree if you now wear office clothes, commute and buy lunch. Then again, you may save little if you now wear jeans and T-shirts, walk or bike and brown-bag.

The bottom line for Linda is that a 70% replacement ratio should be enough to maintain her lifestyle. Probably more than enough. Notice there's no mention of her mortgage, which is now paid off, or her children, who are now grown. Kids and homes are so expensive that they consume a substantial part of the typical breadwinner's take-home pay for much of his or her career. Then, a bit before retirement, those expenses pretty much vanish.

That's a very important point that few really appreciate. In setting your target replacement ratio, do you want to maintain the lifestyle you've been used to for most of your adult life or the one that's affordable for a few years just before retirement? Suppose you earn $50,000. Naturally, you would rather retire with a 70% ratio than a 50% ratio; it's better to draw $35,000 a year than $25,000. But, with 3% inflation indexing, funding that difference for 35 years would require about $220,000 of additional savings. So targeting 70% means spending less now, earning more on your investments or working longer. The trade-off is up to you.

Statistics Canada has found that most people retire on less than 70–80% of their pre-retirement income. StatsCan analyzed tax return data for nearly 200,000 retirees across the earnings spectrum. The 1998 study compared their 1995 incomes to those in 1992, their last year of full-time employment, adjusting for inflation. On average, replacement ratios for middle- and upper-income retirees ranged from 45% to 62%. (A $40,000 salary in 1992 would be about $48,000 now.)

Most Retire on Less than 70% of Income	
Pre-Retirement Income (1992)	**Replacement Ratio**
$20,000 - $29,999	62%
$30,000 - $39,999	60%
$40,000 - $49,999	59%
$50,000 - $69,999	56%
$70,000 +	45%
Source: Statistics Canada, 1998	

Why did those with higher pre-retirement incomes have lower replacement ratios? In part, because the lower ratios still produced enough to meet expenses. A 56% ratio on a $50,000 salary yields $28,000 of retirement income. A 45% ratio on a $70,000 salary yields $31,500. Both people pay the same price for a litre of milk. Also, upper-income people often have stocks and mutual funds in addition to tax-sheltered RRSPs and pensions. An unsheltered $1,000 mutual fund redemption can produce a lot more spending money than $1,000 from a pension plan or RRSP. The pension/RRSP payout is fully taxable because it was never taxed before. The unsheltered mutual fund redemption has two components. First, there's a return of capital that's tax-free because the money was previously taxed when it was earned. Second, the fund's growth qualifies as a capital gain, only half of which gets taxed.

We excluded the results for low-income people because they had very high replacement ratios, thanks to government retirement programs that pay flat amounts regardless of prior income. For example, the average replacement ratio was 147% for those who earned less than $10,000 just before retiring. One of the ironies of retirement finance is that the working poor often make more as retirees than as workers.

The bottom line: You'll likely live quite well as a retiree if you replace 70–80% of your pre-retirement income. But you may need as little as 50% to maintain the lifestyle you're used to if you've spent years feeding kids and a mortgage—or saving hefty amounts on your own or through mandatory pension contributions. For fun, why not see just how much of your current income you need to provide only for yourself and your spouse? Worksheet 1, at the end of this chapter, provides a guide.

LIFE EXPECTANCY

How do you parcel out your retirement money so it lasts at least as long as you do? That's not a major issue if you retire as a member of a traditional defined benefit pension plan that guarantees payments for life. Longevity might matter if you're in a defined contribution pension plan. It's definitely a concern if you rely heavily on RRSP withdrawals and unsheltered investments.

Some financial advisors, software programs and Internet calculators budget your income over the years between your retirement date and the average life expectancy for your age and gender. This approach might seem logical, but it carries a good-sized risk of exhausting your money too early.

Life expectancy is a concept that's often misunderstood. It's a probability exercise, not a death sentence. It's not how long you'll live. Rather, it's the point at which half the people of your age and gender are expected to be dead. So you stand a 50% chance of living longer. Indeed, as you age, your life expectancy stretches—because you're a statistical survivor.

For example, a newborn baby girl has an average life expectancy of about 80 years while her 65-year-old grandmother has an average life expectancy of about 85. Does that make sense? Yes. Based on probability analysis, the infant's life expectancy calculations project that of 100,000 girls born the year she was, 50,000 will die before 80 and 50,000 will die after. As time goes by, some of those girls or women die each year, increasing the odds that those still alive will be part of the 80+ club. The grand-mother's life expectancy at birth was well below 80, but she's a statistical survivor. She just kept going and going. As a result, at 65 she has a 50% chance of dying before 85 and a 50% chance of living still longer. It sounds strange, but the older you are, the older you're likely to be—though it'll be ever harder to find someone your age to drink with.

The accompanying table shows the odds of reaching old age. If you're in rea-sonably good health with a reasonably normal lifestyle, consider basing your retire-ment income on living to 90 if you're a man and 95 if you're a woman.

Percentage Chance of Reaching								
Age	80	85	90	95		80	85	90	95
now	for a man					for a woman			
30	42%	25%	11%	3%		62%	45%	26%	10%
40	42%	25%	11%	3%		62%	45%	26%	10%
50	44%	26%	11%	3%		64%	46%	27%	11%
60	47%	28%	12%	4%		66%	48%	28%	11%
65	51%	30%	13%	4%		69%	50%	29%	12%

These odds might be a bit on the low side because they're based on Statistics Canada projections for the entire population. That includes lower-income people, who tend to have shorter life spans, as well as those with serious medical conditions. Health, wealth and lifestyle have a major impact on how long you live. So do your genes; if your parents and grandparents had long lives, there's a good chance you will too. Also, those projections were based on data gathered in the early 1990s. Average longevity has increased since then.

RELATING CONCEPTS TO CASH

Use Worksheet 1, on the next page, to determine your retirement income target. You can also get a rough idea of the total amount of money required to fund that target. Don't be surprised if you need more than $1 million. Don't panic or get dis-couraged, either. Government programs and your employer's retirement plan may provide a great deal of help. The next few chapters explore how much. Then, in Chapter 8, there's a detailed worksheet that zeroes in on what you really should be saving on your own.

WORKSHEET 1

How Much Do You Need for Retirement?

▶ If you expect a major change in lifestyle or have no idea of what you now spend, try the detailed breakdown in Worksheet 2 on the next page. Then go to Section B below.

Section A: Determine your retirement income

Expected annual earnings just before retirement—in today's dollars   _____ (A)

Target replacement ratio in retirement (likely between 50% & 80%)   _____ (B)

Target retirement income (Line A x B)   _____ (C)

Section B: Determine the total capital needed for retirement

Base retirement income (Line C above or Line N from Worksheet 2)   _____ (D)

Payout period—for example, years to age 90 or 95   _____ (E)

Average annual investment return expected during retirement (try 6%)   _____ (F)

Funding factor from Table B-1   _____ (G)

Total capital needed—in today's dollars (Line D x G)   _____ (H)

Years left until retirement   _____ (I)

Average inflation expected between now and then—use 2% or 3%   _____ (J)

Inflation factor from Table B-2   _____ (K)

Total capital needed—in future dollars (Line H x K)   _____ (L)

This is the total amount needed on retirement day to fund your desired income, paid monthly and indexed annually. It includes the value of government benefits as well as your employer's retirement plan—not just your own savings.

Table B-1:

Find the factor for the payout years and investment return you assumed above. This will index your annual income by 3%, the top of the federal government's target range for inflation.

Payout Years	Average Annual Investment Return			
	5%	6%	8%	10%
15	12.866	12.040	10.613	9.436
20	16.394	15.031	12.775	11.008
25	19.598	17.622	14.480	12.140
30	22.509	19.866	15.826	12.955
35	25.152	21.811	16.887	13.541
40	27.553	23.495	17.725	13.964
45	29.734	24.954	18.386	14.268

Table B-2:

Find the factor for the years to go and the average annual inflation rate you expect.

Years	Inflation Rate	
	2%	3%
5	1.104	1.159
10	1.219	1.344
15	1.346	1.558
20	1.486	1.806
25	1.641	2.094
30	1.811	2.427
35	2.000	2.814

WORKSHEET 2

Where Does Your Money Go?

	Now	In Retirement
Shelter		
Rent or mortgage payments	$_____	$_____
Property taxes	$_____	$_____
Insurance	$_____	$_____
Utilities (hydro, heating, water, etc.)	$_____	$_____
Telephone, cable TV, Internet	$_____	$_____
House & lawn maintenance	$_____	$_____
Furnishings & fixtures	$_____	$_____
Other	$_____	$_____
Food		
At home	$_____	$_____
Away from home	$_____	$_____
Clothing		
New clothes	$_____	$_____
Maintenance (dry cleaning, laundry, etc.)	$_____	$_____
Personal expenses		
Grooming (haircuts, cosmetics, etc)	$_____	$_____
Other	$_____	$_____
Daily transportation:		
Total auto-related expenses	$_____	$_____
Public transportation	$_____	$_____
Recreation		
Movies & live theatre	$_____	$_____
Hobbies, publications & education	$_____	$_____
Vacations	$_____	$_____
Pets	$_____	$_____
Other	$_____	$_____

cont'd

Medical
    Health professionals $_____ $_____
    Drug store items $_____ $_____
    Health insurance premiums $_____ $_____
    Other $_____ $_____

Miscellaneous
    Gifts $_____ $_____
    Charitable donations $_____ $_____
    Life insurance premiums $_____ $_____
    Other insurance premiums $_____ $_____
    Personal loan payments $_____ $_____
    Other $_____ $_____

Taxes
    Federal-provincial income tax $_____ $_____
    Payroll deductions for C/QPP & EI $_____ $_____
    Union or professional dues $_____ $_____
    RRSP & pension contributions $_____ $_____
Total monthly costs $_____ $_____ (M)
Target retirement income (Line M x 12) $_____ $_____ (N)

Go to Section B on Worksheet 1

Are You on a Tricycle or a Bicycle?

With all the attention they get, it's easy to think that RRSPs are the main part of the retirement income system. That might be true for some. For most, though, the system is just that—a system. It has several elements. How many elements will matter to you, and each one's relative importance will depend on your situation—especially your employment and savings pattern before retirement and your income requirements as a retiree. Let's take a look at where current retirees get their money.

The Income Mix for Today's Older Canadians				
Based on interim 1999 tax return data released in 2001				
Income Source	**Age Group**			
	60-64	**65-69**	**70-74**	**75+**
Old Age Security	0%	15%	18%	19%
Canada/Quebec Pension Plan	10%	17%	18%	17%
Tax-exempt income (e.g., welfare & low-income supplements)	4%	5%	5%	7%
Employment Insurance	1%	0%	0%	0%
Pensions, RRIFs & DPSPs	18%	23%	30%	23%
RRSP withdrawals	3%	3%	2%	2%
Investments, rental income and RRSP annuities	14%	16%	18%	25%
Employment & business income	45%	17%	7%	2%
Other income (includes some RRIF withdrawals)	5%	2%	2%	2%
Source: Canada Customs & Revenue Agency		*May not equal 100% due to rounding*		

These figures are for huge groups of people. Individual circumstances vary widely. Also, the pattern will likely change in the future. Many of today's retirees—mainly women—rely heavily on government benefits because they did not, or could not,
have pension plan membership or RRSPs. While today's workers have much better
coverage, the key point is that your retirement income will most likely come from a
variety of sources.

Think of the retirement income system as a tricycle with one wheel for government programs such as Old Age Security, another for employer-sponsored retirement
plans and a third wheel for your own savings such as an RRSP. Instead of a tricycle,
many will head into retirement on a bicycle with just two wheels because they don't
have employer plans. It's extremely unlikely that you'll be on a unicycle with just one
source of income unless you're very poor or maybe a recent immigrant.

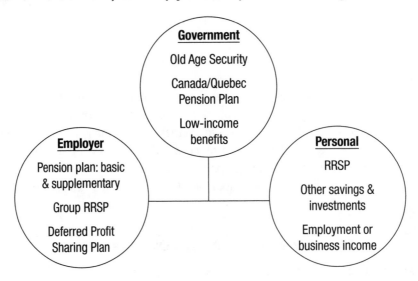

THE GOVERNMENT WHEEL

The government wheel has three spokes. The first is Old Age Security (OAS), discussed in detail in Chapter 3. You qualify for benefits when you're 65 if you've been
in Canada for at least 10 years. The maximum benefit—based on 40 years of residence—is worth about $5,400 a year, fully indexed for inflation and taxed as ordi-
nary income. OAS was designed as a universal program, but benefits are now phased
out for higher-income retirees. This "clawback" hits those with net income above
approximately $57,000, but it's gradual—you lose the full benefit only if you have
more than about $93,000 of income. At the other end of the spectrum, low-income
retirees get supplemental benefits which are tax-free.

The second spoke of the government wheel is the Canada Pension Plan or Quebec Pension Plan, discussed in detail in Chapter 4. These are almost universal programs in that they cover virtually everyone who has been in Canada's paid

workforce. You qualify for C/QPP retirement benefits if you've made at least one contribution during your career. The maximum benefit is about $9,600 a year, fully indexed for inflation and taxed as ordinary income. How much you actually get will depend on your earnings record and when you elect to start receiving payments. That can be as early as age 60, but the maximum is available only if you wait until 65.

Many people feel they can no longer count on government to fund their retirement. The reality is that you never could—unless you were poor. OAS and C/QPP are meant only to provide an inflation-indexed anchor. By design, they replace no more than 40% of the average national wage. The average wage is now about $40,000 and maximum OAS and C/QPP total about $15,000. So the more you need in retirement, the more you must count on other sources. This chart shows how much of your retirement income would come from OAS and C/QPP if you qualify for maximum benefits.

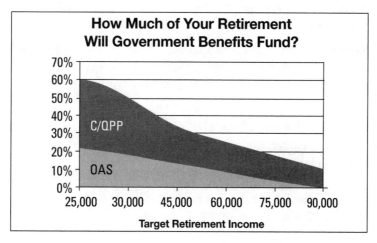

Financial advisors often ignore OAS when doing retirement plans for middle- and upper-income people. OAS is one of the federal government's biggest and fastest growing program expenditures. As you'll see in Chapter 3, Ottawa has already tried three times to rein it in. Just one of those proposals—the clawback of benefits from higher-income recipients—actually took effect.

What about CPP? Canadians love to dump on the Canada Pension Plan and seem to take perverse delight in proclaiming they don't expect to collect one cent from it. The reality is that you stand an excellent chance of getting what you've been promised. CPP may well be Canada's most misunderstood government program, and its long-term prospects were never as bleak as many think. We'll explore that in Chapter 4.

The third spoke of the government wheel comprises special supplements for low-income retirees. The main one is the federal Guaranteed Income Supplement (GIS). It's part of the OAS program cited above and worth an additional $6,400 tax-free. Several provinces and the northern territories pay supplements too. The provincial payments are fairly low. For example, an Ontarian who qualifies for GIS can also get a maximum provincial payment of $83 a month.

THE EMPLOYER WHEEL

There are several ways in which employers help their employees fund retirement:

- **Formal Pension Plans:** Just over 40% of Canadian employees are covered by Registered Pension Plans (RPPs). We discuss these plans in full detail in Chapter 6 and Part Two. If you're a long-serving public employee, your pension plan might meet all of your retirement income needs. If, on the other hand, you work in the private sector and have changed employers often, it's likely that your pension plan will play a relatively minor role. Increasingly, employers are creating supplementary pension plans because outdated rules mean their tax-sheltered RPPs can't fully meet the needs of higher-income employees. We discuss them in Chapters 5 and 14.

- **Group RRSPs:** G-RRSPs are spreading like wildfire. They're easy to administer because they face much less regulation than RPPs. They're also easier to understand. Your employer might have one instead of, or in addition to, a formal pension plan. See Chapter 6.

- **Deferred Profit Sharing Plans (DPSPs):** These plans, also discussed in Chapter 6, play a relatively minor role in the retirement funding system. Unlike formal pension plans and Group RRSPs, they're tied directly to the employer's profits, and employee contributions are not allowed. The annual funding limits are also lower than those for pension plans and RRSPs. If your company has a DPSP, odds are it's in addition to a Group RRSP.

THE PERSONAL WHEEL

This wheel consists of the money you generate on your own. First comes your RRSP. These plans were introduced in 1957, but got off to a slow start. They caught on only in the 1970s after all sorts of financial institutions were allowed to handle them, they really took off in the 1990s after new rules substantially increased contribution limits. Today, thanks to generous tax breaks, the RRSP is Canada's most common investment account. RRSPs offer three tax breaks. First, your allowable contributions are tax-deductible. Second, earnings on that money compound tax-free until withdrawn. Third, with decent planning and luck, you'll ideally withdraw the money at a lower tax rate than it would have faced when earned. The second break—long-term tax-deferred compounding—is actually the most valuable, though people typically focus on the upfront deduction.

The second spoke in this wheel consists of non-RRSP savings and investments. At the end of 2000 Canadians held just over $1 trillion in taxable deposits, bonds, stocks and investment funds, according to Investor Economics Inc., a Toronto-based consulting firm. That was nearly twice as much as individuals held in tax-deferred RRSPs and Registered Retirement Income Funds. Though larger, the taxable accounts are much more concentrated among the affluent.

The third spoke in the personal wheel generates a lot of money, but is commonly overlooked in retirement planning. It's employment and business income. Nearly 62% of those aged 60–64 and 29% of those aged 65–69 reported employment or business income for 1997, the most recent year for which detailed tax data is available. Those earnings provided 16% of income for the 65–69 age group. It may sound awful now if you're a stressed-out Boomer, but there's a good chance that you'll continue to work during the first 10 to 15 years of your retirement. Changes in the nature of work and the structure of the workplace favour casual, part-time and contract jobs. Healthier lifestyles and medical advances are extending our physical and mental ability to keep going. Meanwhile, demographic patterns point to a shortage of workers—especially skilled workers—by 2030 when all Boomers will be at least 65. More and more, people view Freedom 55 as the freedom to keep working—at the pace they want. Not only people, but employers. IBM Canada, for example, has an innovative "phased retirement" program under which early retirees are brought back for project assignments. In 2001 Statistics Canada launched a similar program as a pilot for the federal government. We'll no doubt see much more of this in coming years.

Can a House Be More Than a Home?

Many people assume they'll free up cash as retirees by selling their homes and buying or renting cheaper accommodation. That might work, especially if you're near retirement and have a good idea of what you want out of life. But think hard before counting on it. Here's why:

- Real estate is cyclical and Canada's urban residential markets can be quite volatile. So you might not be able to sell when you want, at least for your desired price. That's especially true with cottages and rural properties.

- Don't underestimate emotion. We've seen several cases in which sentiment beat out common sense as retirees held onto homes that were too large and costly to maintain. Reverse mortgages offer a solution, but are currently available only in urban areas. A financial organization advances a loan that is typically used to buy a life annuity. The annuity pays monthly income that's effectively tax-free. The loan and its compounding interest need not be repaid until you die or move, at which time it would be covered by proceeds from the home's sale. A reverse mortgage is akin to gradually selling your home while still living in it.

cont'd.

- Make sure you really will trade down. Many of today's retirees have wound up with condominiums or houses in retirement communities that proved to be just as expensive as the homes they sold.

- Don't assume it's cheaper to live in a small town unless you've really done it—especially if you're eyeing a rural setting that lacks most of the amenities city folk take for granted. If possible, give your intended retirement locale a test drive by renting before you buy. If you plan to sell your city home and retire to your vacation property, keep the city home for a year or two in case you find cottage living too lonely and arduous in winter. The same goes if you plan to retire in a foreign country. While the cost of living may be lower, you might still wind up returning to Canada because you miss family members and long-time friends or you're concerned about health care. ▲

WORKSHEET 3

Where Will You Get Your Retirement Money?

Check off the sources of income you're going to include in your retirement plan. The Maybe column is for income that you might receive but don't count on.

	Yes	No	Maybe
Government programs:			
Old Age Security (OAS)			
Canada or Quebec Pension Plan (C/QPP)			
Guaranteed Income Supplement (GIS)			
Provincial low-income supplement			
Other			
Employer-related programs:			
Registered Pension Plan (RPP)			
Supplementary Employee Retirement Plan (SERP)			
Group RRSP			
Deferred Profit Sharing Plan (DPSP)			
Other			
Personal plans:			
RRSP			
Taxable savings & investments			
Sale of home and/or vacation property			
Employment or business income			
Other			

Government Benefits:
Cash for Life

More than 95% of Canadians now 65 or older collect government pensions, according to income tax data. And, as we saw in Chapter 2, benefits from Old Age Security and the Canada or Quebec Pension Plan can replace up to 40% of pre-retirement income for someone who was earning the average national wage. Yet a survey done for Human Resources Development Canada in 2000 found that only 11% of working Canadians felt they had a good understanding of these plans—and 43% couldn't even name them. It's no wonder that many Baby Boomers don't think they'll get anything.

As we noted earlier, government programs won't fully fund your retirement unless your earnings have been quite low. Their job is to provide only a basic income that's fully indexed for inflation and guaranteed for as long as you live. The inflation protection is a key safeguard since few private sector employer pension plans and no RRSPs or RRIFs are automatically indexed. The longevity guarantee cushions the growing number of people who rely mainly on RRSPs and defined contribution pension plans, both of which can be exhausted if not prudently managed.

There are two primary government pension programs. The first is Old Age Security (OAS). It covers virtually everyone and includes a Guaranteed Income Supplement (GIS), spouse's allowance and survivor's allowance for low-income recipients. The second program is the Canada Pension Plan (CPP) and the very similar Quebec Pension Plan (QPP). Together, CPP and QPP cover almost everyone in the paid workforce. OAS and CPP are administered by the Income Security Programs (ISP) section of Human Resources Development Canada.

Want More Info on Government Programs?

HRDC's web site (www.hrdc-drhc.gc.ca) has application forms and a great deal of useful information. If you don't have an Internet-equipped computer, your local library or school might have a public access terminal and someone to help you. HRDC also has a toll-free telephone information line at 1-800-277-9914. The Quebec Pension Plan is provincially administered. The web site is at www.rrq.gouv.qc.ca and their toll-free phone line is 1-800-463-5185.

This chapter looks at OAS and its low-income supplements. The next chapter looks at CPP and QPP. In each case, we describe how these programs work and what you can expect. We also comment on your likelihood of collecting it. At the end of the chapter we offer some help in determining how much extra you should be saving if you really don't think you'll get anything.

	Old Age Security (OAS)		
	Basic pension	**GIS**	**Allowances**
Covers	Canadian citizens & residents	Low-income OAS recipients	Spouses of OAS recipients Widows & widowers
Maximum yearly pension (approx)	$5,400	$6,400	Spouse: $9,500 Survivor: $10,500
Taxable	Yes	No	No
Inflation-indexed	Full. Adjusted each 3 months	Full. Adjusted each 3 months	Full. Adjusted each 3 months
Full benefit age Earliest eligibility age	65 65	65 65	Paid only if 60-64
Income-based benefit reduction	Yes	Yes	Yes
Payable outside Canada	Under certain conditions	6 months max	6 months max
Reduces employer pension	No	No	No

WHY DOES OAS EXIST?

OAS can trace its roots to a right-wing nineteenth-century German aristocrat who once declared that his chief ambitions were to smoke 100,000 cigars over the course of his life and drink 5,000 bottles of champagne. Otto von Bismarck—the "Iron Chancellor"—ruled Germany with a heavy hand in the 1880s and sought to undermine growing socialist sentiment by creating the world's first publicly funded pension plan in 1889. The eligibility age was set at 70 at a time when average life expectancy for a newborn was just 37. The pension age was lowered to 65 in 1916.

As the state pension concept spread, Canada's House of Commons began discussing it in 1906 but bogged down amid concerns that welfare was a provincial responsibility. In 1927, Parliament passed the *Old Age Pensions Act* authorizing Ottawa to fund half the cost of provincial pensions for those 70 and older. The maximum monthly benefit was $20, equivalent to about $225 now. But recipients had to meet means tests that in some provinces ruled out all but those in desperate straits. A means test is different from an income test because it looks at what you own, not what you earn. It took 10 years for all provinces to create pension plans—after federal funding was raised to 75%. By 1949 the monthly benefit was $40, worth about $325 now, but the hated means tests remained.

War-weary Canadians demanded a better deal and the Liberals under Louis St. Laurent launched today's version of OAS on January 1, 1952. The maximum monthly benefit was still $40 for those 70 and older, but eligibility was based on residence, not means. Those 65 to 69 could qualify under a means test that was phased out in 1966–71 as the general eligibility age was gradually lowered to 65, today's level.

In the late 1940s and early '50s officials faced two big problems in designing a pension plan that covered all Canadians. With no means tests, costs were sure to balloon—and governments in those days tried to run on a shoestring. How could the program be financed amid likely public demands for ever higher benefits? Finance officials wanted OAS to be self-funding like unemployment insurance, but there was no way to collect premiums from homemakers and low-income workers who did not file tax returns but would be due pensions. So, the government earmarked part of the Manufacturer's Sales Tax (forerunner of the GST), raised the corporate income tax rate and levied a small tax on individuals—the Old Age Pension Tax that many of today's seniors remember. But even with a hefty tax hike in 1959, the deficit-plagued program was still in the red. The OAS fund was wound up in 1972 and the special levies were rolled into the regular tax rates. Today, OAS is funded from the federal government's general revenues.

HOW DOES OAS WORK?

OAS has two sets of rules. One set determines if you are eligible for a pension. The other determines the amount. The most basic rule—which applies to everyone—is that you must be at least 65 years old. It's best to apply at least six months before your sixty-fifth birthday, to allow time for processing. Here's a summary of the other rules in flowchart form:

OAS: Will You Get a Full Pension?

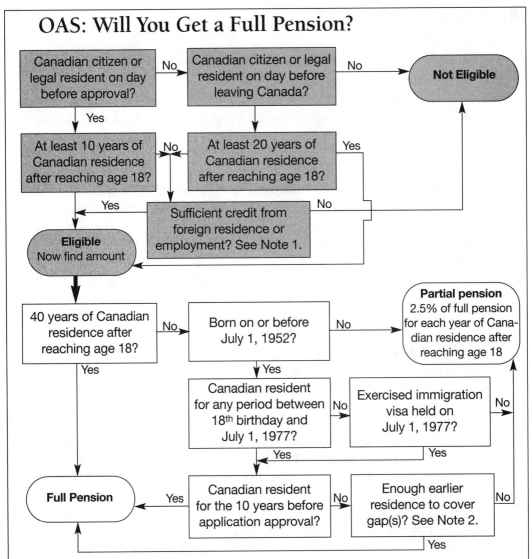

Note 1: Canada has social security agreements with approximately 50 countries. See Appendix A. While the terms vary, your credits are combined so you get a Canadian pension, a foreign pension or both. Alternatively, those who work outside the country for Canadian employers and certain international organizations might be able to count that time as Canadian residence for themselves and their families. Certain conditions apply; consult HRDC. To use these provisions, apply for OAS even earlier than the six months suggested in this chapter.

Note 2: You must have lived in Canada for at least one year before your application's approval. If you meet this test but lack the 10 consecutive years required, you can count residence as an adult —18 or over—from before that 10-year period. This works on a 3-to-1 basis. Suppose you lived outside Canada at age 60-61. That two-year gap can be covered if you lived in Canada for six years between 18 and 55.

HOW MUCH CAN YOU EXPECT?

The full OAS pension is about $5,400 a year. Payments are made monthly and increased every three months for inflation as measured by the Consumer Price Index. OAS benefits are not reduced if the CPI falls. As the flowchart states, partial pensions pay 2.5% of the full pension amount for each year of Canadian residence. With 20 years of credit, you're due 50% of the full amount.

WHAT ABOUT THE CLAWBACK?

In 1989, Finance Minister Michael Wilson imposed a repayment requirement, or "clawback," on OAS recipients with *net* income over $50,000.

This "high-income" group comprised just 4% of recipients at the time, but the $50,000 threshold was only partially indexed for inflation so more middle-income retirees got hit every year. For 1999—10 years after its start—the clawback kicked in at net income of $53,215—the equivalent of $42,318 in 1989. At that rate, inflation would have wiped out OAS for nearly all Baby Boomers! Fortunately, Finance Minister Paul Martin fully indexed the income tax system in 2000. The clawback threshold—approximately $57,000 for 2002—will now rise right in line with inflation.

The clawback applies to individual, not combined, income for couples. The base is the "net income"—total income minus tax deductions—that's determined at the end of Page 2 in the T1 income tax return.

Financial advisors and the media fuss over the clawback, but it's gradual and only those with truly high incomes lose all of their OAS. The clawback claims 15% of the amount by which your net income—including OAS—exceeds the threshold. If full OAS is $5,400—the approximate level for 2002—you need about $93,000 of net income to lose the whole amount.

WORKSHEET 4

How Deep Does the Clawback Bite?

Target retirement income (in today's $)	$	_____
Minus clawback threshold	−	57,000
	=	_____
Times clawback rate	×	0.15
Clawback bite	=	_____

The clawback is now estimated, based on your previous tax returns, and deducted at source. An adjustment is then made after you file your tax return for the current year. If the automatic deduction creates hardship, you can ask the Canada Customs and Revenue Agency to reduce it.

10 Ways to Ease or Avoid the Clawback

1. Make spousal RRSP contributions now to provide for income splitting in retirement.

2. Pay off all debts before age 65 to reduce your income needs. Similarly, make as many major purchases before 65 as seems practical—for example, a new car.

3. Ensure you claim all tax deductions. They reduce clawback exposure by reducing "net income."

4. Review investments. Canadian corporate dividends increase clawback exposure because net income includes 125% of the amount you received but not the offsetting dividend tax credit. Capital gains reduce clawback exposure because just half of the gain gets taxed. Investigate royalty and income trusts which pay tax-advantaged distributions.

5. Reduce your income by taking C/QPP early and sharing the benefits with your spouse.

6. Time the receipt of income to alternate between high- and low-income years.

7. Consult a professional advisor about putting investments into a holding company, alter ego trust or joint spousal trust.

8. In your 70s consider a prescribed annuity which pays tax-advantaged income or a reverse mortgage which effectively pays tax-free income.

9. As you age, give away assets you don't need to secure your lifestyle.

10. Leaving Canada? Some countries have treaties with Ottawa that protect their residents from the clawback. Also, retirees in the U.S. pay U.S., not Canadian, tax on their OAS. Consult a tax advisor.

CAN OAS BE RECEIVED OUTSIDE CANADA?

Yes —if you've had 20 years of Canadian residence since turning age 18 or equivalent foreign credit. Otherwise, payments are suspended after six months and resumed on your return. Obviously, you must notify HRDC before you leave and when you come back.

CAN YOU COUNT ON GETTING OAS?

Interesting question. As Chapter 2 noted, financial advisors often ignore OAS when doing retirement plans. OAS is one of the most costly federal programs, and Ottawa has already tried three times to cut it back. The first attempt was the Mulroney government's 1985 bid to remove full inflation-indexing for OAS benefits. The government retreated under heavy fire from seniors' groups and instead hiked the gasoline tax. Next came their 1989 clawback of benefits for higher-income recipients. That did take effect and proved quite potent since it was not until 2000 that the income threshold was fully indexed for inflation. In 1996, the Chrétien government tried to replace OAS with a Senior's Benefit that would have boosted payouts for low-income recipients while reducing or eliminating them for middle- and upper-income retirees. This proposal attracted thunderous opposition and was scrapped in 1998.

When he killed the Senior's Benefit, Finance Minister Paul Martin said OAS could continue in its current form only if future governments keep their debt loads in check. So we might see another assault in the future. One likely move would be to revive the Senior Benefit's bid to base the clawback on *combined* income for couples. Social groups fought that on grounds that OAS/GIS is the only money that many of today's retired women can call their own because they were full-time homemakers or held casual and part-time jobs without pensions. This justification may fade over time because so many working-age women now hold paid jobs and have pension rights that previous generations lacked.

Then again, OAS may face no change at all. Seniors are politically powerful and vigorously defend their benefits. Aging Baby Boomers will start swelling their ranks in 2012, making cutbacks increasingly harder to sell with each passing year. Some pessimists warn that the sheer number of Boomers will make the program unaffordable and force cutbacks. Optimists point out that the basic pension is taxable, so part of the Boomers' benefits will cycle right back to the federal treasury.

You're probably safe if the total target retirement income for you and your spouse falls below $60,000 in today's money. One cautious planning approach is to ignore OAS or cut your expectation by half. You then create a cushion in case assumptions for your own spending and investing prove too optimistic. It's notoriously difficult to make accurate long-range financial projections.

WORKSHEET 5

What Can You Expect from OAS?

Use the flowchart that appeared earlier in this chapter to determine your eligibility. Then complete this worksheet using today's dollars.

If you qualify for full pension:	$5,400	A
If you qualify for partial pension:		
Qualifying years from flowchart	_____	B
Line B × .025	_____	C
Partial pension (A × C)	$ _____	D
Clawback from Worksheet 4	$ _____	E
OAS pension [(A or D) − E]	$ _____	F

LOW-INCOME SUPPLEMENTS

The OAS program pays three types of supplements to low-income retirees: the Guaranteed Income Supplement (GIS), spouse's allowance and survivor's allowance. These low-income benefits are simple in concept but complex in implementation. You might want to skip to the next section—on the Canada and Quebec Pension Plans—unless you or someone you care about has a target retirement income (excluding OAS) that's below one of these approximate levels, expressed in today's dollars:

- Single pensioner: $13,000

- Two pensioners married or living common-law: $17,000 combined income

- Pensioner and non-pensioner married or living common-law: $31,000 combined income

- Widow or widower: $18,000

The Guaranteed Income Supplement and related allowances top up the basic OAS pension to provide seniors with a minimum guaranteed annual income. Full benefits provide a single pensioner with about 30% of the average national wage. A couple winds up with about 50%.

Guaranteed Income Supplement

GIS began operations on January 1, 1967, one year after the Canada and Quebec Pension Plans began. It was created to help retirees of the day who were too old to qualify for meaningful C/QPP benefits. Planners thought the program would run just 10 years, the time required for the coming wave of retirees to qualify for full C/QPP benefits. But they misjudged the nature of poverty among older Canadians. What was intended to be a stopgap has endured as an essential part of the social safety net. About one-third of today's OAS pensioners get GIS. This group is dominated by elderly single and widowed women. Many could not accumulate their own retirement savings because they were full-time homemakers or held casual jobs without pension or C/QPP coverage. Often, if their husbands had employer pensions, antiquated rules let the benefits die when the men did. Today's working-age women face much better prospects. They are more likely to hold jobs with pension and C/QPP coverage, and current survivor rules for employer-sponsored pension plans are more fair. So the need for GIS may diminish over time. But that need is unlikely to disappear because Canada has many cash-strapped single mothers and working poor who simply can't save on their own.

There are two supplementary benefits, called allowances, for low-income people who are at least 60 but not yet 65, when they become eligible for OAS and GIS.

Spouse's Allowance

The first supplementary benefit is for someone whose spouse already gets OAS and GIS. It used to be called the Spouse's Allowance (SPA) and was created in 1975 to put these couples in line with those who both receive OAS and GIS. The payment was originally only for married couples. Now it's simply called the Allowance and is also paid to common-law couples, including those of the same sex, who have spent at least one year together.

Survivor's Allowance

The second benefit is now formally called the Allowance for the Survivor. It's for low-income widows and widowers aged 60–64. It began in 1979 when the Spouse's Allowance was extended to widows and widowers of OAS recipients. In 1985, a survivor's allowance was created for all low-income widows and widowers. Common-law couples, including same-sex partners, are covered under the same criteria that apply to the SPA benefit.

How Do These Supplements Work?

GIS is paid only to OAS recipients. Interestingly, qualifying for GIS can also increase your OAS benefit. Suppose you're due a partial OAS pension because you don't have 40 years of Canadian residence. When you qualify for GIS, you get a top-up so the combined OAS/GIS payment is the same as for someone who gets full OAS plus normal GIS.

The spouse's allowance and survivor's allowance are paid only to those aged 60 to 64. At 65, those benefits are replaced by the regular OAS and GIS payments the allowance recipients then become entitled to on their own.

You apply for GIS and either allowance the same way as for OAS. Indeed, you use the OAS application form from HRDC. You can submit it as early as 12 months before you reach the eligibility age. The following table summarizes the rules. Unfortunately, they're quite complicated. Unlike OAS, these benefits are tax-free and all of the conditions are intended to ensure they go to those who need them most.

Low-Income Benefits: Do You Qualify?		
	Guaranteed Income Supplement	Spouse's Allowance	Survivor's Allowance
Eligible at age	65 if receiving OAS pension	60–64 if other spouse receives OAS & GIS	60–64 if spouse is deceased
Residency	Canadian citizen or legal resident with 10 years Canadian residence after 18 or equivalent foreign credit under a social security agreement. Special rules for immigrants who fall short.		
To apply	Use OAS application kit from HRDC web site or telephone information line. Apply 6–12 months early. If income is too high but then falls, contact HRDC; you can apply any time.		
Definition of couple	Legally married or two people of opposite or same sex in conjugal relationship for at least 12 months. HRDC web site has statutory declaration for common-law couples to sign.		
Income test based on	Single: Own income Couple: Combined income	Combined income	Own income
Note income exclusions	Prior year's income is usually used. If current year's income will be less due to retirement from employment, ask HRDC to use an estimate. *Test excludes certain types of income: OAS/GIS benefits, up to $500 employment income and C/QPP & EI premiums that recipient has paid, C/QPP death benefits, federal/provincial family allowance, social assistance payments based on a means or income test.*		
Income-based benefit reduction	Single: $1 per $2 of other income Couple: $1 each per $4 other income If spouse gets no OAS or Allowance, reduction applies only to combined income that exceeds OAS pension plus $48. Then it's $1 per $4 of other combined income.	Recipient loses $3 per $4 of other income until reduction = OAS pension amount. Then recipient loses $1 and pensioner loses $1 GIS per $4 of other combined income.	$3 per $4 of other income until reduction = OAS pension amount. Then $1 per $2 of other income.
Annual renewal	Yes—done automatically if tax return filed by April 30. Otherwise, receipient is sent income questionnaire.		
Benefit set	Each July and adjusted quarterly for inflation.		
Benefit stops	• After 6 months outside Canada • Recipient dies • Income is too high • Income information not submitted as requested	• After 6 months outside Canada • Recipient turns 65 • Recipient dies • Separation lasting 3 months • Divorce • If other spouse becomes ineligible for GIS	• After 6 months outside Canada • Recipient turns 65 • Recipient dies, remarries or lives common-law for 12 months • Income is too high • Income information not submitted as requested

How Much Can You Expect?

These tax-free benefits depend on your marital status and income. There are five situations that can affect your income from GIS and other low-income allowances. We've outlined them in the following table, which deals with two people named Pat and Jean. As noted above, Pat and Jean might be legally married or in a common-law relationship without regard to their gender.

The table shows, in approximate terms, the maximum benefits due. GIS and the two allowances are reduced by other income. The bottom row shows how much Pat and Jean can earn before they lose their full entitlements. Many people assume that all income counts. As the previous table indicated, it doesn't. For example, OAS and social assistance payments don't reduce these low-income benefits. But retirement payments from the Canada or Quebec Pension Plan do.

What Pat and Jean Can Expect from the OAS Program					
	Pat is a single* OAS pensioner.	Pat is an OAS pensioner. Jean does not qualify for any benefits.	Pat & Jean are both OAS pensioners.	Pat is an OAS pensioner. Jean gets Spousal Allowance.	Pat dies. Jean gets Survivor's Allowance.
Pat: • OAS • GIS	5,400 6,400	5,400 6,400	5,400 4,200	5,400 4,200	– –
Jean: • OAS • GIS • Spousal • Survivor	– – – –	– – – –	5,400 4,200 – –	– – 9,600 –	– – – 10,600
Total benefits	11,800	11,800	19,200	19,200	10,600
No low-income benefits (just OAS) if other income exceeds	12,700 Pat only	30,800 Combined	16,600 Combined	30,800** Combined	17,400 Jean only
*A pensioner is also coonsidered single if separated, divorced or widowed.					
**Jean's Spousal Allowance stops when combined income is about $23,700.					

Like most other government benefits, these amounts are fully indexed for inflation. But unlike most other government benefits, those adjustments are made every three months, not annually. Indexing works only one way: benefits rise if the cost of living goes up, but do not go down if the cost of living dips.

Provincial Low-Income Supplements

Every province and territory has support programs for low-income seniors. They vary widely and include property tax deferrals, housing assistance, energy grants, transportation subsidies and enhanced health coverage. Often, the programs are run by different departments. Your best source of information might be the constituency office of your member in the provincial or territorial legislative assembly. Or check the Seniors Policies and Programs Database, a multi-government web site at www.sppd.gc.ca. The jurisdictions below also pay cash supplements which do not affect GIS benefits and allowances because they are income-tested provincial social assistance payments. These payments are generally not indexed for inflation.

Province or Territory	Program & Department Responsible	Min age	Max benefit—2001		Telephone & Web Site
			Single	Couple	
Alberta	Alberta Seniors Benefit Community Development	65	$2,640	$3,960	1-800-642-3853 www.gov.ab.ca/mcd
British Columbia	Seniors Supplement Social Development & Economic Security	60	$592	$723	1-800-665-2656 www.gov.bc.ca/sdes
Manitoba	55 PLUS Family Services & Housing	55	$446	$480	1-800-282-8073 www.gov.mb.ca/fs
Newfoundland	Seniors' Benefit Department of Finance	65	$300	$300	709-729-3166 www.gov.nf.ca
NWT	Seniors Supplementary Benefit Income Support Programs	65	$1,620	$3,240	1-800-661-0763 income.learnnet.nt.ca
Nunavut	Senior Supplement Department of Education	65	$1,620	$3,240	867-975-5680 No web site
Ontario	Guaranteed Annual Income System Ministry of Finance	65	$996	$1,992	1-800-263-7965 www.rev.gov.on.ca
Saskatchewan	Saskatchewan Income Plan Social Services	65	$1,080	$1,740	306-787-2681 www.gov.sk.ca
Yukon	Income Supplement (Health & Social Services)	65	$1,200	$2,400	867-667-5674 www.hss.gov.yk.ca

WORKSHEET 6

The Price of Pessimism: OAS

It's easy to say you don't expect to receive anything in government benefits. If you really feel that way, what are you doing about it? Use this worksheet to see how much extra you should be saving to replace that retirement income. **OAS** now pays about $5,400 a year starting at age 65 and fully indexed for inflation. Those who don't qualify for a full pension get 2.5% for each year of Canadian residence after age 18. For simplicity, we assume you'll live to 90 and inflation will average 3% a year between now and then.

OAS pension due at 65 expressed in today's dollars	_____	(A)
What average annual investment return do you expect between 65 and 85?	_____	
Payout factor from 25-year row in Table 1 below	_____	(B)
Lump sum value at 65 in today's dollars (Line A x B)	_____	(C)
How many years between now and 65?	_____	(D)
Inflation factor from Table 2 below—use years in Line D	_____	(E)
Lump sum value at 65 in future dollars (Line C x E)	_____	(F)
What average annual investment return do you expect between now and 65?	_____	
Savings factor from Table 3 below—use years in Line D	_____	(G)
Savings required this year to replace OAS (Line F x G)	_____	(H)

These calculations assume the deposit is made at the start of each year and increased annually by 3% to offset inflation.

Table 1: Find the factor for the investment return you assumed above. Your fund will make a monthly payment just like OAS. The amount will rise by 3% at the start of each year to offset inflation.

Payout Years	Average Annual Investment Return			
	5%	6%	8%	10%
25	19.598	17.622	14.480	12.140

Table 2: Find the factor for the time left until you start OAS.

Years to Go	3% Inflation
5	1.159
10	1.344
15	1.558
20	1.806
25	2.094
30	2.427
35	2.814

cont'd.

Table 3: Find the factor for the years left until you start OAS and the investment return you assumed above. This assumes your deposit is made at the start of each year and rises 3% annually to offset inflation.

Payout	Average Annual Investment Return			
Years	5%	6%	8%	10%
5	.1628	.1582	.1493	0.1410
10	.0668	.0633	.0568	0.0509
15	.0366	.0337	.0287	0.0243
20	.0225	.0202	.0162	0.0129
25	.0147	.0129	.0097	0.0073
30	.0101	.0085	.0061	0.0042
35	.0070	.0058	.0039	0.0025

CPP: Pension Plan or Pyramid Scheme?

Will CPP still be around when I retire—and will I get anything?

Those are invariably the big questions when the Canada Pension Plan comes up in conversation with Baby Boomers and Generation Xers. We believe it will—and you will. But don't just take our word. This chapter looks at the mechanics and background of what's certainly one of Canada's most controversial and most misunderstood government programs. As we go along, we'll address common concerns. Then form your own opinion and use the worksheet at the end of the chapter to see how much extra you should be saving if you're less optimistic than we are.

Canada/Quebec Pension Plan (CPP & QPP)	
Covers	Employees & self-employed
Maximum yearly pension (approx)	$9,600
Taxable	Yes
Inflation-indexed	Full. Adjusted annually
Full benefit age	65
Earliest eligibility age	60 with benefit reduced
Income-based benefit reduction	No
Payable outside Canada	Yes
Reduces employer pension	Possibly

The Canada and Quebec Pension Plans are twins. QPP covers those who work in Quebec. CPP covers those who work elsewhere in Canada (plus members of the Canadian Forces and Royal Canadian Mounted Police who are stationed in Quebec). The CPP and QPP rules are similar and integrated so you don't lose credits when moving into or out of Quebec. The eligibility rules for benefits you collect depend on where you live at the time you apply.

Nearly half the respondents in a federal survey done in 2000 thought everybody gets CPP. Not so. CPP and QPP only cover those in the paid workforce. Full-time homemakers are the largest group not covered, although they can share their spouses' retirement payments and collect as much as a 60% survivor's benefit when their spouses die. Officials have considered homemaker pensions from time to time, but bogged down over who would pay for them. The Mulroney government went as far as proposing that homemakers get CPP credits funded by contributions from their spouses, but didn't follow through. Also exempted from coverage are migrant workers, members of certain religious orders, workers younger than 18 and those paid less than $3,500 a year.

CPP and QPP do more than help fund retirement. They provide active workers with disability coverage. Indeed, disability benefits comprised 20% of CPP's outflows in the mid-1990s and were one of the triggers for significant changes in 1998. Even with tighter rules, more than 273,000 people under 65 were collecting CPP disability benefits in 2001. More than 21,000 of them were under 40. C/QPP also provide a form of life insurance by paying survivor benefits. And there's a one-time $2,500 death benefit, originally intended to cover funeral costs.

The payments in this table are maximums. How much you or your spouse would get depends on your earnings record. The disability and survivor benefits for your children are flat rates. So is the $2,500 death benefit.

What Do CPP and QPP Pay?

Approximate Maximum Annual Amounts

Benefit	CPP	QP
Retirement	$9,600	$9,600
Disability	$11,600	$11,600
Plus each child under 18 gets*	$2,300	$800
Survivor**		
Spouse under 45, no children***		$4,800
Spouse under 45 with children***	$5,300	$7,700
Spouse 45–54 or younger		$8,000
Spouse aged 55–64		$8,600
Spouse aged 65+	$5,800	$5,800
Plus each child under 18 gets*	$2,300	$800
Death benefit (paid once)	$2,500	$2,500

* CPP pays child's benefit to age 25 if a full-time student

** You can receive a survivor benefit from your spouse on top of your own retirement or disability benefit. But total payments cannot exceed the plan's maximum retirement or disability benefit.

*** QPP pays a disabled survivor under 45 the same amount as one 45–54.

C/QPP benefits are taxable. Those paid for children are taxed in their hands. Retirement, disability and survivor payments may reduce entitlements to low-income government benefits such as GIS. C/QPP disability payments normally get factored into payouts by employer-sponsored disability plans. C/QPP retirement benefits may also reduce benefits from an employer's pension plan; see Chapter 13.

C/QPP benefits are fully payable outside Canada. But a 25% non-resident withholding tax will apply unless a tax treaty between Canada and your new country of residence sets a lower rate. For more details, phone the Canada Customs and Revenue Agency at 1-800-267-3395 or visit their web site at www.ccra-adrc.gc.ca.

There are two types of indexing for the retirement, disability and survivor benefits. The benefit amounts for new claimants rise annually in line with the average national wage. Once you start getting a benefit, the amount you receive is adjusted annually for inflation. As with the OAS program, adjustments only go up; benefits are not reduced if inflation dips. The $2,500 death benefit is not indexed at all.

CPP now sends each member an annual statement detailing his or her earnings, contributions and the benefits built up thus far. QPP issues such statements on request. If possible, check old tax slips to verify the contributions shown, especially those from the distant past when record keeping was done mainly on paper. A fellow we know found his CPP record understated contributions for one year in the 1970s when he had several employers. A quick letter got that fixed.

Here are key highlights of the eligibility rules for C/QPP benefits. If you're interested in the disability or survivor coverage, you can get more details from the HRDC and QPP web sites and telephone information lines—see the start of Chapter 3.

- **Retirement pension:** CPP and QPP members qualify if they've made just one contribution. Your actual pension depends on how much and how long you've contributed. While a single contribution would qualify you for a pension, it would be very small.

- **Disability payments:** The eligibility rules are stricter than those for private sector disability insurance. CPP says your disability must be long-term or potentially fatal and serious enough to prevent you from working regularly at *any* job. QPP says your disability must be potentially permanent and prevent you from holding a "substantially gainful" job, but also accepts claims from those aged 60–65 who can no longer do their own jobs. CPP members are eligible if they've made contributions in four of the past six years. QPP requires at least two years of contributions. Both plans convert the disability pension to a retirement pension at 65. Those under CPP would probably then see their benefits cut because the retirement pension will be based on maximum pensionable earnings at the time the disability occurred.

- **Survivor payments:** CPP and QPP cover legally married couples no matter how long they've been together. CPP covers common-law couples, regardless of sex, after one year together. QPP requires three years together or one year if they have a child by blood or adoption. In both plans, the deceased must have contributed for at least three years. In addition, if your contributory period spanned more than nine years, you must have made contributions for whichever is less: one-third of that time or 10 calendar years. CPP benefits are paid to surviving spouses under 35 only if they have children or are disabled. Otherwise, those payments start only when the person turns 65 or becomes disabled. Both CPP and QPP recipients still receive benefits after remarriage.

If you lack the contribution years required, check with plan officials to see if you can qualify under some special rules. For example, divorced and separated people likely have access to credits from their former partners. And those who've worked outside Canada might get credit for contributions to foreign plans. As noted in our OAS discussion, Canada has social security agreements with about 50 countries. See Appendix A at the back of the book.

CALCULATING YOUR C/QPP PENSION

Your C/QPP retirement pension equals 25% of your average pensionable earnings during your contributory period indexed for average growth in the YMPE over the preceding five years.
Huh?

Okay, let's go step by step. The C/QPP system bases contributions and benefits on something called "year's maximum pensionable earnings"—YMPE. That's a measure of the average national wage—now around $40,000. The YMPE is adjusted every January to reflect any increase in the average wage during the prior year.

Your "pensionable earnings" for each year consist of employment or self-employment income up to the YMPE. Your "contributory period" started in 1966 if you were born before 1948 or your eighteenth birthday if you were born later. It runs until you start collecting your pension or turn 70, whichever comes first. C/QPP have a record of your pensionable earnings for each month during that period.

WORKSHEET 7

Your C/QPP Contributory Period So Far

If born before 1948:		If born after 1947:	
Current year	_____	Current age	_____
Minus 1966	− 1966	Minus 18	− 18
= Contributory period	_____	= Contributory period	_____

To calculate your pension, C/QPP first adjust all of those pensionable earnings so that $1 earned in, say, 1966 carries the same weight as $1 earned this year. Then they exclude a certain number of your lowest income months under three provisions called "drop-outs."

- **General drop-out:** This covers the 15% of your contributory period when earnings were lowest. Thanks to the drop-out, you're not penalized for low income due to illness, unemployment, time in school or any other reason. This can also help those retiring early, as shown in the box. Say your contributory period spans 40 years. This drop-out covers the 72 months with the lowest earnings. That time is excluded in calculating your pension—as long as there are still at least 120 months left to work with.

- **Child-rearing drop-out:** A parent whose earnings fell while caring for a child under seven years old can have that time ignored in the pension calculation—in addition to the general 15% drop-out. That's if the child was born after 1958 and you were a Canadian tax resident during the child-rearing period. Unlike the general drop-out, this provision is not applied automatically; you request it when you apply for C/QPP benefits. Either spouse can use it, but you can't double up for the same period.

- **Disability drop-out:** In addition to the general 15% exclusion, C/QPP computers automatically drop any month for which you received C/QPP disability benefits.

Want to Retire Early?

Fred turned 18 on January 1, 1967. So that's when his contributory period began. But he didn't start contributing until 1970 after leaving school. He then put in the maximum every year. He wants to retire at 54, in 2003, and plans to start collecting CPP as soon as he can—at age 60 in 2009.

	Years	
Contributory period (2009 – 1967)	42.0	A
Minus general drop-out (A × 15%)	– 6.3	B
Pension base (A – B)	35.7	C
Actual credits (2003 – 1970)	33.0	D
% pension due [D/C]	92.4%	

Fred will be due 92.4% of his pension entitlement minus a reduction for starting at 60 instead of 65. With no drop-out, he would have 33 years of credit for a 42-year period and get a 78.6% pension minus the age-60 reduction.

Besides the drop-outs, there's a swap for those who contribute past 65, when they no longer have to. They can count any of those months in place of earlier ones with lower earnings.

After excluding your low-income periods, the C/QPP computers average the remaining earnings. Your retirement pension then equals 25% of that if you start it at 65.

BUT YOU DON'T HAVE TO WAIT UNTIL 65 TO START YOUR PENSION

You can start a C/QPP retirement pension as early as age 60 or as late as age 70. Those who start early lose 0.5% of their benefit for each month before 65. Those who start late get an increase of 0.5% for every month they wait. That works out to 6% per year either way. If you start early, your monthly cheques are smaller but you'll get more of them than if you wait until 65.

What's the best option? The one that makes you feel most comfortable—it's your money; enjoy it! By providing spending money, starting early can help you avoid tapping your RRSP or RRIF. You then prolong the tax-sheltered growth of those plans.

Taking C/QPP Early or Late					
Impact of Early or Late Start			Break-Even Age		
Start	Reduction	Annual	After-Tax Growth Rate		
Age	or Increase	Pension	0%	3%	5%
60	−30%	$6,720	76.7	80.7	86.2
61	−24%	$7,296	77.7	82.1	88.5
62	−18%	$7,872	78.7	83.6	90.9
63	−12%	$8,448	79.7	85.0	93.6
64	−6%	$9,024	80.7	86.5	96.3
65	Base	$9,600			
66	+6%	$10,176			
67	+12%	$10,752			
68	+18%	$11,328			
69	+24%	$11,904			
70	+30%	$12,480			

Want a more technical reply? The Break-even Age on the right side of the table is when the accumulated value of the pension begun at 65 catches up to the one that started early. If you live past that point, you would have been better off waiting for 65. The 0% column assumes all payments are spent, not invested. The others assume the money is invested. Say you're now 59 and debating whether to start CPP at 60. If you'll spend the money and expect to live well past 77, consider waiting. Of course, that sort of defeats the idea of wanting to spend the money, doesn't it? If you're going to invest the money, starting early clearly makes sense.

There is one little wrinkle. To start a pension before 65, you're supposed to "wholly and substantially" stop working before the pension begins. That means you expect to earn less from working than the maximum pension payable to someone 65. The QPP rules also let people start if they're on pre-retirement leave—for example, using up accumulated sick leave. Once the pension starts, there's no penalty if you make more than you expected. Indeed, both plans let you work as much as you want, and there's no clawback as with OAS.

Once a CPP pension starts, you can no longer contribute in the hope of boosting your payout. That is, unless you "withdraw" your pension. That means you stop the pension, repay what you've already received and resume contributions based on your income. In that case, CPP clears your record so you'll be treated as a brand new applicant when you reapply. QPP says you're supposed to keep contributing if you retire but then go back to work and earn more than the $3,500 basic exemption. Those continuing contributions will boost your benefit. QPP also has an interesting feature called "phased retirement." You can reduce your workload starting at 55, but continue to contribute at your previous level. That way, you can slow down but still collect a full pension at 65. You could also start this QPP pension as early as 60 if your phased retirement period earnings are at least 20% below your normal level.

WORKSHEET 8

What Can You Expect from C/QPP?

Line A of this worksheet requires the age-65 retirement projection from your latest CPP or QPP statement. If you don't have it, you can request one from the applicable plan.

Projected pension at age 65	_____	A
If you plan to start it before 65		
Number of months early (min age = 60)	_____	B
Line B × 0.5	_____	C
Pension reduction (A × C)	_____	D
Pension due* (A − D)	_____	E
If you plan to start it after 65:		
Number of months late (max age = 60)	_____	F
Line F × 0.5	_____	G
Pension increase (A × G)	_____	H
Pension due* (A + H)	_____	I

*This projection should increase each year you work and contribute.

SPLITTING YOUR PENSION—VOLUNTARILY OR OTHERWISE

There are two situations in which C/QPP will divide your pension between you and your current or former spouse. Unfortunately, financial advisors and others refer to both as "credit splitting," but they're very different. We'll use the terms that C/QPP use.

If Your Marriage Splits Up, Your C/QPP Credits May Split Up Too

You and your former spouse are entitled to half of the C/QPP credits each other earned while you were together. CPP calls this "credit splitting." QPP calls it "partition."

Credit splitting has no impact if both partners have the same earnings record. It was aimed originally at protecting women who earned less than their husbands—or nothing at all. Suppose Tom has been the breadwinner and Mary has been a full-time mom. Mary is entitled to half the credits Tom earned during their marriage and is thereby assured of some retirement income. Tom is technically entitled to half the credits Mary earned, but there are none since she has not been in the paid workforce.

Normally, the higher-paid spouse winds up with less of a pension while the other winds up with more. But an unfair situation can arise for credits covering time when the couple's children were under seven years old. Tom will lose half his credits for that period and his retirement pension will be reduced accordingly. But those particular credits may not increase Mary's pension at all if she goes back to work, advances to the point where she earns maximum credits on her own and ultimately decides to exclude that low-earnings period under the child-rearing drop-out.

Saskatchewan, British Columbia and Quebec allow couples to specifically opt out of the splitting requirement. Elsewhere, couples might include an opt-out in their separation agreements, but it may not be binding if one later has a change of mind. Either spouse can apply for a CPP split. Joint consent is not required for married couples, though QPP requires joint agreement for splits covering common-law relationships. C/QPP send application forms to each party after a divorce decree is issued. In a common-law dissolution, you must contact them. Usually a split is aimed at getting more money, but it can also help someone with little time in the workforce qualify for disability or death benefits.

Common-law couples, regardless of gender, are eligible for CPP splitting after one year in a conjugal relationship. QPP requires three years, or one year if the couple has a child by blood or adoption.

CPP credit splitting is available only for break-ups after 1977. For 1977–86 it applies only to the divorce or annulment of a legal marriage. The application deadline was three years after the end of the marriage, but that can be waived if both parties agree. In 1987 credit-splitting was extended to separations and to break-ups of opposite-sex common-law couples. Now, credit-splitting is also available for same-sex separations that occurred after July 31, 2000. And there is no longer an application deadline. QPP credit splitting covers marriage dissolutions after June 30, 1989 and common-law dissolutions after June 30, 1999.

The credit split is not affected if either spouse enters a new relationship.

If You're Still Together at Retirement Time, There's a Way to Potentially Save Tax

Financial advisors routinely call this credit-splitting. CPP and QPP call it "pension sharing" or "assignment." It's for couples, married or common-law, who are both at least 60. This is aimed at helping those with a meaningful disparity in their credits. The two of you are allowed to share the credits both built up during your time together. Credits earned while on your own can't be shared.

Take Rob and Tina. They have lived together for 80% of their contributory periods. Without pension sharing, Rob would get—and be taxed on—a maximum C/QPP pension of about $9,600 a year. Tina, who has earned a lot less, would be due about $4,000 based on her credits. The box shows how pension sharing can shift their income. They split 80% of Rob's benefit and 80% of Tina's. As a result, $2,240 ends up getting taxed at Tina's rate instead of Rob's. Notice that it does not increase the total pension paid; it just reallocates it.

	Rob	Tina
No sharing	$9,600	$4,000
If shared:		
Own 20%	1,920	800
80% from Rob	3,840	3,840
80% from Tina	1,600	1,600
Total with sharing	$7,360	$6,240

BUT NONE OF THIS MATTERS IF CPP GOES BROKE, RIGHT?

Okay, let's get down to the heart of the matter—the future of CPP. It's easier to discuss the future if we first look at the past.

Canada went through the 1950s with a booming economy but widespread poverty among the elderly. Many were not well educated and spent their adulthoods in poorly paid farm and non-union factory jobs—that is, when they could work at all. They came of age as World War I broke out and then endured the Great Depression and World War II. They raised families without medicare and had no unemployment insurance coverage until the '40s. Times were tough and many entered their "golden" years with little in the way of savings. Even those who could save earned little interest on their money, since war and depression kept bank and bond rates at very low levels during much of their adulthood.

Canada had one public pension plan, Old Age Security, which was funded entirely by the treasury. As the economy—and wages—grew, some felt that, like other industrialized countries, we should also have a "contributory" plan funded by employees and employers. The Liberals under Lester Pearson promised one in their 1963 election campaign.

Pearson's cabinet set two imperatives. First, the government had to move on its campaign promises within its first 60 days. Second, the new pension plan had to get money to the country's retirees as quickly as possible. Meanwhile, Quebec was already working on a plan of its own. It had to be accommodated. So did the other provinces since the new Canada Pension Plan was going to be sponsored by both the federal and provincial governments.

Unlike OAS, the new plans were to be funded by contributions shared equally by employees and employers with the self-employed paying both parts. Significantly, they were designed to run on a "pay as you go" (PAYGO) basis—the decision that underlies almost all of today's controversy.

What C/QPP Costs

These contribution rates were in effect in mid-2001 and are due for review in 2002. They apply to employment income up to the Year's Maximum Pensionable Earnings (YMPE).

Year	Employee	Employer	Combined
2001	4.30%	4.30%	8.6%
2002	4.70%	4.70%	9.4%
2003	4.95%	4.95%	9.9%
2004+	4.95%	4.95%	9.9%

Here's how 2001's maximum contribution was calculated:

YMPE	$38,300
Less basic exemption	− 3,500
Contributions due on	$34,800
Contribution rate	× .086
Total amount due	$ 2,992.80
Employee paid	$ 1,496.40
Employer paid	$ 1,496.40

Employees get an income tax credit that equals 20–25% of their contribution. The employer's share is a tax-deductible expense.

Self-employed people who are not incorporated pay both portions. They get a tax credit for one half and, starting in 2001, a tax deduction for the other half.

CPP and QPP are not like employer-sponsored pension plans, which must set aside money to prefund promised benefits. C/QPP's PAYGO funding is an intergenerational transfer. Retiree benefits are financed primarily by contributions from active workers. In effect, money arrives in the morning and goes out in the afternoon. Remember that the '60s were a time of prosperity, big government programs—and, significantly, families. Birth control and the women's movement were relatively new.

Most people—including CPP's architects—expected the young people of the day to produce children as their parents had. They did not expect the Baby Boom to be followed by a Baby Bust.

With an expanding economy, little or no concern about inflation, and the prospect of increasing contributions from a growing army of workers, PAYGO made sense at the time. The prevailing view in Canada and elsewhere was that companies must prefund pensions to protect workers from the risk that the employer will go out of business, but PAYGO was fine for public plans because governments don't go out of business.

There was, however, one dissenter in cabinet. Defence minister Paul Hellyer, an ardent nationalist, was wary of PAYGO. Pearson gave him 10 days to produce an alternative. Ironically, left-winger Hellyer produced a concept championed today by several right-wing groups. In effect, he called for mandatory RRSP contributions by individuals and their employers. Investment decisions would be up to the individual. With foreign content restrictions, Hellyer saw this as a way to substantially reduce foreign ownership of Canadian industry and predicted that it could ultimately clear the way for Ottawa to phase out OAS. But his idea drew little, if any, discussion.

CPP and QPP were thus born on January 1, 1966. Benefits would be funded by contributions, not by a pool of investments. Contributions not needed to pay benefits would be kept in reserve. QPP's reserve was to be invested in stocks, bonds, real estate and venture capital projects by the provincial government's money management arm, the Caisse de dépôt et placement du Québec.

There's a widespread belief that CPP's money was squandered on "cheap" loans to the provinces. Each province was able to borrow reserve money based on its proportion of contributions. Each loan was issued for 20 years and priced at the interest rate the federal government would have had to pay—so the loans were nowhere near as cheap as people think. In any event, because the CPP and QPP reserves were meant only to provide a cash flow cushion, not to finance benefits, much of the debate about those loans to the provinces is irrelevant. Also, the CPP reserve now has a different management strategy; more about that later.

Initially, the C/QPP contribution rate was set at 3.6% of covered earnings, and planners thought it would eventually top out at 5.5%. This contribution rate was shared equally by employees and employers. The 3.6% rate held until 1987, when it was apparent that the original economic and demographic assumptions were not panning out. The rate then started rising 0.2% per year.

By 1991 it was clear that Baby Boomers were not having enough children for the PAYGO transfer to function in the twenty-first century. Remember that PAYGO has current workers supporting current retirees. In the 1990s, there were about five workers for every retiree. That ratio may fall to three-to-one by 2016 when C/QPP will be 50 years old. In 1991, Ottawa and the provinces agreed on a new schedule of increases for the next 25 years, starting in 1992. At their next review, in 1996, the sponsoring governments considered a grave warning from the CPP's chief actuary that, without changes, the employee-employer contribution rate would have to rise from 5.6% in 1996 to 14.2% in 2030, when all Baby Boomers will be at least 65. The big culprits:

changed demographics and economics, enrichment of benefits and higher-than-expected disability payouts.

The general view in government was that it would be unfair to burden future workers and their employers with such a high rate in order to support Baby Boomers in retirement. A feeling emerged that the rate should be held below 10%—even though the schedule set in 1991 already called for it to exceed that. The publication of an excellent discussion paper and cross-country hearings then set the stage for legislation that made key changes aimed at keeping the rate below 10%:

- Planned increases in contribution rates would be accelerated so that employees and their employers pay 9.9% in 2003. Curiously, the media reported this as a new level even though the previous schedule called for a 9.9% rate in 2015 and further increases after that. Ottawa and the provinces also agreed to review the plan every three years instead of every five.

- Accelerated contribution rates will produce a huge surplus—upwards of $100 billion by 2010. The reform legislation provided for a new arm's length investment board to manage that money the way employer pension funds are run—with holdings in stocks and other investments as well as government bonds. The board is dominated by well-respected members of Canada's investment and corporate communities; they are not government hacks. Instead of serving only as a cash flow cushion, the idea is to build up the fund over time and use it to subsidize future contributions. The hope is that if the portfolio averages 4% a year after inflation, the combined employee-employer contribution rate can be held at 9.9%, the so-called "steady state" rate. A 4% return after inflation is a common target for pension plans.

- As mentioned earlier, the reforms tightened up the disability program that had become a significant expense. There were also several subtle changes that effectively increase contributions while reducing the value of benefits. First, the bottom-level income that's not subject to contributions was capped at $3,500. It was previously indexed at 10% of the average national wage. The cap means the exemption's value will diminish over time. The same goes for the $2,500 death benefit—it used to be indexed for inflation, but is now frozen. Also, wage indexing used to calculate your benefits is now based on growth in average earnings over the past five years instead of the past three.

By and large, actuaries—the people with the best understanding of PAYGO plans like CPP—feel these reforms are enough to put and keep the plan on track. So:

- **Is CPP going broke?** No. It can't go broke because its primary asset is the ability to tax employees and employers. The issue is not solvency, but rather how high future contributions should be. Talk of bankruptcy stems from 1996 warnings that, without changes, the reserve that QPP built up in its early years would run out in 2006 while CPP's would run out in 2015. Changes were made and took effect in 1998.

- **Will young workers be allowed to opt out and just have mandatory RRSPs?** Highly unlikely. Current retirees and workers have been promised about $600 billion in benefits. The PAYGO design counts on future workers to fund those promises. Unlike OAS, C/QPP do not get direct government funding. While individually directed plans might make sense in today's environment, what do you do about the unfunded promises already made? Several proposals for privatizing CPP simply sidestepped that issue. Others conceded that there would have to be a special tax to provide the needed money. Would young workers really be ahead if they have to make mandatory RRSP contributions, buy mandatory disability coverage and pay a special tax? (Chile, which pioneered the concept of privatizing social security, used budget surpluses to cover a much lower level of unfunded promises.)

- **Won't the next generation just refuse to pay?** Interesting question. C/QPP contributions are required by law, backed up by the muscle of the federal and Quebec tax departments. Due to the program's joint sponsorship, it's not easy to rewrite the rules. Change requires approval of the federal parliament plus two-thirds of the provinces with at least two-thirds of the population. As we suggested in discussing OAS, seniors have traditionally been a powerful political force. One of the proposals in the 1996–97 reform discussion would have forced current retirees—who get a great deal—to ease the plan's financial crunch by foregoing part of their inflation indexing for 10 years. It wasn't adopted. The seniors' lobby will, of course, grow even stronger as Baby Boomers age.

Return on Money Contributed to CPP		
Born	**Nominal return—%**	**Inflation adjusted return—%**
1910	31.4	23.1
1920	21.3	13.6
1930	15.0	9.0
1940	10.7	6.1
1950	7.8	4.2
1960	6.2	3.1
1970	5.5	2.4
1980	5.4	2.3
1990	5.1	2.1
2000	5.1	2.0
2010	5.0	2.0
2020	5.0	1.9
2030	5.0	1.9
Source: 17th Actuarial Report		

The key lies in keeping the plan on track. The CPP actuary has projected the "internal rate of return" on contributions from employees and employers. Based on a wide variety of assumptions, this projection estimates the benefits that will be received and compares that value to the money put in by the employee and employer. It actually understates the return because it does not factor in the tax deductions and credits on contributions. For example, in 2000 an Ontarian who made the maximum $1,329.90 contribution for an employee got $310.80 in federal and provincial income tax credits for that year.

Those born before 1940 got a great deal because they qualified for full benefits with fewer contributory years. But, according to the projections, even today's infants stand to get back more than they and their employers will put in—can the same be said for other government programs? Of course, this holds only if the assumptions pan out; that's why one of the more important changes made in 1998 was to require reviews every three years.

- **Will there be a clawback as there is for OAS?** Who knows? We do know that OAS is controlled entirely by the federal government while CPP is run jointly with the provinces. So it's much harder to change the CPP rules, as noted above. Also, OAS is directly funded by the federal treasury and the clawback was imposed as part of the Mulroney government's effort to eliminate yearly budget deficits. CPP and QPP are funded by employees and employers. As well, C/QPP benefits are tied directly to a person's contributions. While Ottawa did levy an Old Age Pension Tax on individuals in the '50s and '60s, it never tied those payments to the payment of a set benefit.

- **Will the eligibility age be raised?** A number of actuaries have long urged going from 65 to 67 or even 70. That was considered, but rejected, during the 1996–97 CPP reform discussions even though it would have saved a lot of money. In 1983, the United States decided to go from 65 to 67 but the phase-in was set to start only in 2002, providing 20 years for people to prepare. Canadian officials have suggested that people should get no less than five to 10 years' notice. Meanwhile, as the Baby Boomers age, the window for such change gets smaller.

If CPP and QPP were being designed today, they would likely look much different. But it's really a case of "in for a penny, in for a pound." The intergenerational transfer required by PAYGO financing, the huge amount of unfunded promises and the need for federal-provincial agreement makes major change difficult and probably unlikely.

WORKSHEET 9

The Price of Pessimism: C/QPP

It's easy to say you don't expect to receive anything in government benefits. If you really feel that way, what are you doing about it? Use this worksheet to see how much extra you should be saving to replace that retirement income. **C/QPP** pay a maximum retirement benefit of about $9,600 a year, fully indexed for inflation. That's if the pension begins at 65. You can start as early as 60, but the amount is reduced by 6% for each year before your sixty-fifth birthday. A pension begun at 60 is therefore 30% less than one begun at 65. For simplicity, we've ignored the value of C/QPP disability coverage while you're still working. As with the OAS calculation at the end of Chapter 3, we assume you'll live to 90 and that inflation will average 3% a year between now and then.

C/QPP pension due at 65 expressed in today's dollars	_____	(I)
Reduction/increase for early/late start—use 6% per year	_____	(J)
Reduction or increase (Line I × J)	_____	(K)
C/QPP pension due at planned start, expressed in today's dollars (Line I − or + J)	_____	(L)
What average annual investment return do you expect during payout years to 90?	_____	(M)
Payout factor from Table 1 on next page: use 30 years for age-60 start, 25 for age-65.	_____	(N)
Lump sum value at start in today's dollars (Line L × N)	_____	(O)
How many years between now and planned start?	_____	(P)
Inflation factor from Table 2 on next page—use years in Line P	_____	(Q)
Lump sum value at start in future dollars (Line O × Q)	_____	(R)
What average annual investment return do you expect between now and start?	_____	
Savings factor from Table 3 on next page—use years in Line P	_____	(S)
Savings required this year to replace C/QPP pension (Line R × S)	_____	(T)

These calculations assume the deposit is made at the start of each year and increased annually by 3% to offset inflation.

cont'd

Total Savings Needed to Replace OAS & C/QPP

Annual savings needed to replace OAS (from Line H of
Chapter 3's worksheet 6 $ _____

Annual savings needed to replace C/QPP (from Line T above) + _____

**Total savings needed...deposited at the start of each year
and increased annually by 3% to offset inflation.** $ _____

Table 1: Find the factor for the payout years and investment return you assumed above. Your fund will make a monthly payment just like C/QPP. The amount will rise by 3% at the start of each year to offset inflation.

Payout	Average Annual Investment Return			
Years	5%	6%	8%	10%
25	19.598	17.622	14.480	12.140
30	22.509	19.866	15.826	12.955

Table 2: Find the factor for the time left until you start C/QPP

Years to Go	3% Inflation
5	1.159
10	1.344
15	1.558
20	1.806
25	2.094
30	2.427
35	2.814

Table 3: Find the factor for the years left until you start C/QPP and the investment return you assumed above. This assumes your deposit is made at the start of each year and rises 3% annually to offset inflation.

Payout	Average Annual Investment Return			
Years	5%	6%	8%	10%
5	.1628	.1582	.1493	0.1410
10	.0668	.0633	.0568	0.0509
15	.0366	.0337	.0287	0.0243
20	.0225	.0202	.0162	0.0129
25	.0147	.0129	.0097	0.0073
30	.0101	.0085	.0061	0.0042
35	.0070	.0058	.0039	0.0025

The Tax Shelter Umbrella

We're about to reveal one of Canada's most closely held secrets—information known only to pension consultants, a handful of government officials and a few academics. By making this secret public, we just might end one of the great myths about Canada's retirement savings system.

ARE RRSP LIMITS TOO HIGH?

Several years ago, a fellow we know was having dinner with some friends, all members of the generous Ontario Teachers Pension Plan. It was right after RRSP season and those teachers were outraged.

"RRSP limits are too high," they complained. "They're only for the rich and deprive government of tax revenue needed for schools and other services."

"Should your own pensions be cut back?" our friend asked.

"No!" the teachers replied.

Our friend then asked if they were aware there's a direct tie between RRSP contribution limits and the funding limits for pensions. They weren't. He explained how this tie works. When he finished, those who were still awake agreed that RRSPs are not at all a sop to the rich.

This chapter will examine this little-known tie and help you determine whether your tax-sheltered savings limit is high enough for your needs.

RRSPs and employer-sponsored Registered Pension Plans (RPPs) fall under the same federal tax legislation. In each case, there's no income tax on earnings set aside for retirement or on that money's investment growth—until the cash comes out of the plan. Ottawa and the provinces forego revenue today so future retirees can be substantially self-reliant and less dependent on the public purse.

Naturally, there has to be a limit on how much revenue governments pass up now, and this limit should ideally be fair to everyone—those with pension plans and those with just RRSPs.

Does This Tally Add Up?

Each fall the federal Finance Department estimates the cost of retirement savings tax breaks. It's usually Ottawa's largest "tax expenditure" and rather controversial.

Left-wing groups and unions play up the estimate for RRSPs, but ignore or minimize the one for pension plans. Right-wing groups and employers argue these breaks are not a "tax expenditure" at all; the tax bill is deferred, not cancelled. Governments are in effect stockpiling tax bills that will come due years from now and help fund medicare and other services aged Baby Boomers will require.

The Finance estimate substantially overstates the short-term revenue loss due to pension/RRSP tax breaks, according to the Canadian Institute of Actuaries. Its 1995 analysis is rather technical, but one part is easy to understand. Finance assumes that if there were no tax breaks, everyone would put the same amount of money into bonds that pay interest which is fully taxed. Nobody would pay down their mortgage or other debts. Nobody would go for more lightly taxed capital gains and dividends. Do you buy that?

Finance has issued explanatory notes acknowledging the flaws, but those notes are never cited in media coverage of the estimate.

Ottawa tackled this by basing the whole system on the funding allowed for defined benefit (DB) pension plans, such as the one for the teachers above. DB plans are the most traditional form of pension arrangement. They promise a predetermined level of retirement income. The other tax-assisted plans, such as RRSPs, don't.

DB plans do not have fixed contribution limits like those for RRSPs and defined contribution (DC) pension plans which work a lot like RRSPs. If officials imposed fixed limits on DB plans, there would be a substantial risk that those plans would not be able to pay the pensions that were promised. So the employer gets to put in whatever's required to meet the promise while Ottawa protects the tax base by limiting how generous that promise can be. Currently, the maximum annual pension that a DB plan can pay is $1,722.22 for each year of service.

If a DB retiree can get that much, so should someone retiring from a DC pension plan or an RRSP, right? In the 1980s, federal officials determined that, on average, $9 must be invested each year to fund $1 of annual pension from a good DB plan like the one for federal civil servants—and our teachers above. This is called the Factor of 9.

So, how much should a person with no pension plan be allowed to put into an RRSP to match the maximum annual DB pension of $1,722.22 per year of service? Multiply $1,722.22 by 9. You get $15,499.98. Round that to $15,500 for ease of use. That's what the maximum RRSP limit is supposed to be, though the government keeps delaying it—largely because of claims that RRSP limits are too generous.

Maximum Contribution Limits		
RRSP limit applies to prior year's earnings. RPP limit applies to current year's earnings.		
		Defined contribution
Year	RRSP	RPP
2001	$13,500	$13,500
2002	$13,500	$13,500
2003	$13,500	$14,500
2004	$14,500	$15,500
2005	$15,500	Indexed to growth in
2006		average national wage

This tie also exists at lower income levels. Bernard and Bernice each earn $40,000. Bernard's DB pension plan will base his retirement income on 2% of his pensionable earnings—the highest "accrual rate" allowed, and the one used in setting the system's limits. So his earnings for the year entitle him to $800 of annual pension—$40,000 times 2%. The Factor of 9 says this promise is worth $7,200 in tax-deductible funding—$800 times 9. Bernice has only an RRSP. Her limit equals 18% of earned income. That's $40,000 times 18%, or $7,200—the same level of funding that Bernard's pension plan is allowed.

Tax Breaks Are Almost as Old as Income Tax Itself

Tax breaks for retirement savings date back to 1919, when Ottawa granted employees tax deductions for their pension contributions. That gesture—just two years after personal income tax began—cost little since there were few pension plans until 1938. That's when contributions by employers became deductible and many created plans. Despite the tax breaks, though, there were no contribution limits, an oversight that led to a strange situation after World War II.

During the transition to a peacetime economy, Ottawa kept the war's wage freeze and excess profits tax. But with fighting over, employers and unions saw less need for patriotic sacrifice and took money that would otherwise be lost to the excess profits tax and used it instead to beat the wage freeze by introducing or increasing tax-free benefits. So the floodgates opened and in 1947 tax officials imposed limits to stem the flow.

Bernard has a pension plan that's pretty much top of the line. Bernice has none. What about everyone in between?

Canada is a world leader in integrating tax-assisted retirement savings vehicles, thanks to Marc Lalonde. He was the federal Finance Minister in the early '80s. At that time, tax rules favoured those in DB pension plans. They could fund pensions two and half times higher than others'. Lalonde sought to better balance tax-sheltered savings opportunities among those with good plans, those with modest plans and those with no plans at all.

He proposed that everyone get enough tax sheltering so that, on their own or with their employer, they could fund a good pension like those for federal civil servants. A study found that contributing 18% of earned income over 30 to 35 years would do the trick.

Lalonde's 1984 proposals put everyone under the same-sized umbrella, one large enough to tax-shelter 18% of each year's earned income. RRSP limits would rise, ideally, to $15,500 by 1988. Unfortunately, this all proved more complex than expected. The rules were unveiled only in 1989 and enacted in 1990. That's why elsewhere in this book you'll see references to pre-1990 and post-1989 service.

Fitting everyone under the same-sized umbrella means your own RRSP shares the 18% limit with any plans sponsored by your employer. The better the pension plan, the less you get to put into your own RRSP. Finance developed three devices to keep people under that umbrella: the pension adjustment, pension adjustment reversal and past service pension adjustment.

PENSION ADJUSTMENT (PA)

Many people feel cheated because their T4 tax slips contain pension adjustments that reduce the amount they can put into their own RRSPs. Some are indeed getting cheated. Others are being treated quite fairly.

Calculating a DB Plan PA

Sponsors of defined benefit pension plans must calculate yearly pension adjustments with this formula:

$9 x (accrual rate x pensionable earnings)—$600

- $9 is the factor discussed in the text.

- The accrual rate is the pace at which you accumulate a pension. These rates generally range from 1% to 2% of annual earnings.

- The $600 is called the "offset." It's a minimum level of RRSP room. It was intended to reflect the fact that plans vary, yet everyone gets it.

Nadu is in a 1.5% plan and made $50,000 last year. The PA is $9 x (1.5% x $50,000)—$600. That's $6,150. Nadu's tax shelter umbrella covers $9,000—that's $50,000 x 18%. The PA uses up $6,150 leaving $2,850 for personal RRSP contributions.

The PA puts a value on how much tax sheltering there is for your employer's retirement plan(s) and reduces your own RRSP limit accordingly. If you have:

- **No employer-sponsored plan:** There is no PA. You get the full RRSP contribution limit for your income level. That's 18% of the prior year's earned income. The RRSP limit for 2002 is capped at $13,500. To qualify for that, you had to have $75,000 of earned income in 2001.

- **Group RRSP:** There is no PA. Group RRSPs are treated like regular ones. With earned income of $40,000 last year, your 18% umbrella covers $7,200 of income. If you and your employer together put $2,400 into a G-RRSP this year, you can still put $4,800 into your own RRSP.

- **Deferred Profit Sharing Plan:** These plans are similar to RRSPs, but only the employer can make contributions. The PA equals the amount the employer put in for the year. If that's $1,000, your RRSP limit for the following year is reduced by $1,000.

- **Defined contribution pension plan:** These work like group RRSPs in many respects, but are formal pension plans. The PA equals whatever you and your employer put in for the year. If that's $5,000, your following year's RRSP limit is reduced by $5,000.

- **Defined benefit pension plan:** The other plans are easy to value because each member has an account and real money goes into it. That's not the case with a DB plan. A DB arrangement consists of a promise and a pool of money covering all plan members. There is no requirement that a particular amount be deposited for you each year. Your employer simply guarantees you'll get what's promised and at some point puts in the required amount. How do you value a promise? Remember the Factor of 9 we mentioned earlier? That's the key.

The Factor of 9

Canada's entire tax-assisted retirement savings system rests on the Factor of 9—a rather controversial concept among actuaries.

During the early '80s, federal Finance officials were told to figure out a way to better balance retirement savings opportunities among all Canadians. They began by creating a benchmark-defined benefit pension plan that resembled the high-quality one for federal civil servants. They then assumed that the benchmark plan member would spend a full career building credits in that plan. Using economic assumptions that were valid at that time, they projected the pension this person would be due in retirement and how much that pension would cost.

Next they determined year by year the funding required for this benchmark pension—assuming that economic conditions which were then valid would continue. Remember that DB funding is aimed at having enough money to pay the promised benefits—no more, no less. The plan gets little funding for young workers since there are many years for that money to grow. Conversely, it gets substantial funding for those near retirement. For simplicity, Finance averaged that and came up with $9 of yearly funding for each $1 of pension. Hence, the Factor of 9.

That's reasonably simple, but arguably unreasonable. First, it makes no provision for the facts that the value of DB credits varies greatly with age and that many of today's workers will not spend 30 to 35 years with the same employer—the time required to get full value for their pension credits. As a result, the PA calculation over-values credits for young people and under-values them for older people. Second, it assumes all pension plans are as good as the benchmark one. In reality, few private sector pension plans match public employee plans in ancillary features, especially inflation indexing and early retirement. So, to be fair, PAs for those plans should be calculated at a factor lower than $9.

The bottom line: PAs over-value pension credits and wipe out too much RRSP room for most people in private sector DB pension plans and most young people whether in private or public sector jobs. Instead of just using $9, officials and legislators considered creating lower factors for younger workers and those in less generous plans. But they ultimately settled on just the one factor for ease of use. Creating a wide array of factors reflecting a plan's value and the member's age would have produced mind-boggling complexity. It also would have required RRSP limits to be age-based.

All this means that if you're in a private sector DB plan or don't expect to spend your full career in government service, to match the benchmark pension you must not only maximize your RRSP but also invest outside of the pension-RRSP system. The saving grace is that the economic assumptions of the high-inflation '80s were much different from those today. So, depending on your needs, you may well be able to set aside less than $9 a year for each $1 of pension and still do okay in retirement. That doesn't mean the Factor of 9 is fair; it's not if your plan lacks the bells and whistles that your neighbour, the public employee, gets on her plan. It might, however, ease a bit of the sting.

Some employers have restructured their plans to reduce this PA discrimination. One approach reduces the defined benefit coverage and adds a defined contribution pension plan or Group RRSP whose PAs are valued dollar for dollar. Another approach reduces the defined benefit accrual rate that's part of the PA formula. That reduces the PA, but also lowers the future pension amount. The employer makes up for the pension reduction by adding automatic inflation indexing or other features that don't affect the PA. The total package is just as valuable, but wipes out less RRSP room. A third approach is the "flexible pension" which allows DB plan members to put money into a tax-sheltered side fund during their careers. They can use that fund to buy inflation indexing, early retirement and other features that don't affect the PA.

The RRSP Lag

Why are RRSP limits based on earnings and pension plan membership for the prior year? That lag provides time for employers to calculate pension adjustments.

Doug earned $60,000 last year. At 18%, that qualifies for $10,800 of tax-sheltered retirement savings. Last year Doug's employer contributed $3,000 to a Deferred Profit Sharing Plan.

	RRSP only	DPSP & RRSP
Tax shelter limit	$10,800	$10,800
Pension adjustment	– 0	– 3,000
RRSP limit this year	10,800	7,800
DPSP from last year	0	3,000
Total savings limit	$10,800	$10,800

Suppose Doug earns $60,000 this year, but his employer makes no DPSP contributions. His RRSP limit next year will be the full $10,800.

PENSION ADJUSTMENT REVERSAL (PAR)

The PAR restores some or all of the RRSP contribution room the pension adjustment takes away. Sound dumb? Read on.

The PAR kicks in if you leave a Registered Pension Plan or Deferred Profit Sharing Plan before retirement. This most often involves people who change jobs, but PARs are also issued when a defined benefit pension plan is wound up or restructured.

The PAR was created mainly for those in DB RPPs. Those in defined contribution RPPs and DPSPs get PARs only if they leave during the time when the employer can take back the contributions it made for them.

Suppose you change jobs after four years in a defined benefit pension plan. You find you're due $5,000 of pension value that's transferable to another tax-sheltered retirement plan. Yet your pension adjustments for those four years wiped out $15,000 of RRSP room. The PAR provides compensation with a one-time $10,000 boost in your RRSP room.

Your plan sponsor determines the PAR by comparing the pension transfer value to the total pension adjustments it has reported for you since 1990, the first year for which PAs were calculated. The sponsor reports that amount to the federal tax department which then grants the one-time boost in your RRSP limit. Unfortunately, this doesn't fully compensate you because it only restores the contribution room you lost—not the growth on that money had it been in your RRSP all along. Still, it's pretty important, right?

Incredibly, Members of Parliament didn't think so in 1990 when they enacted the retirement savings legislation.

The Finance officials who created the system knew many workers would leave DB plans too early to get full value for their pension adjustments. So they included the PAR. But MPs on the House of Commons finance committee found the new system too complex. At the last minute, they advised Finance Minister Michael Wilson to simplify it a bit by killing the PAR and making some other changes. He agreed.

Pension consultants were shocked and Finance officials privately expressed concern. Normally civil servants don't criticize politicians in public. But one told a lawyers' conference that killing the PAR was the MPs' most important change and questioned whether they understood what they were doing, given Canada's increasingly mobile workforce. That official was David Dodge, then the tax policy chief at Finance. He's now Governor of the Bank of Canada.

Dodge had to apologize to the MPs after the media reported his remarks, but history proved him right. The early '90s brought recession and widespread layoffs. Affected employees—especially well-paid young professionals—got pension transfer values far below the RRSP room they had lost to pension adjustments. And they began complaining that they'd been cheated.

In 1995, with Dodge as his top civil servant, Finance Minister Paul Martin said he would implement the PAR if it could be done without losing revenue. In 1997, Martin did just that for those leaving pension plans after 1996. Finance officials wouldn't give PARs to those who left earlier due to a change in the PA formula that was needed to keep the PAR revenue-neutral.

The bottom line: If you leave a DB plan before retirement, a pension adjustment reversal will restore RRSP room you would have otherwise lost. Although there's no compensation for any growth your RRSP missed out on, you're still much better off than those who left DB plans before 1997.

PAST SERVICE PENSION ADJUSTMENT (PSPA)

Suppose your employer agrees to retroactively improve the formula used to calculate your pension or lets you buy credits covering time when you were not in the plan. Those are usually good deals because they increase your pension and might let you retire sooner.

But there's a catch if they affect pension credits for service after 1989. As explained earlier, all pension and RRSP funding since 1990 has to fit under one tax-shelter umbrella. The better your pension, the less you can put into your RRSP. So retroactive pension improvements might require you to give up some of the RRSP room you got in the past. The amount involved—called the past service pension adjustment— is the difference between the PAs that were reported and those that would have been reported had the improvements been in place at the time. Your employer calculates the PSPA and the federal tax department applies it.

Certain changes won't count against your RRSP room. Within limits, your plan is free to add inflation indexing, subsidized early retirement and increased death benefits. To get other forms of upgrade, you might have to give up some RRSP room. Whether that's a problem depends on the amount of the PSPA and how much unused RRSP room you have. For example, suppose the PSPA equals $3,000:

Unused RRSP Room	Consequence
$3,000+	No problem. You give up $3,000 of RRSP room you weren't using anyway.
$1,000	No problem. You lose the $1,000 of unused RRSP room you now have. The $2,000 of PSPA that's left will be applied against your future RRSP room. This accommodation is limited to $2,000.
$0	As above, $2,000 of the PSPA can be applied against future RRSP room. To cover the rest, you remove $1,000 from your RRSP as a taxable withdrawal—unless the upgrade is a feature you're buying such as past service credits. In that case, you can transfer the required amount from your RRSP to the pension plan tax-free. Perhaps you have a defined contribution pension plan and/or DPSP in addition to your defined benefit pension. Instead of touching your RRSP, you could do a tax-free transfer from those plans.

IS YOUR 18% UMBRELLA BIG ENOUGH?

The 18% umbrella provides enough tax-sheltered pension and RRSP room to replace 60 to 70% of pre-retirement earnings for someone at about twice the average national wage. The average wage is now about $40,000.

So a defined contribution pension plan and/or RRSP can fully meet your needs if you're paid as much as $75,000 to $80,000 a year. At present, defined benefit pension plans enjoy somewhat higher coverage—up to $86,111 in salary for someone in a high-quality plan. That's the point at which you would qualify for the maximum DB pension of $1,722.22 for each year of service. The accompanying box shows coverage for less generous plans.

Can Your Pension Plan Cover Your Full Salary?

The key is your plan's accrual rate. That's often 2% for public sector plans and 1.5% for private sector plans. The highest pension payable by a DB RPP is $1,722.22 per year of service—$60,278 after 35 years. This table shows the salary that would earn you a $60,278 pension after 35 years and how much of your income that pension would replace.

Accrual Rate	Top Salary Covered	Income Replacement
2.00%	$86,111	70%
1.75%	$98,413	61%
1.50%	$114,815	53%
1.25%	$137,778	44%
1.00%	$172,222	35%

Suppose you have 35 years of service and qualify for your plan's maximum payout. Your pension would be $60,278 a year. Would you believe that's only $253 higher than a retiree in the same situation got back in 1976? Your tax-sheltered pension plan covers earnings at about twice the average wage. Back in 1976, the same plan would have covered earnings at about nine times the average national wage.

The maximum 1976 pension limit was sufficient for all but the most senior executives. But it was frozen during the high-inflation years to 1990. Then the pension cap was raised by a measly $7.22. At that point the maximum pension covered two-and-one-half times the average wage and had 40% of the 1976 pension's purchasing power. Wages have risen since 1990, but the pension cap hasn't. So it now covers just two times the average wage and buys less than a third of what the '76 pension did. Meanwhile, the freeze continues until 2004, after which the cap is slated to rise in line with the average wage.

Is this an issue only for fat cats? Hardly. Due to the longstanding freeze, the pension cap now affects many mid-level managers, designated professionals such as staff lawyers and accountants, technical employees such as computer programmers and super-skilled factory workers.

What if you're paid $100,000 a year? If your target replacement ratio—as discussed in Chapter 1—is 70%, your annual pension should be $70,000. But tax rules cap it at $60,278. So there's a $9,722 gap that cannot be funded on a tax-deductible basis. This is a growing problem for employers—especially now that it's easy for highly trained Canadians to work in the United States, where pension funding limits are about three times higher. Many employers are responding by creating supplementary employee retirement plans (SERPs) that provide pension coverage without tax sheltering. See Chapter 14.

So, Is the System Fair?

Probably much more so than many think. Believe it or not, the design is actually rather elegant by world standards.

For most Canadians, the system has met the objectives outlined in 1989 when the current design was unveiled. The Finance Department then stated: "The aim of the new system of tax assistance for retirement saving is to provide fairer and more flexible limits." It has.

But the system is still short-changing defined benefit pension plan members whose pension adjustments over-value their credits. The belated implementation of the PAR provides substantial relief, but not full compensation.

The system is also still short-changing well-paid Canadians, young and old, because it has ignored more than 25 years of wage growth in determining who is "rich" and undeserving of tax assistance. Due to repeated delays, maximum contribution limits for RRSPs, DPSPs and defined contribution pension plans are still not at the point where they match maximum funding for defined benefit pension plans. That will be addressed, however, over the next few years if the federal government honours its word. The pension cap, essentially frozen since 1976, will also start rising in line with the average wage—finally. But Canadian companies will still be disadvantaged compared to competitors in the U.S. and several other major countries that allow much higher levels of tax-deductible pension funding for well-paid employees.

Employer Plans: Overlooked Value

José and Josie are a perfectly matched couple. José recently retired after 30 years with a company that produces junk mail. Josie retired on the same day after 30 years with a company that recycles the junk mail people throw away. Their jobs and wages were exactly the same, but one wound up with much more retirement income than the other. Why? Because one had a much better retirement plan at work.

People looking for jobs rarely consider their prospective employers' retirement plans. But they should—because that's often the only time they get a choice. Suppose you have job offers from two employers that are very similar in terms of salary, work conditions and other priority items. You're wracked by indecision. Comparing the retirement plans might tilt the balance—especially if you don't plan to stay with either employer until retirement.

What? Why look at a retirement plan if you don't plan to stick around long enough to get a pension? We'll get to that. The point for now is that there are various types of retirement plans and they vary in their pros and cons. This matters to you if:

- You're in a pension plan, make hefty contributions and feel guilty because you lack the cash for your own RRSP contributions; or

- You're job-hunting and want to get the best compensation package for your needs; or

- Your employer is one of the few that offers a choice between joining a defined benefit and a defined contribution plan; or

- You've built up a meaningful amount in your pension and want to integrate it with your own RRSP management; or

- You want to better understand pension plan changes proposed by your employer; or

- Your union is about to enter contract talks and you want to make sure your concerns are addressed.

Retirement plans fall neatly into two camps:

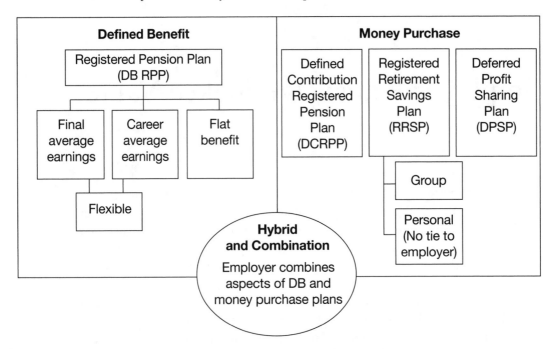

DEFINED BENEFIT REGISTERED PENSION PLANS (DB RPPs)

These plans promise a pre-set level of lifetime retirement income. There's one pool of money; the members do not have individual accounts. The sponsor, usually the employer, is responsible for ensuring the pool will fund the promised benefits.

As formal pension plans, these programs are heavily regulated. The Canada Customs and Revenue Agency ensures they comply with tax rules. Federal pension regulators oversee plans for federal employees, people in the northern territories and those in certain industries such as banking, transportation and telecommunications. Provincial pension regulators oversee the rest. At least every three years an actuary must compare the plan's assets to its liabilities—the promised benefits—and estimate how much money is required to keep the plan solvent. If the liabilities exceed the assets, the sponsor must top up the plan within a certain period of time.

What if the investments have done better than expected and there's a surplus? That has become a highly contentious and legalistic area, which we discuss in Chapter 11 and Appendix E.

Employees in some plans share in the surplus, usually through enhanced early retirement, reduced contributions or benefit upgrades. And some retirees even get cold hard cash; for example, the Canada Mortgage and Housing Corporation plan sent each retiree a fat (but taxable) surplus cheque in 2000. More often, though, employers reduce their own contributions until the surplus is used up. (Quebec allows such "contribution holidays" only if specifically allowed by the plan.)

Supermarket Workers Pressed Their Beef

Until the mid-1980s it was fairly easy for employers to remove surplus funds from DB pension plans. Then, just as the Ontario government was finalizing pension legislation, financier Conrad Black provoked an outcry when he bought the Dominion Stores supermarket chain, ordered widespread layoffs and removed more than $60 million in surplus pension money. An Ontario court later ordered him to repay $56 million and the provincial government sharply curtailed employers' access to pension surplus.

A DB plan might be "contributory" or "non-contributory." A contributory plan requires members to make contributions. The plan can charge no more than 9% of covered earnings and the plan sponsor must pay at least 50% of the cost of the benefit that's ultimately provided. Non-contributory plans are financed entirely by the sponsor; members make no contributions.

DB plans are often "integrated" with the Canada/Quebec Pension Plan. That means the plan's designers took your C/QPP benefits into account when they determined what it will take to replace 70% or so of your pre-retirement income. You might be credited with pension at one rate on earnings that are also covered by C/QPP and at a higher rate for earnings above that level. Or the pension promised by the employer's plan might be reduced at age 65 to reflect the start of C/QPP benefits. That's not necessarily a dollar-for-dollar reduction; it depends on the plan's design and whether you actually get the maximum C/QPP benefit. Integration is discussed in Chapter 13.

What if you leave the plan before retirement? If you leave before the vesting date—usually two years—you lose the employer's contributions but get back your own with interest in line with GIC rates. If you leave after the vesting date, you're entitled to the present value of the pension you've earned. Note that the employer's 50% share applies to the value of the payout, not the annual funding. If you're below 40 or so, you may have contributed more than half of the value of the pension you've earned. The excess contributions are refunded with interest. We'll look at that later in this chapter when we consider what's the best plan for you. It's also discussed in Chapter 15. The key point for now is that DB plans are really designed for those who put in many years with the same employer.

DB plans vary in how they determine a member's pension. Here are the main structures.

Final Average Earnings Plans

These are the most common DB RPPs. The pension is based on average earnings for the last few years of work—often, the final five years. Some plans use the best five consecutive years during the 10 years before retirement. That helps those who gear down near the end of their careers. It also protects those who receive a sizeable part of their pay in the form of a bonus. If their pension was based only on their final five years, they'd really suffer in retirement if those years fell during an economic downturn. Top-of-the-line plans—the best allowed—use average earnings for the best three years. Suppose you're in a "final five" plan with average earnings of $60,000, a 2% accrual rate and 35 years of service. Your pension would be $42,000—that's $60,000 x 2% x 35—though the actual amount might be somewhat less if your plan is integrated with C/QPP.

These plans are hard to understand because they consist of a promise that bears little relation to your current situation if you're far from retirement. On the other hand, they've produced many happy retirees because the payouts are typically based on those years with the highest earnings. In many cases they generously subsidize early retirement so members can stop work sooner than expected and collect a full pension or something close to it.

What Earnings Are Pensionable?

Life used to be so easy! We got straight salary or hourly wages. Now, many get a good-sized chunk of their pay through a performance bonus or commissions. If you're one of them, does your employer's retirement plan recognize that?

Career Average Earnings Plans

These are similar to final average plans except that the earnings base spans your whole career. For example, your annual pension might be determined by adding up 1.5% of each year's earnings. That's easy to understand and, unlike the final average plan, lets you determine your pension at any point. But treating each year equally fails to account for inflation and promotions, so the pension could be unduly low. To address that, these plans typically update the earnings base periodically. For example, your earnings for 2000 might be used for all years before then. If a plan is updated often, the pension will resemble the one that would have been due from a final average plan. If updates are sporadic, the pension could be quite a bit less.

Year	Earnings	Pension @1.5%
1996	$40,000	$600
1997	$41,000	$615
1998	$45,000	$675
1999	$48,000	$720
2000	$51,000	$765
2001	$53,000	$795
Pension due so far		$4,170

Flat Benefit Plans—Multi-Employer Plans

These are typically plans for workers, such as plumbers, carpenters, electricians and labourers, who are hired through their union for short periods of time. Acting through an association, employers negotiate with the union on how much to contribute for each hour worked. The contributions go into a pension fund that's administered by a board of trustees. This board has union representatives and usually, but not always, employer representatives too.

The classic arrangement was aimed at treating workers equally by paying a fixed amount of monthly pension for each year of service. For example, a retiree might get $50 a month for each of his 30 years on the job. So the monthly pension equals $1,500. Basing the pension on time, not pay, means two workers with different wages could get the same retirement income.

In theory, these plans are easy to understand. In practice, many have become complex with different payout rates for various job categories. Also, payout rates are continually renegotiated to reflect inflation and the changing state of the industry. Depending on the bargaining, those updates might not be retroactive. So, for example, your monthly pension might be $30 for each year of service before 1985, $40 for each year between 1986 and 1995, $50 per year for 1996-2000 and $60 for each year after 2000.

There's a big difference between these plans and other defined benefit plans when it comes to deficits. Normally, the employer who sponsors a DB plan must ensure there's enough money in the fund to pay the promised benefits. That's not the case with a multi-employer plan. If a deficit arises, the trustees must wait for the next round of bargaining to see if the union and employer association will agree to increase the contribution rate. Until that rate is raised enough to cover the shortfall, the trustees will have to scale back the benefits granted for service going forward, and in an extreme case might even have to reduce benefits already earned. Recognizing that the pension trustees can't automatically call on the employer, the plan's actuary typically builds an extra cushion into the calculations for the plan's funding. The flipside of all this is that any surplus fully benefits the plan members, not the employers.

These plans have a very clear trade-off between wages and pension contributions. The employers effectively lump both into one payment for each hour of work. So higher pension contributions mean less pay now. That can create conflicts between older workers with long service who want better pensions and younger workers who want bigger paycheques. Usually, the pension trustees have the plan's actuary work out various options which maybe put to a vote by union members.

Flexible Pensions

This is a new wrinkle that is catching on slowly. It responds to the pension adjustment problem discussed in the previous chapter: the PAs that reduce personal RRSP room often over-value credits in defined benefit plans. In addition to a basic DB pension set-up, a flexible pension has a tax-sheltered savings account for each member. The member contributes to that account and toward the end of his or her career uses the fund to buy features such as unreduced early retirement and automatic inflation indexing. Those features can greatly enhance the value of the person's pensions, but don't count against his or her own RRSP room.

Protecting Your Retirement Kitty

One RPP feature often overlooked is that pension legislation protects your money from creditors. They can claim your pension income as it's paid, but not before. This applies to both defined benefit and defined contribution RPPs. The shield does not, however, protect you from a spousal claim on marital breakdown. Also, Manitoba and Saskatchewan let family maintenance officers raid a pension plan if the person falls too far behind in child support.

RRSPs are creditor-proof in Prince Edward Island and to a very limited extent in Quebec and British Columbia. Otherwise, they're protected only if you invest through a life insurance company and meet certain rules for beneficiary designations and the timing of contributions.

The Uniform Law Conference of Canada—a group of lawyers—has drafted model legislation that would creditor-proof all RRSPs. But there's no sign of when, or even whether, Ottawa and the provinces will enact it.

MONEY PURCHASE PLANS

These plans do not promise a pre-set level of retirement income. Indeed, the pension cannot be determined very much in advance of when you stop work.

The term "money purchase" probably sounds strange. It means you accumulate a sum over time and at retirement use that to buy an annuity which pays monthly income for life. You purchase a stream of money. Get it? In reality, the term's outdated since this camp also includes vehicles such as RRSPs and DPSPs that need not be turned into formal life annuities. A better name might be WYSIWYG—pronounced wiz-i-wig—an old computer acronym that stands for "what you see is what you get." In contrast, a DB plan is WYPIWYG: "what you're promised is what you get."

Each money purchase member has an individual account. Usually he or she makes the investment decisions, although it's up to the employer to provide the options. The person's retirement income will depend on how much goes into the account and how well it's managed. So you might do better or worse than someone in a defined benefit plan.

Money purchase set-ups are easier to understand than DB plans because they consist of individual accounts with real money as opposed to a promise from a pooled fund.

Defined Contribution Registered Pension Plans (DC RPPs)

These are formal pension plans that face federal-provincial regulation. The name says it all. It's the annual contribution that's defined, not the retirement benefit. The plan sponsor, typically an employer, must put in money every year. Often that's about 5% of your covered earnings. The sponsor might require you to put in money too.

In some plans the sponsor decides how its contributions are invested. More often, though, you make the investment decisions for both your contributions and the sponsor's. Usually, the sponsor has a contract with a financial organization which offers plan members several investment funds and perhaps guaranteed deposits. It's up to you to decide how to spread the money among those options.

Increasingly, plan sponsors provide educational sessions and materials to help members make those decisions. And, increasingly, employees want someone to guide them; but that's a touchy area for employers who fear workers might sue if they provide advice and the accounts don't do well. Many employers arrange for employees to meet with third-party financial advisors. In 2001, pension, securities and insurance regulators agreed to set guidelines that will better define the employer's responsibilities, but it will likely be years before those standards are finalized and adopted across Canada.

DC RPPs avoid three of the big issues that plague their defined benefit cousins. First, at any time you can see exactly what your account is worth. Second, there's no problem with pension adjustments wiping out too much RRSP room since your PA equals, dollar for dollar, the contributions you and your employer put in. Third, there are no battles over surplus ownership—you reap the full rewards if your investments do very well and suffer if they tank.

At retirement, whatever's in the plan must be used to provide income for as long as you live. That's often through the purchase of an annuity. An annuity is a contract with a life insurer or the pension plan itself. You pay that organization a lump sum and then receive monthly income in return. The prospect of converting the account to an annuity all at once creates another element of uncertainty, since the purchase price for a life annuity changes as interest rates change. To hedge that risk, you could convert gradually during the five years before retirement, purchasing deferred annuities that delay their payouts until your retirement date. Alternatively, your plan might allow you to roll the money into a more flexible Locked-In Retirement Account (LIRA), Life Income Fund (LIF) or Locked-In Retirement Income Fund (LRIF).

Minding the Store

Here are some key questions to ask about a DC RPP or Group RRSP.

- If the investment options are limited to certain funds, how were they chosen? Is there a process for reviewing them? Who does that and how often?

- What are the fees and expenses for each investment option? Do you get a break compared to what people pay on their own?

- If the plan offers guaranteed deposits, do they pay higher rates than those available to anyone at the retail level? Have plan administrators assessed the financial stability of the company that issued those deposits? What happens if that company fails?

Group RRSPs (G-RRSPs)

Group RRSPs are spreading like wildfire because they let employers provide retirement plans at little or no administrative cost or effort. They're especially popular with small companies, but large employers offer them too, often as a supplement to the regular pension plan. Employees like them because they're easy to understand and let each person make his or her own investment decisions.

G-RRSPs are weird creatures. They can be structured to walk and talk like pension plans, yet they don't fall under pension plan regulation. In the first case of its kind, New Brunswick's pension board decided in 1999 that the provincial pension act should govern a G-RRSP that replaced two formal pension plans at Saint John Shipbuilding Ltd. But the provincial cabinet overruled them and specifically exempted RRSPs—individual and group—from pension legislation. British Columbia and Saskatchewan specifically exclude them too. The issue hasn't been pressed elsewhere.

Federal tax officials don't recognize group RRSPs aside from an oblique reference or two. Technically, every RRSP is a personal plan. A Group RRSP is simply a collection of personal RRSPs administered by one financial organization under an agreement with the account holders' employer.

Some Group RRSPs are set up very loosely because the employer simply wants to help employees save on their own. Participation is voluntary. The employer provides no money; it just allows a financial organization to sign up employees and collect contributions through payroll deductions. This might be a good deal if the financial organization waives its RRSP administration fee and offers a good range of investment products with sound advice. It might be a lousy deal if the product choice and service are poor. Payroll deductions are certainly convenient and you get your tax break sooner since there's no income tax withheld from the money used for periodic contributions. But you can duplicate that on your own by authorizing any financial organization to take direct contributions from your bank account, and then requesting a "source deduction waiver" from the tax department, as discussed in Chapter 7.

Other employers structure Group RRSPs more like defined contribution pension plans and kick in money, perhaps 5% of pay. This is tricky since the federal *Income Tax Act* allows RRSP contributions only by employees. The boss gets around this by raising your pay on condition that the money go directly to the RRSP. There's no tax on that bump-up because it becomes part of your regular tax-deductible RRSP contribution. But there is a bit of cost for workers who earn less than about $40,000. That's because the bump-up is subject to Canada/Quebec Pension Plan and Employment Insurance premiums. Those paid more are unaffected since they already pay maximum C/QPP and EI.

As soon as the money goes into your plan it's yours. Federal RRSP rules let you make withdrawals whenever you want, but many employers put controls on the RRSPs they subsidize. You might have to agree to keep the plan intact until age 55. Or, any withdrawal might require the employer's consent. Otherwise, the company will suspend further contributions—it can't take back the money already put in.

Note that RPP rules require an employer to make pension contributions and restrict its ability to change the plan's terms. That's not the case with a G-RRSP. An employer can unilaterally halt contributions or change the plan's terms unless the deal was clearly made part of the compensation package and the employees have the wherewithal to make sure it's honoured.

As with a DC RPP, the investment decision-making is up to you, though your employer might limit the range of options. Your employer might offer education and arrange for you to consult an outside advisor, but you're the one who ultimately determines whether the plan wins or loses. We mentioned above that pension, insurance and securities regulators are working on guidelines that better define the employer's responsibilities for DC pension plans. The project also covers Group RRSPs.

While RPP payouts must be structured to provide lifetime retirement income, there are no controls on what you do with your RRSP money once you've satisfied your employer's lock-in, if any. That's great for people who are reasonably astute and interested in estate planning. It's potentially disastrous for those with no discipline.

Personal RRSPs

While these are part of the money purchase camp, there's no tie to your employer. The next chapter will focus on some tips and tricks to help grow your plan. For now, let's consider your personal RRSP in the context of your overall retirement planning.

The first and perhaps most controversial point we want to make is that you may not need your own RRSP—if you're in a high-quality pension plan and can reasonably expect to put in enough time to qualify for sizeable benefits. For example, police officers, nurses, teachers and many civil servants have good defined benefit pension plans, in part because they pay high contributions. They also tend to have strong job security. And many public employee plans across Canada are so similar that members can transfer credits at full value. Members of certain unions also have good pension plans and strong job security.

Take Bob, a fellow we know. Like many Baby Boomers, he job-hopped for much of his career as a systems analyst. But he was a civil servant and able to move from ministry to ministry without affecting his pension accumulation. He ultimately retired at the grand old age of 50 on a fully-indexed pension that easily met his needs.

This is one reason why it's important to have an income replacement ratio target, as discussed in Chapter 1, and to understand your pension plan, the subject of the second part of this book.

If your plan is good enough to meet your retirement needs and you're committed to staying in that line of work, consider becoming—and staying—debt-free, instead of making RRSP contributions. In a way, the pension adjustment calculation already makes this decision for you. If you're in a very good pension plan you get little in the way of RRSP contribution room.

Our second point concerns how you invest your own RRSP money. One of the keys to growing your RRSP is asset allocation—how you divide money among stocks, bonds and short-term deposits. In financialese, those assets are called equities, fixed-income and cash. You might hold them directly, or indirectly through investment funds. Every investment fund, whether sold directly to the public or limited to use in employer-sponsored plans, publishes material that explains how it is run and what it holds. There are many books that discuss asset allocation. Your bank branch might have a free worksheet, and there are some interactive web sites. But, as good as they are, these materials tend to treat RRSPs in isolation.

We suggest you first view your total wealth and decide the percentages you want in stocks, bonds and cash without regard to particular accounts. That includes taxable assets as well as tax-sheltered retirement savings. Only then decide on the investments a particular account should hold, considering that account's purpose and tax treatment. In particular, coordinate your own RRSP with your employer's retirement plans.

Employer Plan	Guideline
Defined benefit RPP	DB members can invest their own RRSPs more aggressively than others because the DB plan guarantees a set level of retirement income. So make sure your financial advisor is aware of your DB plan and how much you can count on it. Consider it part of your fixed-income allocation. (Since the DB plan sponsor carries all investment risk, the plan's own investment management is irrelevant at this point— odds are you'll neither gain if the fund does well nor lose if it does poorly.)

Employer Plan	Guideline
Defined contribution RPP Group RRSP Deferred Profit Sharing Plan	Your retirement payout is unknown and you carry the investment risk. So these are much like your own RRSP. Using your overall allocation, coordinate their holdings with those in your own plan. Show your advisor what's in these plans to avoid having mismatched investments.

Deferred Profit Sharing Plans (DPSPs)

DPSPs are not too widely used. Those that exist are like a defined contribution RPP in some ways and a Group RRSP in others.

The plan is subject to federal tax rules but not pension legislation. This might change. Pension, insurance and securities regulators view DPSPs as "capital accumulation plans"—just like Group RRSPs—and are working on defining the responsibilities that employers who sponsor them have to their plan members.

The employer is the only one who can make contributions. Before 1991 employees could make non-deductible contributions, but now employee money can go in only if transferred from another registered plan. Since funding is one-sided, the contribution limit is half that for a DC RPP. The money goes right into the DPSP. There is no salary bump-up as with a Group RRSP, so the contributions are not subject to C/QPP or EI premiums.

Unlike an RPP, the employer does not have to contribute each year. Indeed, one reason why an employer might have a DPSP is to keep the cost of its retirement plan funding in line with its profits.

As with other money purchase plans, the employer's contribution is included in the employee's pension adjustment dollar for dollar.

The employer can reclaim its contributions if the employee leaves within 24 months of joining the plan. After that, all contributions immediately become the employee's property.

Plan members cannot lend the employer money through notes or bonds, but can invest in its common stock. Indeed, the employer's stock might be the only investment option—these plans lack the safeguard that prohibits a formal pension plan from putting more than 10% of its assets into any one stock. On leaving a DPSP you can take the stock with you and not face capital gains tax until you actually sell it.

A retiring employee can take his or her money as a lump sum; it need not be structured to provide periodic income. That's a big difference between this type of plan and an RPP. Here are some other important differences:

- DPSP proceeds must start to be paid out no later than 90 days after you leave the company or die. The only deadline for an RPP is that the pension must start before age 70.

- The DPSP payout can be made in instalments over as many as 10 years. Aside from death benefits, RPP payouts must generally be spread over the recipient's lifetime.

WHICH PLAN IS BEST?

That depends on your age, career path, retirement needs and investment ability.

Here's a set-up that's pretty much perfect—for the employee, not the employer. The employer sponsors both a defined benefit and a defined contribution pension plan. But you don't have to enter the DB plan as soon as you're eligible—the usual requirement. Instead, you join the DC plan and then switch after age 40. The RRSP pension adjustment calculations and mechanics of DB funding are such that people generally do better under a defined contribution plan during the first part of their career, when they're most likely to change jobs. The table starts tilting during your 40s, and the value of DB plan credits then jumps sharply after you turn 50. By then you're also less likely to quit for a job elsewhere. Once you join the DB plan, you can transfer money from your DC account and buy past service credits. Your DB credits then cover you full time with the employer and you maximize your guaranteed pension.

This setup would give you the utmost in flexibility and security. Unfortunately, virtually no employers offer it, due to its potentially high cost and complex administration.

Instead, let's assume you're limited to just one plan: a defined benefit RPP, defined contribution RPP or Group RRSP. As you'll see, each has pros and cons. All we can do is help you key in on the points that matter most to you.

Which Plan Is Easiest to Understand?

A money purchase plan—either defined contribution RPP or Group RRSP. You see exactly how much you and your employer put in each year and how much the account is worth. The pension adjustment that reduces your own RRSP limit simply equals the contributions that went into the plan the year before. You know what you'll be due if you leave before retirement. Of course, as you approach retirement you can estimate what your income will be, but won't know for sure until the big day comes—and perhaps not even then unless you buy an annuity.

Which Plan Offers the Greatest Security?

The standard answer is a defined benefit RPP. Your pension is pre-set and guaranteed by your employer. It might be automatically indexed for inflation or adjusted periodically on an *ad hoc* basis. You do not have to know anything about investing, since the plan sponsor is fully responsible for managing the money. But:

- This assumes you'll spend a lengthy career with that employer or one with a plan so similar that it will accept your credits.

- This also assumes your plan will be kept solvent. That's not a concern for public employees, but there have been a few cases in which private sector plan members got reduced benefits after their employers went bust.

Which Plan Is Best for Mobile Workers Who Change Employers?

Most often, a money purchase plan. You're due whatever's in your account when you leave—assuming you're past the point when the employer can reclaim its contributions. The RRSP pension adjustments for your time in the plan fairly reflect the value of your pension membership. Often you can transfer your account's investments intact. Group RRSPs are particularly good for highly mobile workers because the employer's contributions vest immediately—they can't be taken back. Also, the money can be transferred to your own RRSP. In most cases, RPP money can be transferred only to another locked-in vehicle, either your new employer's RPP or an RRSP-like Locked-In Retirement Account. Frequent moves could leave you with a bunch of fairly small LIRAs.

Which Plan Offers the Best Deal for Retirees?

Tough question!

If you're prudent and disciplined, you can do very well with a DC pension plan or Group RRSP—even if you're not an investment genius. Indeed, you'll likely do better over the long term if you shun highly aggressive investments and frequent switching. Remember, though, that your employer makes no guarantee that you'll accumulate enough to retire comfortably. If you're not careful, or if you're just unlucky, a market meltdown near the end of your career might force you to work longer than you want or retire on less.

While a well-managed DC plan or group RRSP can meet your needs, especially in combination with a personal RRSP, it's hard to beat a good final average DB pension plan with inflation indexing—providing you put in enough years to earn a full pension or something close to it. (Many private sector plans are not automatically indexed, but the sponsors have good records of *ad hoc* adjustments.) This can be a fantastic deal if there's a generous early retirement provision. Subsidized early retirement is one of the big advantages of a DB plan. That might be offered periodically when the employer wants to downsize. Or it might be built into the plan, perhaps as a way to use up surplus funds.

Which Plan Is Best for Your Spouse?

That depends on the longevity of your marriage and you.

First, your marriage. If legally married, your spouse is entitled to half the wealth you accumulate during the marriage. Common-law spouses get somewhat weaker protection; it varies across the country. Appendix C at the back of the book summarizes their status under pension legislation. It's easy to split a DC pension or Group RRSP account on divorce or separation because the precise value is known. DB pension credits have been the subject of some very messy and expensive court battles because there are various ways to value them.

Now, your life. What happens when you die? The Group RRSP is the simplest situation because it's just like your own RRSP. Whatever's in the account can be rolled tax-free to an RRSP for your spouse or be used to create income for a dependent child or grandchild. The real concern here is whether you feel your spouse can adequately manage a lump sum. (If you have no such beneficiary, the plan is collapsed and taxed as part of your final year's income.)

A defined contribution pension plan is a bit more complicated. If you die before retirement, the account balance goes to your named beneficiary, if any, or to your estate. If you make it to retirement day, your account gets converted to a life annuity or to an RRSP-like fund that's locked in under pension legislation. The annuity purchase requires two decisions. First, you and your spouse must decide if he or she wants payments to continue after your death. If so, your monthly pension will be reduced; see Chapter 17. Next you must decide if you want to guarantee full benefits for the first five, 10 or 15 years. If so, your monthly pension will be reduced. If you die during the guarantee period, your spouse gets the value of the remaining payments. Then, depending on the answer to the previous question, the survivor's pension kicks in or payments stop altogether. If you and your spouse answer no to both questions, you receive your full pension but all payments stop when you die; your spouse gets nothing.

A defined benefit pension plan is still more complicated—of course! If you die before retirement, the plan sponsor must calculate the value of the pension you've earned just as if you've changed jobs. Then, depending on the plan and the pension legislation that governs it, your beneficiary or estate gets 60% to 100% of that amount. If you make it to retirement day, you and your spouse face the two questions posed above for those converting DC pension plans to annuities.

HYBRID AND COMBINATION PLANS

These arrangements seek to provide the best of both camps—the pre-set guaranteed pension of a DB plan with the flexibility of a money purchase plan.

Hybrid plans go back 20 to 30 years or so. At that time employers were converting defined contribution plans to defined benefit structures—the reverse of what's happening now. Why? Canada had gone through a period of low interest rates and low stock market returns. Employees in DC plans were finding they were not accumulating enough to provide adequate retirement income. Faced with unhappy long-serving employees who could not afford to retire, employers began building in guarantees. For example, a retiree would get whichever was greater: the pension that could be bought with the DC balance or a pension based on 1% of final average earnings. Thus the hybrid plan was born. It was a DC plan with a DB floor.

Today, DC is in fashion. During history's longest bull market, employees decided they wanted high stock market returns to benefit them, not their employers. Employers, meanwhile, came to see the DC plan as a way to make their pension costs predictable by shifting investment risk to the employees. But consider that we may be in a new period of relatively low interest rates and relatively low stock market returns—the climate that years ago put the chill on DC plans. Does this mean employers will start converting DC plans to DB, or introducing hybrid plans? The more likely approach is the combination plan, a setup that's already widespread.

A combination plan has a DB element and a DC element. The DC element might be a formal DC pension plan, a Deferred Profit Sharing Plan or a Group RRSP that's either mandatory or voluntary. There are many variations.

With a hybrid plan, your pension is based either on the DC value or the DB formula. With a combination plan, you get one pension based on the DB formula and a separate payout from the DC pension plan, DPSP or Group RRSP. They operate independently, side by side, under the overall 18% tax sheltering limit discussed in Chapter 5.

Hybrid and combination plans change the risk sharing equation. The hybrid plan reduces the risk to the employee inherent in the DC structure by having a defined benefit provision kick in to cover shortfalls. The combination plan effectively shares the risk by providing part of the pension at the employer's risk and part at the employee's.

Who Bears the Risk?

Fourteen-year-old Casey watched her father as he read his pension handbook. The company plan was a combination—one part defined benefit and one part defined contribution. She read the definitions and when her father asked if she understood them, Casey replied "Yes, it's just like that dress I want."

"What do you mean?" asked Dad.

"Well," said Casey, "if you give me $100 to buy the dress, that's defined contribution. But if you promise to pay for the dress no matter what it costs, that's defined benefit."

"Okay, which kind do you prefer?" asked Dad.

"What you've got—the combination plan. You give me $100 towards the dress and you promise to pay for the shoes, whatever they cost."

As Casey was so quick to note, though Dad was funding her purchases she was bearing some of the risk. If he was prepared to fully underwrite the cost, she could pick any dress. If, on the other hand, he would only cough up a specified amount, there was a chance that she would not get the one she really wanted.

Under a defined benefit plan, the employer usually bears the risk of the cost being higher than originally anticipated. The normal arrangement is that the employer or plan sponsor is ultimately responsible for underwriting any shortfalls. The risk to the employee or plan member is that the employer may, through bankruptcy or other business failure, prove unable to do the funding required. Statutory funding requirements reduce but cannot entirely eliminate the latter risk.

Under a defined contribution plan the risk sharing is different. The employee has the security of seeing the contributions as they are made but bears the risk that the investment returns will be less than expected and that, as a result, the retirement benefit will be inadequate. There is also some risk to the employer. If sufficient care is not taken in selecting investment managers and options as well as communications to employees, the employer may be held responsible for any failure of the plan to perform as expected.

WORKSHEET 10

Pension Plan Shopping List

This worksheet has several uses. You might be job-hunting and interested in comparing various employers' plans, you might have a choice of plans at your current workplace. Or you might want to use it to get a handle on the plans you're now in.

Money Purchase Plans	Plan 1	Plan 2
Type (DC RPP, G-RRSP or DPSP)		
When can you join		
Contributions: • How much do you pay • How much does employer pay • Based only on salary or also bonus/commissions/overtime • When do employer contributions vest		
Investments: • Education sessions or materials • Advice • Good range of options • High-quality funds • Low management fees • Transfer funds intact if you leave early		
Retirement income options		
G-RRSP & DPSP: • Withdrawals restricted • Creditor-proof (Automatic for DC & DB RPP)		
Defined Benefit Plans	Plan 1	Plan 2
• When can you join		
Contributions: • How much do you pay • Based only on salary or also on bonus/commissions/overtime • When do employer contributions vest		
Pension calculation: • Accrual rate (2% maximum) • Earnings base (e.g., average income for final 5 years)		

Defined Benefit Plans *cont'd*	Plan 1	Plan 2
• Inflation protection		
• Integrated with C/QPP		
• Earliest age for pension		
• Earliest age for unreduced pension		
Governance:		
• Who runs plan: employer, union or both?		
• Is the fund now in surplus or deficit?		
• Does the plan document give members any rights to surplus?		

Your Own Plan: RRSPs, RRIFs and Annuities

"Every time you see one of those RRSP commercials, think of Walter."

Prime Minister Jean Chrétien made that comment in 1999 as the House of Commons mourned the death, at age 94, of Walter Harris. Harris, a distinguished lawyer from Ontario, created Registered Retirement Savings Plans when he was Finance Minister in the government of Louis St. Laurent. That was in 1957, the end of his 17 years in Parliament.

The idea was to help people who did not have pension plans. Each year they were allowed to contribute 10% of their earned income to a maximum of $2,500. Adjusted for inflation, $2,500 then equalled more than $16,500 in 2001.

It's hard to imagine now, but it took about 20 years for RRSPs to catch on. At first, the market was pretty much confined to deposits with life insurers. Mutual fund companies offered RRSPs in the mid '60s, but few Canadians were then interested in mutual funds—that's also hard to imagine now. It took the entry of the chartered banks and their marketing muscle in 1975 to really popularize what is now the most widely held investment account in Canada.

The RRSP has evolved into a marvellously flexible instrument, especially since 1990 when the retirement savings system was redesigned. If you have no employer-sponsored retirement plan, your RRSP enables you to create your own with a sizeable level of tax-sheltered funding. If you have an employer plan, you can use your RRSP to supplement it. Indeed, the less generous your employer's plan, the more you're allowed to put into your own RRSP.

It's easy to get information on the basic RRSP rules; virtually every financial organization has free guides available from their offices and web sites. So we're just going to present a grab-bag of tips and tricks, some of which are not well known.

Costs Matter

Fees and other expenses eat into your returns whether you're running an RRSP, a RRIF, an unsheltered investment account or a defined contribution pension plan account. For every dollar they claim, you give up $1 *plus* all of its future compound growth. Unfortunately, there's no way to entirely avoid fees and expenses. But you can be aware of what you're paying and seek decent value.

This particularly applies to mutual funds and segregated funds whose management fees are deducted from each fund you hold; you're not actually billed. (The fund's performance return is based on the portfolio's value after the fees are taken out.) These fees and most other fund expenses form the "management expense ratio" (MER). A 2% MER means fees and expenses consumed 2% of the fund's average assets during the year covered. That may not seem like much, but it is—check the box.

If you invest $1,000 in a fund that averages 10% growth before deducting fees and expenses.....		
MER	Value after 20 years	Average net return
0.0%*	$6,727	10.0%
1.0%	$5,553	8.9%
1.5%	$5,042	8.4%
2.0%	$4,575	7.9%
2.5%	$4,150	7.4%

* Shown only as a base for illustration
No fund has a 0% MER.

Significantly, MERs include compensation for your financial advisor. Those fees—paid out by the fund companies—can be a good investment if your advisor provides good service. Be aware, though, that poor advisors get the same fees as good ones, and make sure you deal with someone who earns that money—as well as your trust. Good advisors don't shy away from explaining their compensation—because they honestly feel they're worth it.

TIPS FOR RRSPS

1. *How much can you put in?* Each year's limit is shown on the Notice of Assessment that was issued after your previous year's tax return was processed. You can also get it from the Canada Customs and Revenue Agency's computerized telephone line at 1-800-267-6999 or through their web site. The tally consists of all your unused RRSP room since 1991, the first year for which unused RRSP room was allowed to be carried forward. CCRA computers automatically update your usage when processing your annual tax return.

2. *When is the contribution deadline?* In a way, there isn't one. There used to be a contribution deadline when each year's RRSP limit was "use it or lose it." Now, unused room from any year is carried forward for use in the future. So, there's

really a deduction deadline. You get 60 days after each year to make a tax deductible contribution for use on that year's return. Deductible contributions for 2001 and 2002 must be made by March 1 of the following year. One for 2003 must be made by February 29, 2004.

3. *Should you really make your full contribution each year?* That depends on your priorities in life. Retirement funding rests on the premise that you will build up a fund over the course of your career. Basically, you could:

   • Contribute early on and then, if desired, scale back later—perhaps to focus on raising a family. Compound growth then funds much of your retirement.

   • Contribute a steady, relatively modest amount every year.

   • Contribute a lot in your later years.

   Ali, Ben and Charlie started work at the same time. Ali contributes $1,000 to an RRSP at the start of every year from age 20 through 29 and then stops. At 8% average compound annual growth, his total investment of $10,000 will be worth $249,830 at the end of the year in which he turns 65. Ben contributes just over half as much each year—$553—but does so over his full career. He pretty much matches Ali but at more than twice the total cost. Charlie delays saving until age 45. To pretty much match Ali, he must invest nearly $3,000 a year—or more than seven times Ali's cost overall. Financially astute readers will point out, though, that due to inflation Charlie will find it easier to invest $1 than Ali does. If we adjust their outlays for average inflation of 3% and express them in age-20 dollars, the totals are $8,786 for Ali, $14,112 for Ben and $29,494 for Charlie. Still a big difference, though not as great as the unadjusted totals suggest.

	Annual Cost	Total Cost	Value at Age 65
Ali	$1,000	$10,000	$249,830
Ben	$553	$25,431	$249,901
Charlie	$2,893	$75,218	$249,813

4. *What's the minimum age for starting an RRSP?* There is none. Anyone who reported earned income in the prior year gets RRSP room. Suppose your 13-year-old earns money baby-sitting or mowing the neighbour's lawn. Though the child doesn't earn enough to pay tax, have him or her file a tax return. The child need only enter the earnings as "other income" on line 104. CCRA will then count 18% of the amount reported as RRSP room. Usually, the child will simply let that room build up until he or she is old enough to owe tax and wants a deduction. But see tip number 6 about the tax deduction carry-forward. You can use

that tip if you can find a financial organization that will let a minor open an RRSP. Technically, a minor can't sign a contract, but in this case many companies bend the rules as a goodwill gesture.

5. *What's the maximum age for having an RRSP?* You must "mature" your RRSP by the end of the year in which you turn 69. That's December 31—not your sixty-ninth birthday. See "Tips for RRIFs and Annuities" later in this chapter.

6. *Suppose your income varies greatly from year to year. You made a lot last year so you have a high RRSP limit this year, but you expect this year's earnings to be quite low. Should you contribute now or wait until you're back in a high tax bracket when your RRSP tax deduction is worth more?* Contribute now to get your money growing on a tax-sheltered basis. You can delay claiming your deduction until a year when it's worth more. Do that by completing Schedule 7 when you file your tax return. CCRA then keeps track of your undeducted contributions. Please don't confuse this with an over-contribution. You're putting in your allowable amount but opting to wait for your tax break.

7. *What if you put in too much?* Contributions during the first 60 days of the year can be allocated to the prior year, the current one or divided between the two. If that doesn't solve the problem, be aware that you can over-contribute by as much as $2,000 without penalty. That's a cumulative limit, discussed more fully in the next tip. If you've already used your $2,000 cushion, you'll face a steep penalty of 1% per month on the new excess contribution unless CCRA grants permission for you to withdraw it.

8. *Is a deliberate $2,000 over-contribution worthwhile?* Yes—if you understand the mechanics. Otherwise, you may face double taxation. There's no tax deduction when the cash goes in, so it's after-tax money. On withdrawal the money gets taxed again. In the meantime, though, it compounds on a tax-sheltered basis. To avoid the double tax bite, view this as an advance contribution. Report the over-contribution on Schedule 7 so CCRA knows about it. In a future year, have them count it as a normal contribution within the RRSP room you then have available. Say you make a $2,000 over-contribution at age 40 in 2002 and it compounds at 8% until age 60 in 2022. Then, during your first year of retirement, you apply it against the RRSP limit from your last year of work. You thus use the $2,000 in cash from 2002 as a contribution in 2022 and get a tax deduction for it. Meanwhile, 20 years of growth has added $7,322 to your plan.

9. *You say you can't afford regular contributions, let alone extra ones.* First, if you're in a good pension plan you may not need an RRSP. Second, if you have no pension is it that you can't afford RRSP contributions or that you choose not to afford them? The pension plan members among your neighbours—especially public employees—are likely contributing 6–8% of their pay to their plans. Do their lifestyles appear to be lacking?

Consider starting a monthly investment plan with a mutual fund company or financial institution. That's likely the best—certainly the easiest—way to make fair-sized contributions since the money is automatically taken from your bank account or paycheque. After a few months you probably won't even notice. Significantly, you can request a "source deduction waiver" so your employer does not withhold tax on the money going into the RRSP. Employers with Group RRSPs do this routinely, but you can do it for your own plan by filing form T1213 with the federal tax department and, if applicable, form TP-1016 with Revenu Québec. These forms are available from the tax department web sites or by telephone. What if you make a big contribution at the start of each year instead of monthly? That qualifies for reduced withholding too.

Here's How to Use the Upfront Deduction to Boost Your RRSP Contribution:

$$\frac{\text{Available cash}}{1 - \text{marginal tax rate}}$$

Monthly investment plan: Figure out how much pay you can do without—say $300 per month. That's your "available cash." If your marginal tax rate is 40%, divide $300 by .6. That's $500. So you could put in $500 monthly—$300 from you and $200 from the tax deduction for your contribution.

RRSP loan: Suppose you have $600 on hand and your marginal tax rate is 45%. Divide $600 by .55 to get $1,091. That's your break-even contribution—$600 of cash plus $491 in borrowed money. Use the $491 tax refund on the contribution to repay the loan.

Alternatively, wait for January or February when financial companies routinely grant cut-rate RRSP loans with no payment due for two or three months. That leaves time to file your tax return and get your refund. Use the refund to pay off the loan. Ideally, submit your tax return through CCRA's TELEFILE telephone service or their NETFILE computer link and have the refund sent directly to your chequing account. That way, you might get your refund within two weeks. Repay the loan immediately to minimize your interest cost—which is not tax-deductible the way it is with other investment loans. Many financial institutions offer multi-year RRSP loans for those with lots of unused contribution room. Consider that if you really lack discipline. Otherwise, you might do better by simply starting a monthly investment plan with contributions that equal what the loan payment would have been. Ask your financial advisor or banker to project both scenarios over 10 and 20 years and compare the results.

There is one caveat about the RRSP tax deduction. A $1,000 RRSP contribution won't necessarily save $400 in tax for someone at a 40% marginal tax rate. The value of your RRSP tax deduction equals the tax rate that would otherwise hit that income. The lower the rate, the less you save. Suppose you're just $400 inside the 40% bracket and the other $600 falls one bracket below, where it's taxed at 35%. Your RRSP tax savings will total $370—40% of $400 and 35% of $600. This can shock those who make huge catch-up contributions that drive their taxable income down through several brackets.

10. *You earn much more than your spouse.* Should you make spousal contributions to his or her RRSP? Maybe. Spousal contributions are a long-term strategy aimed at saving tax in retirement by equalizing a couple's future income. You're allowed to put part or all of your RRSP contribution into a plan for your spouse. This does not increase your limit; you just use it differently. You still get the tax deduction, but the money and its earnings are taxed in your spouse's hands when taken out. These contributions do not affect your partner's own RRSP limit. Your spousal contribution immediately becomes your partner's property, but would be subject to asset splitting rules under provincial law if your marriage breaks up. Be careful: common-law couples don't always fall under those asset-splitting rules.

Sometimes the Lower Income Partner
Should Consider Making Spousal Contributions:

- He or she has a good pension plan while the other has none.

- His or her RRSP is far larger due to an earlier start or better investing.

- He or she expects a large inheritance that can be put away for retirement.

- Both have jobs now, but the other plans to take time off for child-rearing or some other purpose. Or, the other plans to quit and start a business.

The spousal contribution must sit in your spouse's plan for two years past the end of the year in which the contribution is made. Otherwise the withdrawal is taxed in your hands. The spouse can avoid this by having one RRSP for spousal contributions and another for personal contributions than can be withdrawn any time. The holding period is waived if the couple break up and live apart, or if one dies or becomes a non-resident for tax purposes. The hold is also lifted if the spouse transfers the money to a RRIF and makes only minimum withdrawals, or to an annuity that cannot be commuted for three years. There's also no holding period on spousal contributions used for the RRSP Home Buyers' Plan.

Spousal Holding Period		
Contribute	**For**	**Hold Until**
Dec. 30, 2002	2002	Dec. 31, 2004
Jan. 2, 2003	2002	Dec. 31, 2005
Jan. 2, 2003	2003	Dec. 31, 2005

11. *Can you still roll job severance money into your RRSP?* Yes, but only the severance for service before 1996. The rollover limit is $2,000 for each year with your employer and any related one. A partial year—even one day—counts as a full one. You can roll an additional $1,500 of severance money to your RRSP for each year before 1989 that's not covered by vested pension credits. Many employees, for example, must wait one year before they can join the pension plan. This rollover must be done within 60 days after the year you leave your job. The best procedure is for your employer to pay the eligible amount directly to your plan so no tax is withheld. Be careful: you could lose this entitlement if you quickly go back to work for your employer as an "independent contractor."

12. *Isn't it better to pay down a home mortgage than to make an RRSP contribution?* That really depends. As we've suggested elsewhere, those who are reasonably confident that their pension plans can meet their retirement needs might be best off by focusing on debt reduction instead of RRSP contributions. Internet users can easily try a mathematical comparison courtesy of the "Mortgage versus RRSP" calculator at www.retireweb.com. But the numeric results would likely play second fiddle to other considerations. For example, it's not wise to have all of your wealth tied up in your house. Homes are illiquid and subject to cyclical market demand. Second, an RRSP can serve as a last-resort emergency fund. The only way to get cash from your home equity is to borrow against it, and that may not be possible if you're in a financial crunch. Third, you will need more than a paid-off home in retirement; you will also need money for expenses. Remember that the RRSP's most powerful feature is long-term tax-sheltered compounding. Fourth, a mortgage pay-down strategy might work if, after clearing the home loan, you continue to pay out that entire monthly amount as RRSP contributions. But, invariably, people increase their lifestyle spending once the mortgage is gone. Financial advisors often suggest an approach that's less than optimal but which addresses both desires: put the cash into your RRSP and use the resulting tax deduction to pay down your mortgage.

13. *Would you be better off by skipping the RRSP and investing for capital gains?* There is growing interest in this now that only half of a capital gain gets taxed. That means the capital gains tax bite on a stock sale or mutual fund redemption in

retirement would be much less than the hit on an RRSP or RRIF withdrawal. Going this route also means you face no restrictions on where and how you invest, you can borrow against your portfolio and you will have full control over the timing of your retirement income.

There are, however, negatives. First, there is no tax deduction on the money you set aside. So you'll be able to invest much less than you would with an RRSP unless you borrow money in order to put the same amount to work. Investment loans—also called leverage—magnify returns, both up and down. Market downturns can be incredibly stressful because you run the risk of losing more money than you started with. Consider leverage only if you have a strong stomach, fully understand the downside and can afford to keep your loan in good standing during tough times. There are also some pitfalls in the tax rules for deducting interest on investment loans. Basically, you lose that deduction on a pro-rated basis if you start taking money from your account for non-investment purposes such as living expenses.

The second negative is that you will need a great deal of discipline as an investor. That's because you'll face capital gains tax every time you switch your holdings. That tax hit can really depress your long-term accumulation. This alternative strategy is best for those with the patience to do buy-and-hold investing, especially with index mutual funds or exchange-traded funds. As well, several fund companies offer corporate structures that allow you to switch among funds in the same family without triggering capital gains tax. But you're then confined to that family.

The examples of this strategy that we've seen tend to assume the unsheltered account will vastly outperform the RRSP. The reasoning is that the unsheltered account faces no foreign content restrictions. But, as you'll see in tip number 14, your RRSP can effectively be 100% foreign. Also, be careful about investing in aggressively run mutual funds. They tend to pay high capital gains distributions every year or so. Tax on those distributions will sap your long-term growth.

If you're seriously considering this strategy, see if your financial advisor has software that does Monte Carlo simulations. The standard procedure for doing investment projections involves assuming one average annual rate of return. That's easy to do and requires no special software; it's the approach we've used for the worksheets in this book. But it presents a grossly inaccurate picture for the leveraged investor, who is far more vulnerable to market downturns. A Monte Carlo simulation varies each year's returns on a random or programmed basis to more accurately depict market behaviour. The Monte Carlo results might suggest that, based on probabilities, the leveraged strategy does not beat the RRSP by enough to justify the added risk and effort.

TIPS FOR BOTH RRSPS AND RRIFS

14. *Does the foreign content limit mean 70% of your money must be in Canada?* Not at all. Your plan could easily be 100% foreign if you wish; it just takes a little finagling. First, be aware that the 30% foreign content limit applies to your plan's "book value," not its market value. The book value changes whenever you put in money or trade securities. The financial organization that holds your plan must track it—you don't have to, but you should check with your advisor before buying or selling any foreign holdings. Now, some ways to legally exceed that limit:

    • Does your plan hold mutual funds? If so, each Canadian fund is allowed 30% foreign content on its own. Suppose your RRSP or RRIF book value is $100,000. You could put $30,000 into investments that are purely foreign. The other $70,000 could go into a Canadian fund that's fully using its own foreign content limit. So you'd have $30,000 of foreign content directly and $21,000 indirectly—that's 30% of the $70,000 Canadian fund holding. At this point, with minimal effort, your RRSP or RRIF is as much as 51% foreign. (Segregated funds could previously be 100% foreign yet still count as Canadian content. They're slated to come under the 30% rule on January 1, 2002.)

    • Many investment funds are designed to reflect foreign stock and bond movements yet qualify as Canadian content. They make it easy for your plan to go 100% foreign. Some are low-cost index funds. Others are clones of actively managed foreign funds with somewhat higher management fees than the funds they mimic.

    • A wide range of Canadian companies are essentially foreign because much of their operations and/or revenues are outside of Canada. Examples include transportation manufacturer Bombardier, telecommunications manufacturer Nortel and insurer Manulife. Canadian-based natural resource companies typically export much of their oil, gas and lumber—commodities which are priced in U.S. dollars. So they're essentially foreign too. Note that Canadian equity mutual and segregated funds routinely hold shares of Canadian companies with strong foreign operations or revenues. So those funds really have more foreign content than the 30% they're technically allowed.

    • A wide range of government and corporate bonds are denominated in foreign currencies yet count as Canadian content. Those bonds react to economic developments in the country of their currency, not Canada.

- To encourage venture capital investing, the government will increase your foreign content limit by $3 for each $1 of RRSP money you invest in a labour-sponsored investment fund or shares of a privately-held company that meets certain criteria. The rules for this bump-up are complex; consult your financial advisor.

15. *Should you always name your spouse as RRSP or RRIF beneficiary?* That has long been the standard advice, but it might not be your best move since it handcuffs your executors and survivors. Let's review your options:

   - **Name your spouse:** The full value of your plan can then be rolled into your spouse's without facing tax. But what if your marriage breaks up and you forget to change the designation? What if you die very early in the year with little income in your own name? Part of your RRSP or RRIF could then be liberated at little or no tax. Or, what if you leave a large charitable bequest whose tax credit offsets much of the tax that would have been due had your plan been simply cashed out?

   - **Name dependent children or grandchildren:** If the child is healthy, your money can be used to buy an annuity that will pay regular income until he or she is 18. If the child is physically or mentally infirm, your money can be rolled into an RRSP or annuity that can support that child for life. In all of these cases, tax applies to the child's periodic payments, not to the lump sum transfer from your plan.

   - **Name one or more registered charities:** Your plan's value would be paid tax-free to the organization(s). Your estate would face tax on the withdrawal, but gets an offsetting charitable donation tax credit.

   - **Name your estate:** This provides the most flexibility by leaving the disposition of your plan to your executors. They can assess your family's needs and tax position and then, by filing CCRA form T2019, do any or all of the above tax-sheltered transfers. They might even find it's best to cash out part of your plan and pay the tax so your heirs get money with no strings attached. Your province will levy a probate fee when the RRSP or RRIF is paid to your estate. Those fees are not a big deal in most provinces. Ontario has the highest rate—1.5% of the amount transferred. That might be a small price to pay for the flexibility your heirs get. If this choice appeals to you, it's best to have your will explicitly authorize your executors to dispose of the plan as they see fit. Otherwise, one heir might challenge payments to others. Also have your will authorize your executors to make a spousal RRSP contribution to use up any RRSP room still available. That can be done up to 60 days after the end of the year. It will generate a tax deduction for your final return and, of course, fatten your spouse's plan.

By the way, make sure you fill out a new beneficiary designation when you convert your RRSP to a RRIF. Technically, that conversion creates a brand new plan even if the account number is the only thing that gets changed. Tax officials won't let a designation made for an RRSP be automatically carried over to a RRIF.

16. *If your self-directed RRSP or RRIF has an annual administration fee, should you pay it within the plan or outside?* These fees, often $100-$150, used to be tax-deductible if paid outside the plan. Unfortunately, that's not the case anymore. Those under 50 years old should pay the fee themselves to maximize their RRSP growth. Those older are likely best off having the plan pay the fee; effectively that's the same as getting to withdraw $100 to $150 tax-free.

TIPS FOR RRIFS AND ANNUITIES

17. *You're in your 60s and wondering what to do about your RRSP.* You must convert your RRSP to an income vehicle by the end of the year in which you turn 69. You have four options:

- Take the proceeds as cash. The amount is added to your income and taxed accordingly.

- Convert the account to a Registered Retirement Income Fund (RRIF). This is the most popular choice. Think of a RRIF as an RRSP in reverse. With an RRSP, you get to put in a certain tax-deductible amount each year. With a RRIF, you're required to take out a certain taxable amount each year. That need not be in cash; you can remove securities whose value at the time of transfer equals or exceeds the required withdrawal. There's no maximum limit on RRIF withdrawals, so you could run out of money if you're not careful. You can have more than one RRIF.

- Buy an annuity which guarantees payments for a fixed term or for as long as you live. You then no longer have to worry about making investment decisions. Security is the prime reason for buying an annuity. Make sure the issuer is rock solid. If it's a life annuity, make sure the monthly payout is fully covered by the Canadian Life and Health Insurance Compensation Corporation (CompCorp). That limit is currently $2,000 per month per issuer. For more details, call 1-800-268-8099 or visit www.compcorp.ca.

- Combine any or all of the above. For example, you could divide money between a life annuity and a RRIF. The annuity would provide a guaranteed base income. More flexible RRIF withdrawals would offset inflation and provide cash for special needs.

18. *You can start a RRIF only when you're 69, right?* Wrong. You can start a RRIF at any age, but still have to make a mandatory withdrawal each year—the rates for those 50 and older are in the table below. Instead of starting a RRIF before 69, you could simply make RRSP withdrawals. You'd face withholding tax on each withdrawal, but you wouldn't be forced to take out money if you don't need it. With a RRIF, there's no withholding tax on the minimum withdrawal but that withdrawal must be made whether you need it or not—and, while there's no withholding tax on the withdrawal, it's still part of your income for the year and will face tax when you file your return. Suppose you start a RRIF for some reason and then change your mind. You can switch it back to an RRSP until the mandatory conversion deadline.

19. *Once past 69, you can no longer make RRSP contributions, right?* Wrong. If you have RRSP room, either from the past or because you still have earned income, you can make tax-deductible contributions to an RRSP for your spouse as long as he or she is below the maturity age. What if your spouse is older or you have none? There's a little fandangle that's best described by example. Suppose you just turned 69 and will have $40,000 in earned income this year from a property rental. At 18%, that will create $7,200 in RRSP contribution room for you next year—when you'll be too old to use it. So, just before winding up your RRSP this December, make a $7,200 over-contribution. If you've already used up your $2,000 penalty-free over-contribution cushion, you'll face a 1% fine for being too far over in December. The penalty meter will click off on January 1 when, based on your earned income for this year, the system will automatically create $7,200 in new RRSP room. So a $72 penalty for December ends up producing a $7,200 tax deduction for the following year.

20. *How can you reduce the impact of the RRIF withdrawal?* When you set up the RRIF, you must make a one-time decision on whether to use your age or your spouse's in the minimum withdrawal calculation. Using the age of a younger spouse will reduce the minimum required withdrawal.

    You can also delay the start of your withdrawals by up to one year so your money stays tax-sheltered longer. Suppose you turn 69 on January 1, 2003 and don't need money. Set up your RRIF in late December of 2003 with the first withdrawal set only for the end of December 2004. Each year's minimum withdrawal is based on the plan's value at January 1 of that year. Let's assume your RRIF is worth $100,000 on January 1, 2004 and, for simplicity, that you have no spouse. Your minimum withdrawal the following December would be $5,000.

Minimum RRIF Withdrawals

Amount is based on age and plan value at January 1

Age	Rate	Age	Rate	Age	Rate	Age	Rate	Age	Rate
50	2.50%	59	3.23%	68	4.55%	77	8.15%	86	10.79%
51	2.56%	60	3.33%	69	4.76%	78	8.33%	87	11.33%
52	2.63%	61	3.45%	70	5.00%	79	8.53%	88	11.96%
53	2.70%	62	3.57%	71	7.38%	80	8.75%	89	12.71%
54	2.78%	63	3.70%	72	7.48%	81	8.99%	90	13.62%
55	2.86%	64	3.85%	73	7.59%	82	9.27%	91	14.73%
56	2.94%	65	4.00%	74	7.71%	83	9.58%	92	16.12%
57	3.03%	66	4.17%	75	7.85%	84	9.93%	93	17.92%
58	3.13%	67	4.35%	76	7.99%	85	10.33%	94+	20.00%

21. *Is there any way to qualify for the $1,000 pension income tax credit if you have no pension from work?* People who collect pensions from RPPs are entitled to a tax credit that, for many, offsets the tax due on $1,000 of pension benefits each year. If you don't have $1,000 of pension income and you're 65 or older, you can claim this credit on $1,000 of RRIF proceeds. That $1,000 can even be part of your required withdrawal. (There's also a way to qualify for the pension tax credit with non-RRSP/RRIF money. It's basically for those who like to invest in GICs. Get the GIC from a life insurer instead of from a bank, trust company or credit union. That deposit is technically considered a "deferred annuity" and the interest it pays qualifies for the pension tax credit.)

Will It Be STEW for You?

STEW stands for the options that await people who do a retirement planning exercise and find they won't have enough money to realize their dreams. Those options are:

- **Save more.** Retirement funding is a balancing act. You trade off some of life's pleasures today for a comfortable standard of living down the road. The sooner you start, the easier it is. That's because compounding investment earnings will provide much of the money you need. Also, you'll get used to living on that much less. As we noted earlier, public sector employees pay high contributions for the pension plans that are so envied by others. They're required to set aside as much as 6–8% of each year's income. If they can do it, you can too. If you have trouble saving, see a financial advisor. They have all kinds of tips and tricks.

- **Take less.** We find that people commonly have an exaggerated view of how much income they'll need in retirement. Make sure you understand the points we made in Chapter 1 about your income replacement ratio. In particular, be aware of how much of your current income goes for retirement savings, union dues or professional fees, Employment Insurance, Canada/Quebec Pension Plan contributions and work-related spending such as commuting and office clothes.

- **Earn more.** That is, on your investments. Getting a pay raise usually doesn't fill the gap since our lifestyle spending invariably seems to rise as our paycheques go up. Think about how you invest. Does your standard approach to retirement savings amount to making a last-minute RRSP contribution and then investing the money in whatever's hot at the time? Or maybe you selected some mutual funds years ago and have no idea of how they've been doing. A little bit of effort—reading an investment book or speaking with a financial advisor—might make a big difference.

- **Work longer.** Why do you want to retire? Do you hate your job or is it that you'd like to do other stuff? Work need not be an on-off proposition. The past 20 years have seen a revolution in the workplace with mushrooming use of part-time, casual and project employees. That has generally been seen as a bad news story because it has led to widespread layoffs and almost killed the concept of job security. But it's also a good news story for those able and willing to adapt. You might find that working one day a week is all it takes to make early retirement possible.

In any event, don't even consider STEW until you've done a retirement funding projection. That's the job of this chapter. It consists mainly of a five-step worksheet that wraps up everything we've discussed so far. The end result provides an idea of how much you should be saving now to be able to fund the retirement you want.

Frankly, though we put a lot of effort into developing this worksheet, you'd be better off using a computer with good software. Computers make this type of exercise much less tedious. More importantly, you can easily try different assumptions until the results make sense for you.

Some employers provide such software with the terms of their pension plans already built into the programming. If your employer is among them, that's fantastic. Put that software to good use and let the head of human resources know if you found it helpful. Employee feedback counts for a lot when organizations review spending on such initiatives. Many financial advisors also have sophisticated software for retirement projections. See if yours does.

Be careful about do-it-yourself retirement calculators on the Internet and even software sold in stores. Some are really little more than toys. Most are "black boxes"—the creators have not disclosed the assumptions that drive the calculations. It's not uncommon to put the same data into two programs and get different results. If you can access the Internet, check out the free Gross Replacement Ratio calculator at www.retireweb.com. If you're willing to part with a few bucks for a handy-dandy tool, many financial advisors sing the praises of RRIFmetic. It's a $79 program available on the Internet at www.fimetrics.com or by phone at 1-800-663-4088.

Not Cast in Stone

Your retirement funding projection should not be cast in stone. Review it periodically, perhaps every year when you're about to make your RRSP contribution. Then revise it if required. That's another reason to use a computer.

You'll no doubt find that your wants and needs change over time. Even if your wants and needs don't change, your financial position will. Most projections—including the one in this chapter—are based on annual rates for inflation, investment returns and earnings that are *averaged* over many years. That makes calculations simple, but can prove woefully wrong unless you regularly review those assumptions to make sure they're still reasonable. In particular, assumptions for average annual investment returns fail to reflect the positive and negative impacts of stock and bond market volatility. If you have a computer spreadsheet, use the average annual rates to plot how much money you should have at the start of each year between now and retirement. Then do an annual reality check, comparing your savings to the projection. If you're ahead by a wide margin, consider reducing your investment portfolio's risk exposure. If you're behind, work out a plan to top up your account and/or review your investment management.

Reasonable Returns

Projecting investment returns is more art than science. Actually, it's more luck than art. Many financial advisors now use 8% as the average annual return expected during the pre-retirement accumulation phase from a balanced stock and bond portfolio. Conservative advisors may knock that down to 6% in retirement.

There's a general rule-of-thumb that over time stocks produce a 6% real return—that's 6% above the inflation rate. The same rule-of-thumb holds that bonds produce a 3% real return over time. If it's any help, most large Canadian pension funds—which hold both stocks and bonds—now target a 4% "real" return. That's 4% on top of inflation, or about 6–8% overall.

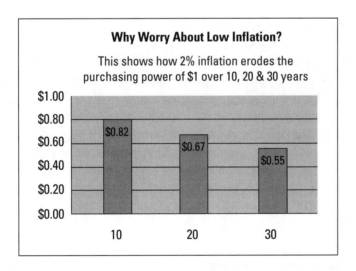

If you want to see actual historical figures, check the Report on Canadian Economic Statistics produced yearly by the Canadian Institute of Actuaries. It's in the Publications section of their web site at www.actuaries.ca. This compendium provides year-by-year data since 1924. For example, the chart on page 94 shows the average annual inflation and investment returns (%) for five-year periods during the last half of the twentieth century, the era when most Baby Boomers were born, grew up and established themselves in the workforce.

Period	Inflation (Consumer Price Index)	Canadian Stocks	US Stocks in CDN $	Long Canada Bonds	91-Day T-Bills
1950-1954	2.99	21.10	20.53	2.38	1.11
1955-1959	1.84	9.54	14.50	-1.73	3.02
1960-1964	1.48	12.73	13.39	6.20	3.58
1965-1969	3.84	7.29	4.94	-0.51	5.53
1970-1974	6.54	-0.29	-4.00	6.59	5.51
1975-1979	8.58	22.29	18.52	5.05	9.25
1980-1984	8.11	10.27	17.50	12.29	14.18
1985-1989	4.39	14.23	17.14	13.69	10.07
1990-1994	2.54	4.47	12.65	9.85	8.08
1995-1999	1.66	16.98	30.09	12.43	4.96
Source: Canadian Institute of Actuaries					

Be careful about extrapolating from these or any other historical averages. As you can see, the 1970s and '80s saw abnormally high inflation, as measured by the Consumer Price Index. Meanwhile, 1980-99 brought history's longest bull market for stocks. Surveys routinely find that people have overly high expectations for their mutual funds. That may be due in part to the resilience of the bull market that began in 1982 as inflation and interest rates tumbled. Also, mutual fund companies heavily advertise their top-performing funds with little or no mention of the others. Those top performers tend to be volatile specialty funds, not the more pedestrian balanced and large cap equity funds that form the core of most prudently managed portfolios.

Fudge It

It is notoriously difficult to make mid- or long-term financial projections with any degree of accuracy. Hedge your bets by building in a fudge factor. For example:

- Ignore Old Age Security when estimating your retirement income; or

- Don't count any employment income as a retiree even if you intend to keep working; or

- Ignore the capital gains tax break and assume your unregistered stocks and mutual funds will be fully taxed just like your pension and/or RRSP; or

- Don't count an expected inheritance or other windfall.

This is truly more art than science. Some people substantially overestimate their required retirement income or sock away every penny they can. Their thinking is that you can never go wrong by having too much money. But you can go wrong if that overly cautious stance keeps you working longer than you really want, or if your investment program demands so much cash that you wind up living poor in order to retire rich. Remember that retirement funding is a balance between your current and future spending.

WORKSHEET 11

What Should You Be Saving for Retirement?

This worksheet may seem a bit longer than others you've tried. But it's probably much more flexible in that it allows you to retire as early as you want, start C/QPP and OAS at different ages and include continuing income from a business or part-time work. The form might be easier to fill out if you download the full-sized version from URL.

The worksheet divides your planned retirement into three periods based on the receipt of government benefits. That's because every dollar you get from C/QPP and OAS is one less dollar you must provide on your own. So your self-generated income will start at the full requirement, drop when C/QPP kicks in during Period 2 and fall again when OAS starts in Period 3.

- **Period 1:** This is for early retirees—those who plan to retire before they start collecting a C/QPP pension. That's often from age 55 to 60, the earliest age when C/QPP is available. Some prefer to wait to start C/QPP. Suppose you want to retire at 55, but won't start C/QPP until you turn 63. Period 1's duration would then be eight years.

- **Period 2:** This is the period when you're retired and receiving C/QPP but not OAS. That's often from 60 through 64. You become eligible for OAS at 65.

- **Period 3:** This is the traditional retirement period—the time after you turn 65 when you are eligible for OAS as well as C/QPP. This period extends to your "run-out age," the point at which you've planned to have exhausted your retirement money.

If you plan to retire *after* turning 60 and will start C/QPP *before* 65, skip Period 1. If you plan to retire at or after turning 65, skip both Periods 1 and 2.

The worksheet has five steps. You first supply some information about your plans and assumptions. Next you determine, in today's dollars, how much in savings you will need to fund your desired income for each period. You then convert those amounts to future dollars and restate them as one lump sum due on your first day of retirement. Finally, you see what your current savings will be worth at that point and determine how much you should be saving to cover any gap. (Unless otherwise specified, enter all dollar amounts in today's dollars. Steps 3 and 4 take care of adjusting them for future inflation.)

cont'd

Every worksheet and planning calculator must make certain assumptions. It's important that you be aware of them. Please note that:

- We assumed that all savings are tax-sheltered. Relatively few people have substantial retirement savings beyond their RRSPs and employer plans. If you do have such savings, estimate your after-tax rate of return. Then, modify the worksheet so that your tax-sheltered RRSP and pension plan compound at the pre-tax rate while your unsheltered savings compound at the after-tax rate.

- This worksheet does not calculate after-tax income. That's too complicated for a paper-based exercise. Also, people tend to think about their income in pre-tax terms. For example, can you say right now—without checking your return—what your after-tax income was last year? We made no special provision for drawing retirement income from unregistered savings. Relatively few people have substantial retirement savings beyond their RRSPs and employer plans. The tax treatment of those savings is rather complex and unique to each person since the amount of capital gains tax due depends on what you paid for the investment. We simply include those savings with all other retirement savings which will be *fully* taxed on withdrawal. That's a major logic flaw if you have substantial unregistered savings. In that case, see if your financial advisor has retirement planning software that does after-tax income projections. Alternatively, as a very crude adjustment, reduce your target income by one-third for the portion to be funded through capital gains investing.

- We made no provision for living off proceeds from the sale of your home or other valuable property. Some financial advisors leave the home intact and assume it will be sold to fund potentially substantial nursing home costs in the person's final years.

- We made no provision for leaving an estate. The worksheet assumes you want your money to last only until you reach the run-out age.

- We assumed you want your retirement income paid at the start of each month and indexed for inflation at the start of each year. We've provided factors for average annual inflation at 2% and 3%. The current policy of the federal government and the Bank of Canada is to keep inflation within a 1 to 3% range.

- We assumed that your employer's defined benefit pension plan, if any, is indexed for inflation. Generally, plans that are not automatically indexed periodically get *ad hoc* adjustments.

- The worksheet makes provision for continued employment in retirement. For example, you might wish to retire at 55 but work part-time until 58. Or, in Period 3, you might plan on working until age 70.

cont'd

Step 1: We first establish the duration of each retirement period and make a few assumptions. These numbers will be used at various points throughout the worksheet. Those references are printed in italics.

		Line
		Line
Current age	_____	A
Age at start of retirement	_____	A1
Age for start of C/QPP: no earlier than 60	_____	A2
Age for start of OAS	65	A3
Run-out age: the end of your money, perhaps age 90	_____	A4
Years to retirement (A1–A)	_____	B0
Period 1 duration: no government benefits (A2–A1)	_____	B1
Period 2 duration: C/QPP available (A3–A2)	_____	B2
Period 3 duration (A4–A3)	_____	B3
Target retirement income from Worksheet 1 in Chapter 1	_____	C
Average annual inflation: 2% or 3%	_____	D
Average annual investment return:		
• Between now and retirement	_____	E1
• During retirement	_____	E2

Step 2: This step has one part for each period. We calculate how much, in today's dollars, you will need to fund the desired income for that period.

Period 1: Do this section if you plan to retire before you start collecting C/QPP benefits.

Target retirement income (Line C)	_____	1A
Annual defined benefit pension: see employer statement		
(Ignore defined contribution plan balance until Step 5)	_____	1B
C/QPP retirement benefit	0	1C
OAS retirement benefit	0	1D
Total DB pension & government benefits (1B + 1C +1D)	_____	1E
Income shortfall (1A–1E)	_____	1F
Average inflation rate (Line D)	_____	
Duration of Period 1 (Line B1)	_____	
Average investment return (Line E2)	_____	*cont'd*

Funding factor from Table A	_____	1G
Total capital needed in today's dollars (1G x 1F)	_____	1H

If you plan to work in retirement:		
Annual earnings	_____	1I
Average annual increase (Perhaps inflation from Line D)	_____	
How many years will you work in Period 1	_____	
Average investment return (Line E2)	_____	
Funding factor from Table A	_____	1J
Lump sum value of expected income (1J x 1I)	_____	1K
Total capital needed in today's dollars (1H–1K)	_____	1L

Period 2. This section covers the period when you receive C/QPP but not OAS.		
Target retirement income (Line C)	_____	2A
Annual defined benefit pension: see employer statement (Ignore defined contribution plan balance until Step 5)	_____	2B
C/QPP retirement benefit from Worksheet 8 in Chapter 4	_____	2C
OAS retirement benefit	0	2D
Total DB pension & government benefits (2B + 2C +2D)	_____	2E
Income shortfall (2A–2E)	_____	2F
Average inflation rate (Line D)	_____	
Duration of Period 2 (Line B2)	_____	
Average investment return (Line E2)	_____	
Funding factor from Table A	_____	2G
Total capital needed in today's dollars (2G x 2F)	_____	2H

If you plan to work in retirement:		
Annual earnings	_____	2I
Average annual increase (Perhaps inflation from Line D)	_____	
How many years will you work in Period 2	_____	
Average investment return (Line E2)	_____	
Funding factor from Table A	_____	2J
Lump sum value of expected income (2J x 2I)	_____	2K
Total capital needed in today's dollars (2H–2K)	_____	2L

cont'd

Period 3: This section covers the period after you turn 65 and can receive OAS and C/QPP.

Target retirement income (Line C)	_____	3A
Annual defined benefit pension: see employer statement		
(Ignore defined contribution plan balance until Step 5)	_____	3B
C/QPP benefit from Chapter 4 Worksheet or Line 2C	_____	3C
OAS retirement benefit from Worksheet 5 in Chapter 3	_____	3D
Total DB pension & government benefits (3B + 3C +3D)	_____	3E
Income shortfall (3A–3E)	_____	3F

Average inflation rate (Line D)	_____	
Duration of Period 3 (Line B3)	_____	
Average investment return (Line E2)	_____	
Funding factor from Table A	_____	3G
Total capital needed in today's dollars (3G x 3F)	_____	3H

If you plan to work in retirement:

Annual earnings	_____	3I
Average annual increase (Perhaps inflation from Line D)	_____	
How many years will you work in Period 3	_____	
Average investment return (Line E2)	_____	
Funding factor from Table A	_____	3J
Lump sum value of expected income (3J x 3I)	_____	3K
Total capital needed in today's dollars (3H–3K)	_____	3L

Step 3: So far we've determined the capital required for each period—in today's dollars. But there will be inflation between now and the start of those periods. We provide for that here by converting each period's capital requirement to future dollars.

Period 1:

From Step 2 copy Line 1L: Total capital needed	_____	1L
Years from now to start of Period 1 (Line B0)	_____	
Average inflation rate (Line D)	_____	
Inflation factor from Table B	_____	1M
Total capital needed in future dollars (1M x 1L)	_____	1N

Period 2:

From Step 2 copy Line 2L: Total capital needed	_____	2L
Years from now to start of Period 2 (B0 + B1)	_____	

cont'd

Average inflation rate (Line D)	_____	
Inflation factor from Table B	_____	2M
Total capital needed in future dollars (2M x 2L)	_____	2N

Period 3:

From Step 2 copy Line 3L: Total capital needed	_____	3L
Years from now to start of Period 3 (B0 + B1 + B2)	_____	
Average inflation rate (Line D)	_____	
Inflation factor from Table B	_____	3M
Total capital needed in future dollars (3M x 3L)	_____	3N

Step 4: We're almost done. We now have three amounts, each expressed as an inflation-adjusted value at a future date. We're going to bring forward the amounts for Periods 2 and 3 so we can see how much money you'll need at the start of retirement to cover all three periods. To do that, we strip away the investment earnings during Periods 1 and 2.

Period 1: From step 3 copy Line 1N	_____	1P
Period 2:		
From Step 3 copy Line 2N	_____	2N
Duration of Period 1 (Line B1)	_____	
Average investment return (Line E2)	_____	
Discount factor from Table C	_____	2O
Value at start of retirement (2O x 2N)	_____	2P
Period 3:		
From Step 3 copy Line 3N	_____	3N
Duration of Period 1 & 2 (B1 + B2)	_____	
Average investment return (Line E2)	_____	
Discount factor from Table C	_____	3O
Value at start of retirement (3O x 3N)	_____	3P
Total capital needed at start of retirement (1P + 2P + 3P)	_____	F1

cont'd

Step 5: We now know how much you will need on the first day of retirement to provide your target income until your run-out age. In this section we see how much your current savings will grow by your retirement day and then determine how much more you need to save.

From prior section copy Line F1: Total capital needed	_____	F1
Capital available now:		
• Employer's defined contribution pension plan	_____	F2A
• Employer's Group RRSP & DPSP	_____	F2B
• Personal RRSP	_____	F2C
• Other savings	_____	F2D
Total capital available now (F2A + F2B + F2C + F2D)	_____	F2
Years left till retirement (Line B0)	_____	F3
Average pre-retirement investment return (Line E1)	_____	F4
Growth factor from Table B	_____	F5
Value of current capital at start of retirement (F5 x F2)	_____	F6

If F6 is greater than F1, your savings are already more than adequate. Congratulations! If F6 is less than F1, do the next calculation.

Gap to be covered between now and retirement (F1–F6)	_____	F7
Average inflation rate (Line D)	_____	F8
Years left till retirement (Line B0)	_____	F9
Average pre-retirement investment return (Line E1)	_____	F10
Accumulation factor from Table D	_____	F11
Savings needed this year (F11 x F7)	_____	F12

These calculations assume the deposit is made at the start of each year and increased annually to offset inflation. If this year's requirement is $3,000 and your inflation assumption was 3%, next year's deposit would be $3,090 and so on.

cont'd

Table A: Funding Factors

This table shows the amount of capital required to fund $1 of annual income that is paid monthly and indexed for inflation at the start of each year. Suppose you want $1,200 a year paid monthly over five years and indexed annually for 2% inflation. If your invested money earns 6% a year, your funding factor is 4.515. You need just over $4.51 of capital for each $1 of desired income, or $5,418 for the full $1,200—4.515 times 1,200. You would then receive $100 each month for the first year, $102 each month for the second year and so on.

Years of Income	Inflation indexing = 2% Average Annual Investment Return				Inflation Indexing = 3% Average Annual Investment Return			
	4%	6%	8%	10%	4%	6%	8%	10%
1	0.982	0.974	0.966	0.958	0.982	0.974	0.966	0.958
2	1.946	1.911	1.878	1.846	1.955	1.920	1.886	1.854
3	2.890	2.812	2.739	2.669	2.918	2.839	2.765	2.694
4	3.817	3.680	3.552	3.432	3.873	3.733	3.602	3.480
5	4.726	4.515	4.320	4.140	4.818	4.601	4.401	4.216
6	5.617	5.318	5.046	4.797	5.754	5.445	5.163	4.906
7	6.492	6.092	5.731	5.406	6.681	6.264	5.889	5.551
8	7.349	6.835	6.378	5.970	7.599	7.061	6.582	6.155
9	8.190	7.551	6.990	6.494	8.508	7.835	7.243	6.721
10	9.015	8.240	7.567	6.979	9.408	8.587	7.873	7.251
15	12.906	11.313	10.006	8.925	13.782	12.040	10.613	9.436
20	16.438	13.849	11.839	10.259	17.950	15.031	12.775	11.008
25	19.643	15.941	13.217	11.173	21.921	17.622	14.480	12.140
30	22.552	17.667	14.252	11.800	25.705	19.866	15.826	12.955
35	25.191	19.091	15.029	12.230	29.310	21.811	16.887	13.541
40	27.586	20.266	15.614	12.525	32.746	23.495	17.725	13.964
45	29.760	21.235	16.053	12.727	36.019	24.954	18.386	14.268
50	31.732	22.035	16.383	12.865	39.138	26.218	18.907	14.486

Table B: Inflation Factors & Growth Factors

The inflation columns show how much it would take in the future to buy goods and serv-ices that cost $1 today. After five years of 2% inflation an item now priced at $1 would cost just over $1.10 and one priced at $150 would cost $165.60—that's 1.104 times $150.

The investment return columns show the future value of $1 compounding annually at the specified return. For example, $1 invested for five years at 8% would be worth just under $1.47. So $675 invested for five years at 8% would grow to $991.58—that's 1.469 times $675.

After Year	Average Inflation		Average Annual Investment Return			
	2%	3%	4%	6%	8%	10%
1	1.020	1.030	1.040	1.060	1.080	1.100
2	1.040	1.061	1.082	1.124	1.166	1.210
3	1.061	1.093	1.125	1.191	1.260	1.331
4	1.082	1.126	1.170	1.262	1.360	1.464
5	1.104	1.159	1.217	1.338	1.469	1.611
6	1.126	1.194	1.265	1.419	1.587	1.772
7	1.149	1.230	1.316	1.504	1.714	1.949
8	1.172	1.267	1.369	1.594	1.851	2.144
9	1.195	1.305	1.423	1.689	1.999	2.358
10	1.219	1.344	1.480	1.791	2.159	2.594
15	1.346	1.558	1.801	2.397	3.172	4.177
20	1.486	1.806	2.191	3.207	4.661	6.727
25	1.641	2.094	2.666	4.292	6.848	10.835
30	1.811	2.427	3.243	5.743	10.063	17.449
35	2.000	2.814	3.946	7.686	14.785	28.102
40	2.208	3.262	4.801	10.286	21.725	45.259
45	2.438	3.782	5.841	13.765	31.920	72.890
50	2.692	4.384	7.107	18.420	46.902	117.391

Table C: Discount Factors

Use this table to determine the present value of a future amount. Say you need $100,000 in 10 years and figure you can average an 8% annual investment return. What's that in today's dollars? Multiply the $100,000 by the factor .4632. The result—$46,320—is the value that must be invested today at 8% to have $100,000 after 10 years.

Years	Average Annual Investment Return			
	4%	6%	8%	10%
1	0.9615	0.9434	0.9259	0.9091
2	0.9246	0.8900	0.8573	0.8264
3	0.8890	0.8396	0.7938	0.7513
4	0.8548	0.7921	0.7350	0.6830
5	0.8219	0.7473	0.6806	0.6209
6	0.7903	0.7050	0.6302	0.5645
7	0.7599	0.6651	0.5835	0.5132
8	0.7307	0.6274	0.5403	0.4665
9	0.7026	0.5919	0.5002	0.4241
10	0.6756	0.5584	0.4632	0.3855
15	0.5553	0.4173	0.3152	0.2394
20	0.4564	0.3118	0.2145	0.1486

Table D: Accumulation Factors

Use this table if you wish to accumulate a sum over time by making a deposit at the start of each year. We've assumed that each year's deposit is increased by the chosen inflation rate. Suppose you wish to accumulate $100,000 over 25 years, assuming inflation averages 2% a year and your annual investment return averages 6%. Multiply $100,000 by the factor .0142. The result—$1,420—is the amount of your first deposit. The next year's deposit would be 2% higher, or $1,448 and so on.

Years of Income	Inflation Indexing = 2% Average Annual Investment Return				Inflation Indexing = 3% Average Annual Investment Return			
	4%	6%	8%	10%	4%	6%	8%	10%
1	0.9615	0.9434	0.9259	0.9091	0.9615	0.9434	0.9259	0.9091
2	0.4668	0.4536	0.4409	0.4288	0.4645	0.4514	0.4388	0.4268
3	0.3021	0.2907	0.2799	0.2696	0.2992	0.2879	0.2772	0.2671
4	0.2200	0.2096	0.1998	0.1906	0.2168	0.2066	0.1970	0.1879
5	0.1708	0.1612	0.1521	0.1436	0.1676	0.1582	0.1493	0.1410
6	0.1382	0.1291	0.1206	0.1127	0.1349	0.1261	0.1179	0.1102
7	0.1150	0.1063	0.0983	0.0909	0.1117	0.1034	0.0957	0.0885
8	0.0977	0.0894	0.0818	0.0748	0.0945	0.0865	0.0793	0.0726
9	0.0843	0.0763	0.0691	0.0625	0.0811	0.0736	0.0667	0.0604
10	0.0736	0.0660	0.0591	0.0529	0.0705	0.0633	0.0568	0.0509
15	0.0423	0.0359	0.0304	0.0257	0.0396	0.0337	0.0287	0.0243
20	0.0273	0.0219	0.0175	0.0139	0.0250	0.0202	0.0162	0.0129
25	0.0188	0.0142	0.0107	0.0079	0.0168	0.0129	0.0097	0.0073
30	0.0134	0.0096	0.0067	0.0047	0.0118	0.0085	0.0061	0.0042
35	0.0099	0.0066	0.0043	0.0028	0.0085	0.0058	0.0039	0.0025
40	0.0074	0.0047	0.0028	0.0017	0.0062	0.0040	0.0025	0.0015

The Real Nitty Gritty

We hope that if you made it through Part One of this book you now have a pretty good understanding of how the retirement savings system works and where you fit in. Part Two is for members of Registered Pension Plans (RPPs). Think of it as an owner's manual. Issue by issue, we're going to tell you what you need to know to understand how your particular plan works and how well it meets your needs. For example, do you know:

• How early you can retire and how much your pension would be?

• What happens if you change jobs and leave the plan before retirement age?

• What happens if your marriage breaks up?

• What happens if you become disabled—or die?

Pleasant thoughts, eh? If you don't want to think about that, think about this: it's not uncommon for 50-year-old members of defined benefit pension plans to find that their pension credits are worth more than any other family asset, even their home.

Who Makes the Rules?

Pension plans have layers and layers of rules. Most are aimed at protecting plan members. Some protect the plan sponsor. Others protect taxpayers in general by limiting the tax sheltering each plan and its members get.

If your workplace is unionized, the pension plan most likely resulted from bargaining between your union and the employer. If your workplace is not unionized, the employer set the terms and conditions, perhaps with employee input. Either way, government officials got involved too. Lots of them.

Pension plans face two kinds of regulation. First, there are minimum standards for the plan's benefits as well as controls on its operation. This is primarily a provincial responsibility, although the federal Pension Benefits Standards Act governs certain plans; see the accompanying box.

When Ottawa Calls the Shots

Federal legislation governs private sector pension plans in certain industries:

- Banks
- Railways
- Airlines
- Shipping
- Broadcasting
- Telecommunications

As might be expected, federal legislation also governs plans for federal employees and those in federal Crown corporations. As well, it covers public and private sector pension plan members in Yukon, the Northwest Territories and Nunavut.

Each province has its own legislation. Unfortunately, these laws—summarized in Appendix B—vary. In the 1980s, regulators tried, but failed, to standardize them.

Pension industry organizations keep pressing for uniformity. That would save employers and unions a lot of time, money and effort, but the provinces keep finding reasons to go their own ways. This is, after all, Canada.

Ready for a challenge? Suppose you live in Saskatchewan and work in Manitoba for a manufacturing company based in Ontario. Which provincial pension act covers you? Generally, Manitoba's; it's based on where you're employed. Which province ensures the plan is operating properly? That might be Ontario, or Manitoba or any one of the others. Huh? Each plan is registered with one province, the one where the greatest number of plan members are employed. Under a reciprocal agreement, the pension regulators in that province enforce the rules covering all plan members wherever they work. Compare this checkerboard to the United States, where there's just one national pension act and regulator for everyone. Not in Canada, you say? Pity.

The second form of regulation was discussed in Chapter 5, which dealt with the tax sheltering for retirement savings. The federal *Income Tax Act* controls the government's short-term revenue loss on those tax breaks by limiting how generous pension plans can be. Naturally, these rules play a big role in every plan's design. And naturally there's even more complexity; the federal tax rules involve two bureaucracies. The Finance Department writes the rules while the Canada Customs and Revenue Agency—CCRA—interprets and enforces them.

What the Heck Does "Registered" Mean?

Registered Pension Plan... *Registered* Retirement Savings Plan... *Registered* Education Savings Plan. In each case, the R-word means the plan has been registered with the Canada Customs and Revenue Agency. CCRA registers the plan only after officials determine that its terms and conditions comply with the income tax rules. This registration can be revoked if a plan goes offside. The plan then loses its favourable tax treatment.

WHERE DO YOU FIND THE RULES?

Your employer must provide a written description of the plan within 30 to 60 days of your hiring or before you become eligible for the plan. This pension plan booklet is usually called—ready?—the pension plan booklet. But it's often combined with information about your other perks into one employee handbook. Remember the benefits booklet you got when you were hired? That's it. Many organizations also have employee web sites where you can download the material.

Whatever the form, the information given to you must include an explanation of the plan provisions together with a summary of your rights and any obligations you have under the plan.

If you want to go beyond your employer's summary, you are entitled to inspect a copy of the actual plan and any amendments. That's the ultimate authority, but it's filled with dense legalese and could easily run 100 pages. You can also be charged a reasonable fee for photocopying if you want your own copy. Still interested? Ask your employer or the pension plan's administrator. If they don't provide the material, contact the regulator for the jurisdiction in which the plan is registered—see Appendix D.

What Information Can You Get from the Regulator?

Your pension plan's regulator maintains extensive files on the plan's design and operation. The information you can get includes:

- Current plan text and any amendments

- Provisions of any predecessor plan

- Details of employer/administrator responsibilities

- Annual information returns

- Financial statements

- Correspondence between administrator and regulator

- Statement of investment policy and procedures/goals

- Actuarial report

Before contacting the regulator, request this material directly from your employer or the plan's administrator. You'll likely get it sooner.

ANNUAL PENSION STATEMENT

As an active member, you must be provided with a written statement every year that contains information about the pension plan and your personal benefits. You should also get a similar statement when you leave the plan at or before retirement.

What are you supposed to do with that statement? Let's go through one issued for Noah Answer, who works on the computer support help desk at Integrated Widgets.

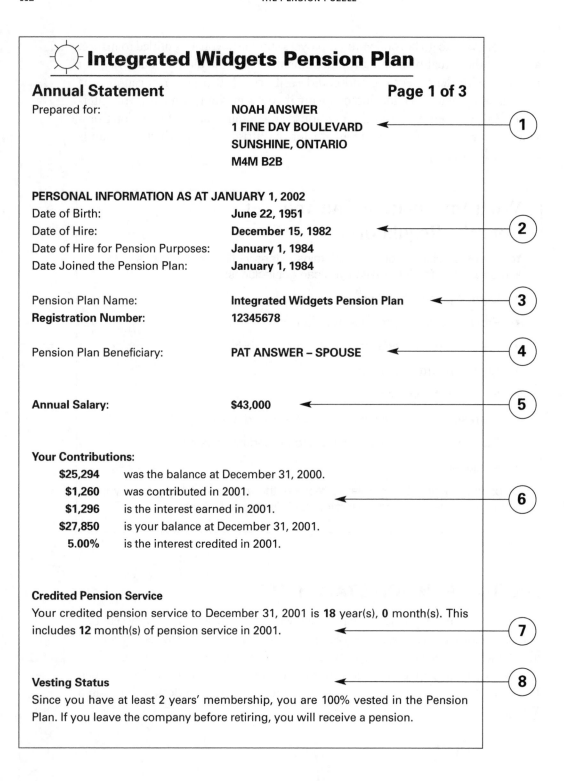

☼ Integrated Widgets Pension Plan

Annual Statement   Page 1 of 3

Prepared for: NOAH ANSWER ①
                                 1 FINE DAY BOULEVARD
                                 SUNSHINE, ONTARIO
                                 M4M B2B

PERSONAL INFORMATION AS AT JANUARY 1, 2002

Date of Birth:	**June 22, 1951**
Date of Hire:	**December 15, 1982** ②
Date of Hire for Pension Purposes:	**January 1, 1984**
Date Joined the Pension Plan:	**January 1, 1984**

Pension Plan Name: **Integrated Widgets Pension Plan** ③
Registration Number: 12345678

Pension Plan Beneficiary: **PAT ANSWER – SPOUSE** ④

Annual Salary: $43,000 ⑤

Your Contributions:

$25,294	was the balance at December 31, 2000.
$1,260	was contributed in 2001.
$1,296	is the interest earned in 2001. ⑥
$27,850	is your balance at December 31, 2001.
5.00%	is the interest credited in 2001.

Credited Pension Service

Your credited pension service to December 31, 2001 is **18** year(s), **0** month(s). This
includes **12** month(s) of pension service in 2001. ⑦

Vesting Status ⑧

Since you have at least 2 years' membership, you are 100% vested in the Pension
Plan. If you leave the company before retiring, you will receive a pension.

1. Your statement is usually sent to your home address to prevent the risk of a co-worker accidentally seeing your personal information.

2. The date of birth and date of hire are shown as they appear in the plan administrator's records. They're used to calculate the pension due at retirement, so make sure they're correct. Why does Noah have a different Date of Hire for Pension Purposes? The IW plan has a one-year waiting period. Noah joined on the first day of the month after his waiting period ended.

3. You'll need the plan's official name and registration number if you ever have reason to contact the provincial or federal pension regulator.

4. Noah was single when he joined the plan and named his mother as beneficiary. When he married Pat, he made her his beneficiary. Make sure you update your beneficiary designations for any change in your family or marital status.

5. Noah checks the salary and notes that it includes his latest increase. If your statement does not include your latest increase, check the statement's date of issue before getting upset. Your raise might have come through after the pension plan ended its fiscal year. Make a note to check that next year.

6. Noah files each pension statement with his other financial information for the year. That way, he can make sure the ending balance for one year matches the starting balance for the next. He can also verify the contribution amount shown by comparing it to his T4 tax slip or pay stubs. The interest rate is about the same as he has been getting on his GICs, so he figures it's okay.

7. The plan gives service credits from the date of joining. Noah has accrued 18 years of credits to January 1, 2002. At Normal Retirement Date—the first day of the month following his sixty-fifth birthday—Noah will have 32.5 years of credits. He might even have 33.5 based on talk that the plan might be amended to count the one-year waiting period.

8. Noah is fully vested so he's entitled to a deferred pension if he leaves the plan before retirement. What's a deferred pension? That means the pension he's due can't start until the plan's early retirement date even though he left the plan long before then. Suppose Noah will be due $1,000 a month starting in 20 years. The transfer value that he can take from the plan now represents the amount that must be invested today to be able to pay that pension 20 years from now. Before he was fully vested, Noah's statements showed the date at which vesting would occur. Some employers have two vesting dates, one for credits earned under current legislation and one for credits earned before then.

9. The IW plan provides for normal retirement at age 65, specifically on the first day of the month following the sixty-fifth birthday. Noah was born June 22, 1951, so his normal retirement date is July 1, 2016.

10. The next few lines deal with calculation of pension benefits, so Noah digs out his pension booklet from his financial folder and reads the section on normal retirement benefits. IW has a combination plan. The defined benefit portion will pay Noah a monthly pension of 1% of his final average monthly earnings for each

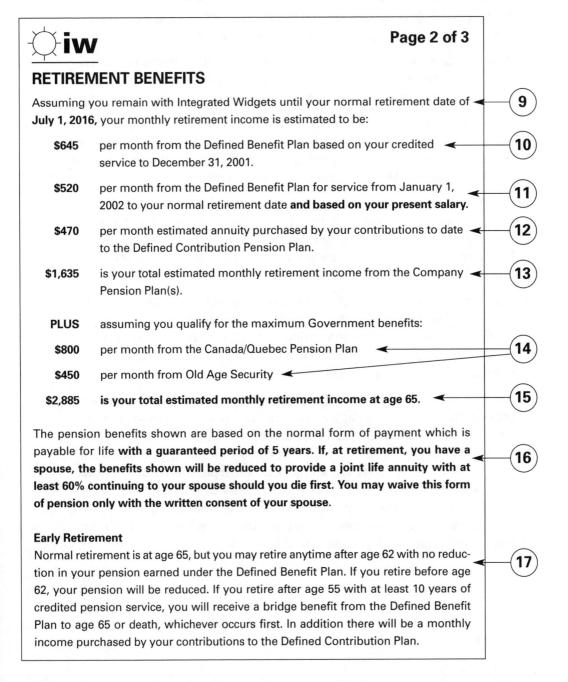

year of credited service. He now has 18 years of credits, so his pension earned is: 1% x 18 x $43,000. That's $7,740 per year or $645 monthly. Noah's golf buddy, Peter, is in a plan with a more complex formula and finds it very difficult to check his pension statement. He keeps complaining that his company should simplify the plan or provide information that employees can understand.

11. If Noah stays with IW until age 65, he will add 14.5 pension service credits to his total and earn a further $520 monthly pension. As with the pension calculation above, this assumes no salary changes before retirement.

12. Noah makes a 3% contribution to the Defined Contribution Plan, the other part of IW's combination plan. IW does not match this contribution. They fund the defined benefit plan while Noah funds the DC plan. At retirement Noah can elect to buy a pension with his accumulated contributions. The plan actuary estimates this pension will amount to $470 monthly. Use such estimates cautiously. They rest on two assumptions that may not pan out. One is for the future investment earnings on the contributions to date. The other is for annuity purchase rates 14 years away. Also note that this estimate does not include the additional pension that can be bought with future contributions.

13. Noah's estimated pension from the company plan totals $1,635 monthly. This is a conservative estimate. It does not factor in any salary increases, which would boost the defined benefit pension and increase his DC contributions. Nor does it include the additional pension he can buy with his future DC contributions.

14. The IW plan is not integrated with C/QPP or OAS. So these are the estimated government benefits Noah will receive on top of his pension. Since Noah's earnings exceed the YMPE, the statement assumes he'll qualify for the maximum C/QPP retirement pension. Noah's better off checking the annual CPP statement he gets from the government since the IW estimate does not reflect Noah's earnings at his previous employers. IW also assumes Noah will be due a maximum OAS pension.

15. Noah figures out that his IW pension and government benefits will replace 80% of his $43,000 salary. That's if he works until 65. That beats his 70% target replacement ratio without even counting his RRSP and some other savings. So early retirement is quite possible.

16. Noah reads the section on the 60% survivor pension and makes a note to call the plan administrator and ask how much the reduction would be to guarantee a 60% survivor's pension for his spouse. These guarantees are discussed in Chapter 17.

17. The IW plan allows retirement at age 62 with no actuarial reduction. Noah plans to take advantage of this. His RRSP will make up for the three years of pension accruals he'll forego. His DC contributions will buy less monthly pension at 62 than at 65, but this statement does not include the further contributions he'll make between now and retirement.

18. The IW plan provides that Noah's beneficiaries will share the value of his accumulated DC plan contributions on his death. That amounts to $27,850 so far. The plan will also pay to Pat—if she survives Noah and is still his spouse—a lump sum equal to the value of his DB pension. She can take that in cash or use it to buy a pension.

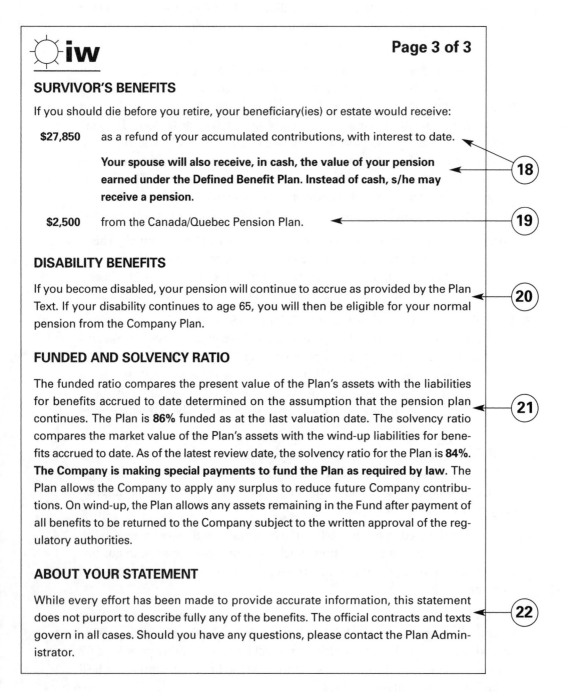

iw   **Page 3 of 3**

SURVIVOR'S BENEFITS

If you should die before you retire, your beneficiary(ies) or estate would receive:

$27,850 as a refund of your accumulated contributions, with interest to date. ◄

Your spouse will also receive, in cash, the value of your pension earned under the Defined Benefit Plan. Instead of cash, s/he may receive a pension. ◄   (18)

$2,500 from the Canada/Quebec Pension Plan. ◄   (19)

DISABILITY BENEFITS

If you become disabled, your pension will continue to accrue as provided by the Plan Text. If your disability continues to age 65, you will then be eligible for your normal pension from the Company Plan. ◄   (20)

FUNDED AND SOLVENCY RATIO

The funded ratio compares the present value of the Plan's assets with the liabilities for benefits accrued to date determined on the assumption that the pension plan continues. The Plan is **86%** funded as at the last valuation date. The solvency ratio compares the market value of the Plan's assets with the wind-up liabilities for benefits accrued to date. As of the latest review date, the solvency ratio for the Plan is **84%**. **The Company is making special payments to fund the Plan as required by law.** The Plan allows the Company to apply any surplus to reduce future Company contributions. On wind-up, the Plan allows any assets remaining in the Fund after payment of all benefits to be returned to the Company subject to the written approval of the regulatory authorities. ◄   (21)

ABOUT YOUR STATEMENT

While every effort has been made to provide accurate information, this statement does not purport to describe fully any of the benefits. The official contracts and texts govern in all cases. Should you have any questions, please contact the Plan Administrator. ◄   (22)

19. Noah's survivors would also be entitled to the standard $2,500 death benefit from C/QPP.

20. Noah doesn't care to think about becoming disabled, but in that eventuality the company long-term disability plan would pay him a benefit until he reaches age 65—and he would continue to build pension credits. The pension would then kick in at 65.

21. This section might give you peace of mind—or some sleepless nights. It summarizes how well the plan is funded and the degree to which it could meet its liabilities if it were wound up now. See Appendix E. IW's plan was fully funded until it began offering unreduced pensions at 62. Noah has noticed that the ratios have been creeping back up in recent years. While not concerned about the current ratios, he looks forward to the day when they'll again be 100%.

22. Okay, here's the fine print. Noah has never bothered to read the official plan text. But he does keep his pension booklet in a file and refers to it from time to time. That and the annual pension statement should keep him reasonably well informed.

CHAPTER TEN

When Can You Join the Plan— and Who Pays How Much?

Employers are allowed to segment their employees and have a separate pension plan for each class. But everyone in that class must be treated equally. For example, there might be one plan for unionized workers and another for non-union staff. Employees who are paid hourly wages might have a different plan from those on straight salary. There might be separate plans for supervisors and managers and yet another plan for the "shop floor" employees who really do the work. (Just kidding!) Executives often have their own plan.

FULL-TIME VERSUS PART-TIME

Is there a pension plan for your class of employee? If so, are you a full-timer? If you are, you must have the option of joining the plan as soon as you have completed two years of continuous employment.

What if you're a part-time employee? Your pension plan eligibility might be based on earnings or hours worked. Pension legislation limits how onerous these conditions can be. But the rules vary among jurisdictions; see Appendix B. For example, suppose you fall under Ontario's legislation. You're eligible for pension plan membership if in each of the past two calendar years you earned at least 35% of the average national wage as measured by Statistics Canada's year's maximum pensionable earnings (YMPE). If you haven't earned that much, you're still eligible if you worked at least 700 hours in each year.

Some employers have separate pension plans for part-timers. In that case, the benefits must be comparable to those provided for full-time employees.

MANDATORY VERSUS OPTIONAL PLANS

Your employer can make pension plan membership mandatory or optional. Many employers make their plans mandatory because many employees—especially younger ones—don't recognize the value of long-term growth and resist the idea of making pension contributions. The employers thus fear these people won't join an optional plan until it's too late to accumulate a reasonable amount of pension. In that case, the soon-to-be-retired employee might accuse the employer of not having made the offer clear enough. With a mandatory plan, the employer ensures that everyone puts away something for retirement.

If your employer does offer an optional plan and you elect not to join, you will probably be asked to sign a statement acknowledging that the option was fully explained before you made your decision. Note that opting out need not be a one-time decision. Generally, pension legislation requires that employees be allowed to join an optional plan at a later date if they passed it up when they first became eligible. Verify this with your employer or the plan's regulator.

SHOULD YOU JOIN THE PLAN IF IT'S OPTIONAL?

Much of this comes down to whether you're a spender or a saver.

If you're a heavy-duty spender, join the plan. It will impose some savings discipline and might be the only way you can put aside money for retirement. If you're under 40, retirement may seem too far off to worry about. The reality, though, is that it creeps up on you—and by the time you recognize the importance of retirement saving, it may well be too late to accumulate what you'll need.

If you're not a heavy-duty spender, do you have the discipline to make fair-sized RRSP contributions? If so, do you have the ability to prudently manage that money? If you feel you do, decide what you consider a reasonable target return and then check how your investments to date have actually performed. Appreciate that the 1980s and '90s produced unusually high returns. If you do have the discipline to adequately fund your RRSP and the ability to prudently manage it, consider these points:

- If the employer matches your RPP contribution, you have an immediate return on your investment. You would hardly turn down a pay raise, so why turn down an offer of a pension contribution?

- RPP contributions produce tax deductions sooner than RRSP contributions. That's because RRSP limits work on a one-year lag as explained in Chapter 5.

- Your RPP is protected from your creditors except for spousal claims on marital breakdown. Most RRSPs are not creditor-proof, as discussed in Chapter 6.

- If you go the RRSP route, recognize that you should put in more than the contributions you would otherwise make to the pension plan. You have to cover the employer's pension contributions that are forgone as well as your own.

- Is the pension plan a defined benefit one? If so, see if you can join later and use your RRSP stash to buy past-service credits. Today you may not need or want the security of a DB pension, but your views might change as you age—especially if you find you want to stay with that organization and the DB plan provides a generous early retirement option. Ask to what extent those past-service credits contain employer funding. If you can buy past-service credits later with a full employer match and if you are confident you can do a decent job of building your own RRSP in the meantime, opting out becomes a neutral to positive choice.

- Is the pension plan a defined contribution one? Be aware that if you later go to buy past-service credits, tax rules will probably prevent your employer from matching your past-service contributions.

- How long do you expect to stay with the employer? Defined benefit pension plans are really designed for those who put in long service. Job-hoppers can do as well, or better, on their own provided they really do make adequate RRSP contributions and generate decent returns. The big question, though, is why do you see yourself as a job-hopper? Assuming your current employer wants a long-term workforce, have you really checked out the mobility and advancement opportunities it offers?

WHO PAYS?
Defined Contribution Plans

As the name suggests, the contributions for a defined contribution plan are determined by a formula. There's always an employer contribution. There is usually, but need not be, a contribution from the employee. The employee's contribution might be a fixed or a varying amount. Typically the employer matches the employee's contribution in whole or part. Note, though, that the employer does not have to pay 50% of the cost of the ultimate pension benefits as it would in a defined benefit plan.

- Hamida contributes 3% of her pay and her employer matches that in full. So she's effectively socking away 6% of what she earns.

- At Werner's company, the employees each set their own contribution rate—as little as 1% of pay and as much as 5%. The company pays a 50% match. Werner set his rate for this year at 3% so his employer will kick in another 1.5% for a total contribution of 4.5%.

- Roger's firm has a non-contributory plan. The company contributes 3% of each employee's pay; the employee puts in nothing.

Defined Benefit Plans

As with a defined contribution plan, the employer must contribute. But this contribution is not a fixed amount. It's whatever is needed to ensure that the promised benefit gets paid. There is generally no requirement that a DB plan sponsor contribute each year—only that contributions are made promptly when needed.

A "contributory" DB plan requires contributions by employees. Much is made of the fact that public sector plans are typically more generous than private sector plans. A big part of the reason is that public sector employees typically make much higher contributions.

A "non-contributory" plan does not require employee contributions; the employer pays the full cost. Non-contributory plans are very common in the private sector. During the growth period of the 1980s many companies took plans that were contributory and made them non-contributory. One reason was that tax rules at the time allowed members of non-contributory DB plans to double-dip. The rules reduced RRSP contribution limits for pension plan members only by the amount they put into the pension plan. If the employer paid the full shot, the employees got no RRSP reduction.

Another reason is that many employers decided to pay the full cost themselves because their employees had grown unhappy with their DB plans. When these plans were created—before inflation took off in the '70s—the contribution rates were often set so that the employer and employee shared the cost equally. But inflation brought high returns. That reduced the plan's overall cost. Many employers responded by reducing the contribution rates for their employees and boosting the interest rates credited on their money. But many employers did not; they reduced or eliminated only their own contributions.

That one-sided approach prompted two key changes in pension standards legislation. First, the legislation now almost universally requires that interest credits be based on either the pension fund's rate of return or on the rates that banks pay on five-year term deposits. The plan can no longer use a fixed return set arbitrarily low. Second, there's a rule that the employer must pay at least half of the cost of the defined benefit. That's not half the value of any one year's contributions, but rather half the value of the benefits as they are about to be paid out. If the employee contributions with interest turn out to have funded more than half of the benefit, the excess must be credited to the employee. This generally can be done by buying extra pension or refunding the money.

So how does the boss decide how much employees pay for a contributory plan?

Generally, private sector employees in final average DB plans contribute about 4% of their pay. Why 4%? That's a rule-of-thumb that came into use many years ago as actuaries concluded that, over time, the funding for a typical DB pension should work out to be 8% of pay. Employers felt it was fair to share that cost, so they set the employee charge at 4%. From time to time, employers have found that at 4% their employees were not paying enough, but they frequently decided it was easier to leave the rate intact and cover the shortfall themselves than to explain why the workers should have to pay more.

Public sector employees typically pay more than 4% for their typically more generous plans. But there's a trend emerging in which governments are sharing control of those plans with their employees' unions. That makes it easier for the unions to win improvements when times are good, but also means their members now share the investment risk that was previously borne entirely by the employer. So, over time, we may see those workers' contribution rates periodically go up as well as down.

Tax rules limit how much employees can be required to contribute to both defined benefit and defined contribution plans. The DC limits are similar to those for RRSPs—see Chapter 5. The DB limit is 9% of pensionable earnings up to a dollar amount that depends on how the plan determines your pension. The dollar cap is rather arcane; if you really want to know what it is for your plan, ask your plan administrator.

The employee contribution rate for a career average plan will typically be lower than for a final average plan. That's because the total cost is likely to be lower unless the plan is updated regularly.

Flat benefit plans are usually funded entirely by the employer.

PAST SERVICE CONTRIBUTIONS

One day you might open your mail and find a letter from your pension plan stating that by a certain date you have the opportunity to buy a certain amount of past service credits. In effect, you get to make a contribution beyond what you're normally allowed. Those credits might be based on service with your current employer a long time ago or even with a former employer. They might relate to periods of pregnancy or parental leave. The issue is not why you're getting this offer, but whether you should take advantage of it. Here are the key questions:

- In dollars and cents, how much will this increase my monthly pension?

- To what extent is my employer sharing the cost of this benefit? Your employer is most likely paying at least 50%, but verify that with the plan administrator. If so, exercising the buy back means you're getting $1 for 50¢. That's an immediate return that's hard to turn down.

- To what extent does it mean I can retire earlier? Suppose you're 50 years old and have 20 years of credit in a plan where you're eligible for an unreduced pension when age plus service equal 80. You're now at 70 so freedom is five years away. Suppose you're offered a past service buy-back for seven years. That would boost your credited service to 27 years so, overnight, you advance to an age-plus-service factor of 77. You're then just three points—one and half years—away from freedom.

All of this sounds great, but where will you get the money to cover your share of the cost? The tax man will help. How much will depend on whether that service applies to years before 1990 or after 1989.

- **Pre-1990 service:** Your cost is tax-deductible, though not necessarily all in one year. You might have to spread your claim over several years and each claim might be capped at or below $3,500. The rules are so complex that you should have a good accountant do your tax return. Significantly, this deduction does not affect your RRSP contribution room. So, you're best off using unsheltered money in order to get those extra tax deductions.

- **Post-1989 service:** This is a good news-bad news story. The good news is that your contribution is fully deductible for the year you make it. The bad news is that the buy-back will generate a past service pension adjustment that will affect your RRSP room, as discussed in Chapter 5. That's no problem if you have unused RRSP room that equals or exceeds the cost of the buy back. You buy your pension credits, claim your tax deduction and lose RRSP room you weren't using anyway. If you don't have enough unused RRSP room, you'll have to remove money from your RRSP to make space in your overall tax shelter for the pension purchase. But that's no problem. Simply transfer that RRSP money to your pension plan and then use it to pay for your buy-back. In this case, you would not get a new tax deduction but you wouldn't lose the one you previously got when you made the RRSP contributions. That's because no tax applies to direct transfers between an RRSP and an RPP. This little dance keeps you neutral in terms of tax breaks, but there's now more money set aside on your behalf because the new pension credits include some employer funding.

We once explained this to a friend who had trouble understanding the significance of getting $1 in pension value for 50¢. She really wanted to put spare money into her RRSP. "If I put the money into my RRSP, I get a tax deduction; isn't that the same?" she asked. No. If you put 50¢ into your RRSP, you'll have 50¢ set aside plus perhaps 25¢ in a tax refund. The pension contribution is deductible just like the RRSP. So if you put 50¢ into the pension plan, you'll have your own 50¢ set aside, plus some amount from your employer—perhaps 50¢—set aside, plus 25¢ or so in a tax refund.

What Happens to the Money?

How do I know my pension money is safe?

How do I know it will still be there when I retire?

How do I know I'll get the pension I have been promised?

All good questions. There are a number of safeguards to protect your retirement savings. Some are controls which put limitations on how the pension plan is administered and the money is handled. Others are disclosure requirements that enable the regulator and plan members to see what's going on.

The key safeguards are that only certain types of people can handle pension money, they must follow clear rules and, except for some government employee plans, the money must be kept separate from the employer's own funds. Generally, your employer must remit any contributions deducted from your pay within 30 days of the end of the month. There are also promptness standards for the employer's contributions.

THE F-WORD: FIDUCIARY

The people and organizations involved in running pension plans are "fiduciaries." That's a legal term. It means they are in a position of trust and are obligated to act in the best interests of those who rely on them—in this case, the pension plan's members and their survivors. Significantly, fiduciaries must not allow their personal interests to interfere with the interests of those they serve. All parties involved in the investment of pension funds are required to follow a "prudent person" rule. This means they must take the same care, and apply the same diligence and skill, that would be expected of a normally prudent person who was looking after the property of someone else. Those with professional qualifications must apply their skills. If they don't, they risk fines and even jail sentences. Your plan has three key fiduciaries:

- **Plan Administrator:** Somebody must be ultimately responsible for the plan's management. In the private sector, that's usually the employer, or actually its board of directors. The board usually creates a pension committee, consisting of a few directors, some of the company's management and perhaps some representatives of the plan members. In the public sector, ultimate responsibility usually lies with the sponsoring government or a body appointed for that purpose. Some private and public plans have shared management; the employer(s) and union form a joint board. Whatever the setup, the actual day-to-day work is done by hired staff or contracted out, but it's the corporate directors, union officers or sponsoring government who are ultimately liable if the work is not done properly.

Don't Confuse the Administrator with the Administrator!

Your colleagues and employer may refer to the "administrator" when talking about the person who does pension calculations, sends out statements and answers your questions. Staff or outside professionals such as actuaries, lawyers, accountants and benefit consultants may be hired to administer the plan, but they do not have ultimate responsibility for it. In effect, the Administrator can delegate day-to-day tasks to these administrators, but not the ultimate responsibility.

- **Trustee/custodian:** Every private sector pension fund must have a custodian to ensure the money is kept separate from the sponsoring employer's money and is only used for pensions. It also keeps the pension fund intact and protected from corporate creditors in case the sponsoring employer or union fails. The custodian is usually an insurance company or trust company. In addition to holding the money, the custodian is supposed to check that any transfer requested by the Administrator, administrators or investment manager(s) complies with the plan's rules and governing legislation.

- **Investment manager:** In a defined contribution plan, each member normally gets to make his or her own investment decisions from a menu of options. Those options are likely set by the staff and consultants who oversee the plan, but the ultimate responsibility lies with the Administrator. Note that the Administrator and his or her administrators have a duty to ensure that the investment managers on the list are above board. But they carry no responsibility for the performance of the investments you pick.

Defined benefit plans are quite different. Again, the Administrator is ultimately responsible, but the actual investment decisions are centralized. The Administrator's pension committee must prepare a written policy setting out how the funds are to be invested by professional money managers.

This policy, required by pension law, is detailed in a document called a Statement of Investment Policies and Goals (SIP&G) or Statement of Investment Polices and Practices (SIP&P). It sets out rules for dividing the fund's money among stocks, bonds and other assets.

The document also sets standards for how the managers select individual securities and may restrict or prohibit the fund from making certain investments. In recent years several unions and social groups have urged pension funds to embrace "ethical" or "socially responsible" investing. These mandates typically rule out certain companies because of what they produce or their records on environmental matters, labour relations or human rights.

There is also an emerging trend in which some pension funds use their clout as large investors to press for change in the companies whose shares they hold. Some huge funds could wield enormous power, but most take a fairly passive stance on voting their shares.

The SIP&G or SIP&P must be updated regularly and, in some jurisdictions, filed with the regulator. The document must be made available to plan members who request it.

Should You Care about Your Plan's Returns?

Some defined benefit pension plans go to great lengths to inform their members about the fund's investments and performance. It may be nice to know what your pension fund holds and how it's doing, but that's largely irrelevant to your financial game plan. That's because your employer is responsible for ensuring the plan can pay the benefits promised. The fund's returns might, however, be very relevant if the plan's rules provide for members to benefit from a surplus, usually through enhanced benefits or reduced contributions.

Your plan's target investment return might seem quite low. Remember that this is normally expressed as a "real" return—the return above inflation.

Do you find your plan's managers too stodgy? Be aware that, unlike mutual fund managers, pension fund managers rarely try for eye-popping returns. They're more interested in doing a bit better than the fund's target while keeping volatility within a range the sponsor finds acceptable.

Do you find your plan's managers too daring? The pension fund has a different risk profile than you do. Its liabilities are spread over many people and a much longer timeframe. The managers can also count on a continuing flow of contributions.

PENSION FUND AUDIT

A pension fund must prepare an annual financial statement and file it with the plan's regulator, usually within six months of the plan's fiscal year-end. This statement includes details of the investments, the fund's net assets and a reconciliation of the changes that occurred during the year. If the fund is above a certain size, usually $3 to $5 million, it must include an auditor's report. Copies of the financial statements must be made available to plan members who request them.

HOW DO YOU KNOW YOU'LL GET THE PENSION YOU'VE BEEN PROMISED?

First, have you really been promised a pension? If you're in a defined contribution plan, your employer promised to make contributions on a regular basis, but has made absolutely no promise about your level of retirement income. That retirement income will depend heavily on how well the money is invested—usually by you—and on annuity rates preceding your retirement date.

If you're in a defined benefit plan, your employer has indeed promised you a pension. At least every three years an actuary must determine the plan's current financial status and project the funding required to meet future liabilities. This actuarial report is then filed with the pension plan's regulator. You're entitled to a copy if you want one. Basically, the actuary gives the plan the equivalent of a medical check-up. In Appendix E we summarize this process and tell you what to look for in the actuarial report.

WHO OWNS THE SURPLUS?

This doesn't affect you if you're in a defined contribution plan because you have an individual account and, subject to the plan's vesting rules, whatever's in it is yours. Defined benefit plans have no individual accounts; there's one pool of money to cover all members and the plan sponsor is responsible for ensuring that pool is large enough to pay the promised benefits as they come due. These plans often find themselves with a surplus because they've done better than expected, and surplus ownership has become a big—and contentious—issue for the sponsors and their members.

Before we get into the question of who owns a DB surplus, it's important to understand what that surplus is. Suppose a plan has $10 million in assets and $9 million in liabilities, the present value of the benefits already promised for payment in the future. The assets exceed the liabilities by $1 million so there's a $1 million surplus. Had the numbers gone the other way, there would have been a $1 million deficit. Odds are that a DB plan will always have a surplus or deficit since it's unlikely that the assets would precisely match the liabilities.

Now, a key point that many people miss: A surplus does not necessarily mean there's extra money in the bank and a deficit does not necessarily mean there's a bill collector pounding on the door. You can't really tell if there's a surplus unless a plan is wound up and all benefits paid. Until then, all you have is an estimate, which depends on a lot of assumptions:

- The ages at which the plan members will retire and the number of years for which they will draw pensions

- The number of members who will change employers or die before retirement age

- The rates at which earnings will increase in future years if the pensions are based on final average earnings

- The future return on the invested assets

Two actuaries valuing the same plan may quite reasonably use different assumptions and therefore arrive at different liability calculations. Even with high-powered computers, this is still largely an exercise in judgment.

The actuary who does the calculations thus strives to minimize the margin of error, not to be precisely correct. Because the security of benefits is paramount, he or she will first arrive at a set of "best estimate" assumptions and then build in margins for conservatism. For example, if the actuary feels the fund's average long-term return will be 7%, the assumption used in the valuation might be 6.5% or even 6%. This reduces the risk that the fund will under-perform and increases the odds that it will do better than expected.

Since employers shoulder the burden if a DB fund under-performs, they feel they should benefit if it out-performs—all that matters to the employee is that he or she gets the pension that was promised. Also, tax rules prohibit employers from making contributions if the surplus is too big. Unions counter that pensions are really deferred wages so any surplus should benefit workers. You'd think this would have been settled and documented when the plan was created. Unfortunately, many older plans did not clearly spell out the options for using a surplus.

Although this surplus is just a snapshot that could easily change, employers and unions view it as real money and squabble over how it might be used. Sometimes they agree to share it. For example, when Eaton's was facing bankruptcy, employees agreed to let the company take $200 million in surplus while they got an equal amount. Ontario's teachers struck a deal with the provincial government that reduced employer contributions while teachers got access to enhanced early retirement benefits. There have also been examples of surplus being used to allow both employees and employers to take contribution holidays.

Often, though, the two sides can't agree. That has led to court case after court case as plan sponsors have attempted with more or less success to unilaterally remove surplus. There does seem to be a trend emerging, in that pension standards legislation now stipulates that employers cannot remove surplus unilaterally unless their right to do so is spelled out clearly in the plan documents. Pension plans that are terminated without surplus rights clearly spelled out in their documents now go through a process aimed at having both sides agree on surplus sharing before any distribution.

Partial Plan Wind-Ups

Ontario and Nova Scotia allow partial wind-ups (for example, a company closes just one factory and terminates just those employees). The pension plan is then deemed to have been split into two parts—one part for the departing workers and one part for those still employed elsewhere. The pension legislation requires any surplus at that time to be allocated between the two parts, but does not make clear whether the surplus allocated to the wound-up part should be divided among the departing employees. At first glance, you might think that would naturally be fair. But consider that such a distribution would create a bonus for those who are leaving, while reducing the cushion for those who are still in the plan. Later on the survivors might find their benefits have to be reduced if, for some reason, the remaining part of the plan gets wound up with a deficit.

Don't feel bad if you can't make up your mind in that quandary. Ontario's pension regulators and courts have been struggling with it for more than four years. The Monsanto case began when Ontario's pension regulator refused to accept a partial wind-up request from Monsanto Canada Inc. because there was no provision for surplus distribution. Monsanto appealed to the provincial Financial Services Tribunal, arguing the surplus could really be determined only if the entire plan was wound up. The company won, but the tribunal's ruling was then overturned by the Ontario Divisional Court. As we write this, Monsanto is waiting for the Ontario Court of Appeal to hear the case. The appeal court's judgment might come in mid-2002 and, if the Ontario government does not step in to change the rules, we would not be surprised if the losing side then tries to take it to the Supreme Court of Canada. Stay tuned!

CHAPTER TWELVE

When Can You Retire?

There are few times in life when your birth date really matters. When you get to drive. When you get to buy booze for the first time—legally. When you turn 30—and then 40—and then 50. And when it comes to your pension plan. Your plan will define three retirement dates:

- **Normal:** This is, well, the normal retirement age. Usually 65. That's the point at which you can stop work and collect the full pension you've earned. You do not need permission from your employer or the pension plan's administrator. Nor do you have to pass GO and collect $200.

- **Early:** This is the earliest point at which you can leave your job and collect a pension. Usually that's age 55 or 10 years before the normal retirement date. As discussed below, the pension you get might be reduced.

- **Postponed:** This covers people who want to keep working. Some love their work too much to leave. Others feel they can't afford to retire. Many pension plans provide for members to continue to accrue credits if they work past the normal retirement age. That means their pension will be higher when they do stop work. Effectively, you can delay your pension until the end of the year in which you turn 69. After that you face income tax—even if you don't draw benefits. Generally, tax and pension legislation prohibit you from collecting a pension and earning credits in the same plan at the same time. Quebec and Alberta provide a notable exception, called "phased" retirement. It's discussed at the end of this chapter.

THE EARLY RETIREMENT "PENALTY"

Many people are aware that their pension is reduced if they retire early. They commonly view this as a penalty. It's not really a penalty, but an adjustment for the time value of money. Indeed, this adjustment might even contain a subsidy, so that early retirees do a bit better than their colleagues who wait for the normal retirement age.

Suppose Michael will be due a pension of $1,000 a month at his plan's normal retirement age, 65. But he wants to retire at 60. That means he'll start drawing benefits five years early. Obviously that will cost the plan a lot more than it expected— unless his benefits are reduced accordingly. It's just like cutting a pizza. If you want six slices, each one must be smaller than if you want four slices. This is called an "actuarial reduction." That is, for the pension—not the pizza.

But My Boss Is Really Generous...

Unfortunately the *Income Tax Act* generally allows unreduced pensions only for those who:

- Have reached 60; or

- Have 30 years of eligible service including time with a related prede-cessor employer; or

- Have age plus service equal to 80.

Those limits are reduced by five years for firefighters, police officers, cor-rections officers, air traffic controllers and commercial airline pilots. There are also breaks for the disabled and those in downsizing programs. See Chapter 13.

In theory, the plan's actuary could do a custom calculation so that, adjusting for time and interest rates, Michael's total benefits work out to be the same no matter when he retires. In reality, many plans save time and actuarial fees by using standard formulas. The *Income Tax Act* requires a reduction of at least 0.25% for each month the plan member retires before the earliest age that qualifies for an unreduced pension. But the formula more commonly used reduces the pension by 0.5% per month—that's 6% per year. This formula is also used by the Canada/Quebec Pension Plans.

Michael would be leaving 60 months before normal retirement so his pension would be reduced by 30% (60 x 0.5 = 30). He would therefore receive a pension of 70% of the full amount—or $700 per month. This 0.5% per month reduction is in fact slightly more generous than a detailed actuarial calculation. So Michael's plan provides a small subsidy if he retires early.

Many plans waive this reduction once a member has reached a certain combination of age and years of membership. There's one point for each year of age and one point for each year of membership. Suppose Michael's plan allows an unreduced pension at 85 points. With 30 years of membership, he could retire at 55 with no reduction—that's 30 + 55 = 85. What if he has just 20 years? He's 10 points short since 20 + 55 = 75. But he earns two points each year—one for the extra year of service and one for the increase in his age. So it would take five years to get the 85 points he needs for an unreduced pension.

A variation on this approach is the "30 and out" formula pioneered by the Canadian Auto Workers union. A member qualifies for an unreduced pension after 30 years, though there might be a minimum age of 50 or 55.

Note that the actuarial reduction is just one of two ways in which early retirement means a lower monthly pension. The other is that each year of early retirement means there's one less year of service counted in your pension calculation. Suppose your plan pays 1.5% of final average earnings for each year of service. You'll get a 45% pension if you retire with 30 years of service, but 37.5% if you leave after 25 years. As well, your earnings during those extra five years might be higher and therefore boost your pension a bit more.

Past Service Pension Credits

If your plan allows it, making extra contributions to buy past service credits can make it possible for you to retire sooner. See Chapter 10.

PHASED RETIREMENT

You may reach retirement age and decide you'd like to continue working at the same job but on a part-time basis. The boss is keen because she doesn't want to lose your expertise. The problem: you'd like to have more income than the part-time work will provide, and you don't see why you should not continue accruing pension credits as long as you work at the same job. Why not draw part of your pension to make up the difference?

The problem is that tax rules prevent you from both receiving and accruing a pension at the same time. Also they require pensions to be paid in equal instalments (except for indexing adjustments) and drawing a partial pension for a period of time would seem to violate this rule.

In 1997 Quebec came up with a way to get around these problems. Alberta later followed suit, and we would not be surprised to see the other jurisdictions join them in coming years.

The "phased retirement" concept is for those within 10 years of their pension plan's normal retirement date. You reach an agreement with your employer to reduce your hours of work and draw annual lump sums from the pension plan to make up some of the lost income. The federal tax department has agreed that these lump sums are the same as commuting part of the pension and thereby avoiding the two problems mentioned above. The provinces, for their part, have waived their restrictions on commuting when it's done for this purpose.

There are, however, restrictions. The lump sums are available only during the term of the work agreement and each year's withdrawal must not exceed whichever is less:

- 70% of the reduction in remuneration; or
- 40% of the YMPE; or
- the total value of the member's pension.

Tom was earning $50,000 annually before he agreed with his boss that, starting in January, he'd work half-time for 18 months and that his pay would be reduced to $25,000. His pension value is quite large so it doesn't figure in this calculation. If we take 70% of his new $25,000 salary we get $17,500. If we take 40% of the YMPE— about $39,500—we get $15,800. So Tom's total income from the job and the pension plan would be $40,800 ($25,000 + $15,800) or 82% of his full-time pay. Not bad for a half-time job. His pension withdrawal for the last six months of his contract would be half the amount shown.

To do this, Tom needs written consent from his spouse. He must also understand that these withdrawals will reduce the pension due from the plan when he retires completely. As well, he must make a new application for his withdrawal each year—pensions and paperwork both start with P!

What Do You Get in Retirement?

The amount, form and predictability of your retirement pension depend on whether you're in a defined contribution plan, a defined benefit plan or an arrangement with both DC and DB elements.

DEFINED CONTRIBUTION PLAN

There are several options for converting a defined contribution pension plan to an income stream. We'll discuss them all, but your particular plan may not offer the full range. Check your booklet.

Purchasing a Life Annuity

This is the traditional way to go and is probably still the most common. A life annuity is a contract with a life insurance company under which they guarantee—in return for a lump sum payment—to make regular (usually monthly) payments to you throughout your lifetime and perhaps also to your survivor(s).

Your plan administrator will check annuity prices at several insurers (the only organizations now allowed to sell life annuities) and then select the best deal, hopefully considering the financial stability of the insurer as well as the annuity cost. A few DC plans offer the opportunity to, in effect, buy an annuity from the pension plan itself—perhaps at a better price than available elsewhere.

What are the advantages of annuitizing?

- It provides security. You're guaranteed that no matter how long you live, you'll receive the monthly income. You can also have this income indexed for inflation if you're willing to take a lower starting amount.

- It means you no longer have to worry about investing; you no longer control the money once it goes to the insurer.

- Your income is protected. If the insurer fails, the Canadian Life and Health Insurance Compensation Corporation—CompCorp—covers up to $2,000 in monthly annuity payments. That's per insurer, so two annuities from two issuers would be covered for $4,000 a month.

- Your capital is protected from creditors, though they could garnishee the payments as they're made.

What are the disadvantages?

- You give up investment control.

- You cannot vary the monthly payments as your needs and tax position change. Your income amount is locked in when the annuity is purchased; you can't benefit if interest rates or stock market conditions subsequently improve.

- When you die, there's nothing for your heirs unless you arranged for a certain number of guaranteed payments and/or continuing income for your spouse.

The amount the annuity pays each month is a function of how it's priced. That depends on:

- Your age when the payments start and the age of your spouse if it's a joint annuity. The ages are important because they determine the expected number of payments the insurer is going to make. The older the age, the higher your monthly income.

- The guarantee for payments after your death, if any. Guarantees tend to increase the number of payments the insurer must make. So, the greater the guarantee, the lower your monthly income.

- Provision for increases in the monthly payments, if any.

- The time delay before payments start, if any. Time delays will reduce the price of the annuity and thereby increase your monthly income. For example, if you're now 50 and buy an annuity that starts payouts only when you're 60, the insurer will have the money invested for 10 years before paying out anything. The earnings on that money allow the insurer to charge less upfront.

- Market interest rates when the annuity is purchased. This tends to have the most impact. This might be easier to understand if you think about a home mortgage. That's actually an annuity for the bank. They give you a lump sum and you give them a stream of monthly payments. Suppose you need $100,000 to be repaid with interest over 25 years. If the mortgage rate is 5% when the bank "buys" this annuity from you, they get $582 a month. If the rate is 6%, they get $640. Now turn it the other way. You have $100,000 in retirement capital. If annuity rates are 6%, the insurer will pay you more each month than if they're 5%.

Unlike a mortgage, the annuity rate is locked in—life annuities do not come up for renewal. So the best time to buy one is when interest rates are really high. What if you're approaching retirement and those rates are fairly low, or perhaps they're acceptable but you expect them to rise? You don't have to wait until retirement to buy an annuity, and you don't have to buy an annuity all at once.

First, assuming you have control over your DC account, you should probably alter the investment mix a few years before retirement to make the portfolio less volatile. Suppose you're now 55 and plan to retire at 60. You might take one-fifth of the money earmarked for annuitization and buy a "deferred annuity" that will start payments at 60. Do the same next year and each year thereafter. You'll wind up with a series of annuities, each priced at the rate in effect at the time of purchase. If you buy the annuities from a mix of issuers, you can ensure that each payout stream is fully covered by CompCorp's limit of $2,000 per month.

Here's a somewhat different approach. Suppose you won't need much pension income at first because you plan to work part-time in your first few retirement years. Or perhaps you want to shop the annuity market through your financial advisor instead of the pension administrator. Transfer money from your DC plan to whatever form of locked-in RRSP your jurisdiction allows and then buy annuities from the RRSP account using the staggered approach above.

Lump Sum Transfer to Another Registered Vehicle

You don't have to buy an annuity at retirement. If you want flexibility in taking your income, prefer to retain investment control and/or place priority on estate planning, you can transfer your DC account value to a locked-in RRSP or similar plan and manage the income stream yourself. Remember that you must start to draw income by the end of the year in which you turn 69. See Chapter 16.

DEFINED BENEFIT PLAN

Defined benefit plans fall into three broad groups: final average, career average and flat benefit. They sound different, but are very similar. The retirement pension formula for each one has three elements: the accrual rate, the pensionable earnings and the amount of service. The only real difference is the way earnings are treated.

Consider three friends: Larry, Moe and Curly. They work at different companies, but just happen to have the same earnings: $45,000 a year. They're also the same age and plan to retire at the same time. (Isn't it amazing how these books always find such neat and tidy situations?)

Final Average Plan

Larry's plan provides a pension based on average earnings in the three years before retirement. Its formula is: 1% x average earnings x years of credited service. If Larry stays until normal retirement age he'll have 30 years of service. So his annual pension would equal 30% of his $45,000 in final average earnings. That's $15,000. Suppose his earnings soar and he winds up averaging $60,000 for those years. He'd then get 30% of $60,000. That's $18,000. So Larry's final average plan automatically factors rising earnings into the pension calculation. Indeed, his pension reflects only the earnings in his final years.

This works very well in times of inflation and for those who earn more just before retirement. It does not work so well for someone whose earnings fall. Some plans cover this by using a longer period, perhaps the best five of the last 10 years. A best-five-in-10 base also protects those with performance bonuses and other forms of variable pay.

Career Average Plan

Moe's plan will base his pension on the average earnings over his whole career. Its formula is: 1% x career average earnings x years of credited service. Every year he earns a pension of 1% of his earnings for that year. When his salary goes up, he earns more pension for the year the increase occurred and those that follow—but not for the years in the past.

At first glance, Moe's plan does not look as good as Larry's since Larry's pension will be based on earnings only during his final years, when they're likely to be highest. But every three years or so, Moe's company updates his past earnings to bring them in line with what he's making now. If the company keeps doing that, Moe's pension will be based on pretty much the same earnings as Larry's.

Career average plans like this used to be very common, but many were converted to final average structures when high inflation forced employers to keep doing updating. Some employers still have career average plans because they're more flexible. The company can incur the cost of updates only as it can afford them instead of committing to the higher built-in cost of a final average plan.

Flat Benefit Plan

Curly is in a flat benefit plan for hourly-paid employees. It pays a monthly pension of $37.50—$450 annually—for each year of service. His $450 pension accrual for the year just happens to equal 1% of his $45,000 annual pay.

Curly earns $25 per hour and works 1,800 hours per year. His pension formula is: 1% x ($25 x 1,800 hours) x years of credited service. Assuming Curly gets no pay raise, he'll wind up with the same pension as Larry and Moe because they'll all have a $45,000 earnings base. That's if Larry and Moe get no pay raise either.

So what's the difference? Larry's plan automatically factored in higher pay by using only earnings for the final years. Moe's plan factored in higher pay through voluntary employer updates. Curly's flat benefit pension is, well, flat—unless his union negotiates a higher rate in the next round of contract talks. That's been the case so far. For example, next year his hourly pay will rise 10% from $25 to $27.50 and his hourly pension accrual will rise 10% from $37.50 to $41.25. The new contract will also boost his past credits to that level. If future bargaining produces similar results and Curly's earnings remain in line with Larry's and Moe's, he'll get much the same pension as they do.

The Big Difference Lies in How the Pension Due Is Adjusted as Earnings Rise over Your Career	
Final average	Adjusted automatically
Career average	Adjusted automatically for the future but needs updates for the past.
Flat benefit	Needs upgrades for both future and past

Reciprocal Agreements

Notice how the credited service was a key factor in each case above. Suppose you're about to change jobs and your current and new employers both have defined benefit pension plans. Or maybe you've already changed jobs and simply left your credits in your old employer's plan.

Ask if there's a reciprocal agreement that will let you transfer your current or old credits to the new plan. That's more likely if you're a public sector employee, and less so if you're in the private sector. But still ask.

This is particularly valuable if the new pension plan is based on final average earnings. Suppose you left a job with 10 years of credit and pensionable earnings of $50,000. The credits in that plan will almost certainly be frozen at that level. Now suppose you can transfer them to your new final average plan at full value. Not only do you have 10 years of credited service right off the bat, but the portion of your ultimate pension that's attributable to the transfer will be based on the final earnings in your new job, not the frozen $50,000.

Integration with C/QPP

Final average plans are often "integrated" with the pension provided by the Canada or Quebec Pension plan. Many people think that's unfair. Let's look at the reasoning.

A final average plan is designed with a target retirement income in mind, say 70% of final average earnings after 35 years service. A plan with a 2% accrual rate meets that target. But if there's no integration, the C/QPP benefits mean the retiree will end up with more than the 70% target and the employer will have spent more than was really required for that person to replace 70% of his or her income.

One way to address this is by having two accrual rates for the pension plan—often 1.3% for earnings that are covered by C/QPP and then 2% on earnings above that. Suppose Bernadette is retiring at 65 after 35 years of service. Her pensionable earnings are $60,000 and she qualifies for the C/QPP maximum, say $10,000.

If she's in a straight 2% pension plan with no integration, she'll get $42,000 from the plan (70% x $60,000) plus $10,000 from C/QPP. That totals $52,000 or 87% of her pre-retirement salary. Now, assuming C/QPP covers $40,000 of earnings, as discussed in Chapter 4, let's see what happens under an integrated plan with two accrual rates:

- Pension on earnings to $40,000 = 1.3% x 40,000 x 35 = $18,200
- Pension on earnings over $40,000 = 2% x 20,000 x 35 = $14,000
- C/QPP pension $10,000
- TOTAL RETIREMENT PENSION $42,200

Bernadette's employer wanted her to retire with a 70% replacement ratio. This arrangement meets that goal. The $42,200 is 70.3% of her $60,000 pre-retirement salary.

There's an alternative form of integration called the "offset" approach. It would first calculate Bernadette's pension at a straight 2% rate and then reduce the amount due by the amount of her C/QPP pension. The result and employee contributions for this approach work out to be much the same as for the two-rate approach above, but the calculations are more complex.

Bridge Benefits

A bridge benefit is a pension payable for a limited period of time. It's used mainly to fill the gap an early retiree faces until OAS and C/QPP kick in at age 65. This does not mean that you have to wait until 65 to start C/QPP. You could double up, collecting both the bridge benefit and a reduced C/QPP pension between 60 and 65. But understand that your total income would then drop at 65 when the bridge ends and C/QPP continues at the previous, reduced level.

Naturally, tax rules prevent you from doing too well on a bridge benefit. They limit the size of any bridge that starts before age 60. Suppose you're retiring at 58 and will be due $15,000 in OAS-C/QPP benefits at 65. Your bridge must be reduced by 0.25% of that OAS-C/QPP total for each month the bridge is paid before age 60. That's 24 months in this case, so the maximum bridge benefit is reduced by 6%. The amount is also prorated if you're highly paid and have less than 10 years of service.

If your plan does not offer a bridge benefit, you can achieve the same result by taking a level income option. Say you can retire at 55 with a $40,000 pension. Full

OAS and C/QPP would boost your income at 65 to $55,000, ignoring adjustments for inflation. You might like to trade some of that higher income at 65 for more money today. If your plan permits, you can request a calculation of the levelled amount. In our example, you might be offered a pension of $47,000 now with a reduction to $32,000 at age 65. The $15,000 from OAS and C/QPP would then boost that reduced income back to the $47,000 level.

Approved Downsizings

Many people get forced into early retirement by layoffs. Tax rules allow those 55 and older to be granted additional pension credits if certain conditions are met.

The downsizing must involve a significant number of employees. That's generally whichever is greater: 50 people or 10% of those employed at the affected location. The program cannot be biased towards the group's high-income earners, and those with similar age and service profiles must be treated equally when it comes to the additional benefits. Tax officials check all of this before authorizing the enhanced pension.

The additional service equals the difference between your age and 65, but there's a seven-year maximum. Joe is exactly 57 and has 20 years of service. His plan's normal retirement age is 65. So he has eight years to go. If his layoff qualifies as an approved downsizing, he can be granted seven more years of service—the maximum—so his pension will be based on 27 years, not just 20.

Joe may also be granted additional early retirement subsidies. The reduction in pension can be set at 0.25% for each month by which his retirement precedes the earliest of the day he reaches 55 (instead of 60), the day he has 25 years of eligible service (instead of 30), and the day on which his age plus eligible service adds up to 75 (instead of 80).

Note that Joe's employer is not required to provide any of these extras. Also, Joe will lose these enhancements if he goes back to work for the same employer or a related one.

Pregnancy and Parental Leave

There are safeguards for people who take time off to care for a new child, natural or adopted. You have the right to remain a pension plan member during your leave, generally for up to one year. If the plan normally requires employee contributions, you must continue to make them. The plan will determine the amount due and likely provide several payment options. You might make periodic contributions during your leave or after your return, or perhaps pay a lump sum once you're back at work. Your employer is required to explain your options. Also, the employer cannot make its contributions conditional on your returning to work.

Flexible Pension Plans

A flexible pension plan allows employees to take a hand in the design of their defined benefit pension. You make voluntary tax-deductible contributions to a side account, which is used at termination or retirement to provide improvements like indexing or increased early retirement benefits. This is particularly valuable if your pension adjustment is so high that it pretty much wipes out your own RRSP limit.

How can you make deductible contributions if you have no RRSP room?

The flexible pension concept is based on the fact that certain valuable features—such as inflation indexing—can be funded without affecting your RRSP limit, because they don't count in the PA calculation. That makes your plan more tax-efficient.

Your Standard Pension...	...Might Be Improved To:
• Actuarial reduction for early retirement	• Unreduced early retirement
• *Ad hoc* inflation indexing	• Automatic inflation indexing
• Pension base = best 5 years' earnings	• Pension base = best 3 years' earnings

This concept also lets you tailor your employer's plan to suit your needs. Which is more important to you—indexing or early retirement benefits? You decide, and spend your contribution account accordingly.

Be aware that employers have not rushed to offer this concept because regulators have been moving slowly in approving it. Also be aware that the growth of your side account needs monitoring. If it grows beyond the amount required to fund all available benefits, your plan might not be allowed to refund the excess.

HYBRID AND COMBINATION PLANS

As discussed in Chapter 6, a hybrid plan is an either/or proposition. Your pension will either reflect the defined contribution options described above, or be based on a defined benefit formula if that value is greater.

A combination plan provides retirement income in two parts. You receive a defined benefit pension. In addition, you have a defined contribution pension account, deferred profit sharing plan or group RRSP.

CHAPTER FOURTEEN

What If You're Highly Paid?

As we explained in Chapter 5, tax rules cap the amount of pension that a tax-sheltered Registered Pension Plan can pay. This means a regular defined benefit plan can't provide the full pension to which many upper income people are entitled.

The key is your plan's accrual rate. The maximum that tax rules permit is whichever is less: 2% of pensionable earnings or $1,722.22 for each year of pensionable service. The maximum pension based on 35 years of service would be $60,278. This table shows the salary that would earn you a $60,278 pension after 35 years and how much of your income that pension would replace.

Accrual Rate	Top Salary Covered	Income Replacement
2.00%	$86,111	70%
1.75%	$98,413	61%
1.50%	$114,815	53%
1.25%	$137,778	44%
1.00%	$172,222	35%

This does not mean your employer can't provide a pension for the income over that limit. Rather, it means this top-up pension can't be funded on a tax-sheltered basis.

SUPPLEMENTARY EMPLOYEE RETIREMENT PLAN (SERP)

As the pension limits have remained essentially unchanged since 1976, SERPs are becoming more and more common. Once provided only to senior executives, they're now being broadened to cover middle management, professionals and other highly skilled workers. Almost all large employers in the private sector and those in the public sector now have SERPs. The plans are less prevalent among smaller employers but the numbers are growing.

The key point to remember is that there are no government limits on what a SERP can pay; that's entirely up to you and your employer. Obviously, the best time to discuss this is when you negotiate your contract before accepting a new job. That's when you have the most bargaining clout and it's also when it's easiest for your new employer to meet your needs. Altering an executive pension in mid-stream can be very complex and expensive.

Documentation

This is a big problem. Documentation of SERPs is, to put it bluntly, poor. Remember that there are no government standards to protect you. The majority of today's SERPs do not have a formal plan document. Sometimes the only document is a resolution passed by the board of directors that's not even shared with the employees affected. Sometimes the affected employees receive nothing more than a one-page letter telling them that they are members of the plan. Clearly, thorough documentation is best for both you and the employer. You'll really appreciate the value of good documentation once you read the section below on funding.

Pension Due

Most SERPs use a defined benefit structure. Many SERPs simply extend the formula for the regular pension plan, but a common design promises a pension of 2% of final average earnings for each year of service. That amount is then offset by whatever's payable from the regular RPP. For example, your pension entitlement might work out to $75,000 a year with about $60,000 coming from the RPP and about $15,000 from the SERP. Or you might simply get a lump sum payment instead of $15,000 a year.

SERPs for senior executives frequently provide benefits above the usual 2% limit (for example, 4% of pensionable earnings). This helps to attract new executives in mid-career who would otherwise not have enough time under the new plan to make up for pension benefits they might forfeit on leaving their previous employer.

The definition of pensionable earnings can make a big difference. Does it just cover your salary or also the performance bonus that might comprise a big part of your pay? Is that averaged over your last three or five years, or perhaps your best consecutive three or five years during your final decade of employment?

Here's a tip on estate planning. A lump sum death benefit from an RPP can be rolled into your spouse's RRSP tax-free, but tax will be due if your spouse receives a continuing pension instead. A SERP payout gets taxed whether received as a lump sum or an income stream. To maximize the RPP's tax advantage, the surviving spouse should consider taking the RPP benefit as an RRSP-eligible lump sum while using SERP payments to put food on the table.

Vesting

Even though this is not required by legislation, most SERPs use the same vesting requirements as the regular pension plan—usually vesting after two years. But SERPs for executives frequently take longer to vest—sometimes not until you reach early or even normal retirement age. This creates "golden handcuffs" that tie you to the organization. It also creates a major risk for you, given the accelerating pace at which companies are dumping executives. With point-of-retirement vesting you may get little or nothing if you leave—or get forced out—early.

A related issue concerns how much you'd get for your vested credits if you left before retirement age. The simplest approach is to commute the SERP's value just as though it were a regular pension plan. So you would get a lump sum that equalled the present value of the benefits earned to date. But there's a significant wrinkle—tax. SERPs are not part of the tax-sheltered retirement system, so this lump sum would be fully taxed in the year it's received. If your payout is $200,000, you could end up with just $100,000. That's unless you have enough unused RRSP room to accommodate the payout or a portion can be attributed to pre-1996 service and thereby qualify as an RRSP retiring allowance.

A well-designed SERP would iron out this wrinkle by providing a tax adjustment. The most common approach increases the payout to cover the tax due. Instead of $200,000, you'd get $400,000 so you net $200,000 after tax. (But you'd still face tax on that money's investment earnings.) Better yet, the payout could be increased to cover the tax due on the lump sum plus the estimated tax due on the investment earnings. That would be great for you, but arguably unfair to your employer who gets no credit for the fact that you'll be able to access some of that money tax-free during retirement as a return of capital. The most fair, though most complex, approach would be to project how much *after-tax* retirement income your SERP credits are supposed to provide. Your payout would then be tax-adjusted to produce a lump sum capable of funding that stream.

Funding

Many SERPs are not pre-funded. All you have is a promise that your employer will top up your pension, either with a lump sum when you retire or continuing payments until you and your spouse die. But what if the company fails? Or what if it's bought by another company that refuses to honour the commitment? If there's good documentation, you could go to court to enforce your claim. Of course, that's time-consuming, expensive and might not yield much if the company has gone under.

In theory, there's nothing to prevent SERP pre-funding. In reality, the federal government has imposed complex and costly rules to make sure there's no tax shelter for either the plan's capital or the investment earnings. These rules refer to SERPs as Retirement Compensation Arrangements, or RCAs.

In its simplest form, the RCA consists of a trust. As with a regular pension plan, the trust secures the money by separating it from the employer's other assets. The contribution is tax-deductible for the employer on the same basis as if it had simply been paid out as salary. But then things get complicated.

Ottawa wants to ensure the RCA trust is not tax-sheltered. So there's a special 50% tax on the contributions. That means your employer would have to shell out $20,000 for the RCA trust to be able to put $10,000 to work. There's also a 50% tax on the plan's investment earnings. So the RCA's $10,000 would not produce the same level of growth as $10,000 in a tax-sheltered pension fund. (Some employers avoid the RCA tax on investment earnings by using life insurance contracts that offer tax-sheltered compounding.)

The 50% levy is aimed at ensuring that the RCA is not a tax shelter; it's not meant to raise extra revenue for the government—or so they say. Thus, down the road, this tax gets refunded as the RCA pays out benefits which are then fully taxed as income for the recipient. But that refund does not include any interest for the time Ottawa had use of that money.

As you can see, the RCA process is expensive and cumbersome. Is it any wonder that so many SERPs are not pre-funded?

Fortunately, there's an alternative way in which your employer might be able to provide the security of an RCA without its cost and complexity. Instead of pre-funding the SERP by putting great big gobs of money into a trust, the employer could simply provide enough cash for the trust to buy a letter of credit. That document obligates the issuer—usually a chartered bank—to pay the pension amount due if the employer can't. The cost of this guarantee is based on the employer's financial standing, but typically amounts to only a small percentage of the amount covered. Significantly, that fee is the only amount subject to the 50% RCA tax. A letter of credit thus provides a relatively cheap way to secure your top-up pension. But—isn't there always a but?—it's not perfect. These guarantees are typically issued for just one year at a time. Usually, renewals are routine, but there's no assurance that a new letter will be issued if your company has run into serious financial trouble—the very time when your pension security really matters.

How Strong Are the Ties that Bind?

Unlike RPPs, SERPs frequently include non-competition clauses as a condition for benefit payments to be made. In an Ontario court case called *Woodward v. Stelco Inc.*, a retired Stelco executive challenged the clause after going to work for a competitor. Woodward called the clause an unreasonable restraint of trade. He lost on grounds that he was an experienced businessperson who understood the terms of the contract and held proprietary information. Courts generally uphold non-competition clauses in cases like that, but the outcome might be different in a case involving employees in a broader-based plan who do not have access to confidential or proprietary information.

SECULAR TRUST

A secular trust is a way to secure a SERP without the RCA's administrative complexity. You and your employer would establish a trust with you as beneficiary. Every year the employer would pay you a special bonus on condition that the money be put in the trust until your retire.

The bonus would, of course, be taxed as part of your income for the year it's received. On one hand, that's better than with an RCA, because the RCA tax is 50% while top marginal rates in most provinces are now below that level. On the other hand, the RCA tax is ultimately refunded as benefits are paid out. The tax on a secular trust bonus is not refunded at all.

An RCA faces a 50% tax on each year's investment earnings with no breaks for capital gains and Canadian corporate dividends. You'd face tax each year on your secular trust's investment earnings, but would get the standard tax breaks for capital gains and Canadian dividends.

As with an RCA, you could avoid the yearly tax on investment earnings by using a tax-effective life insurance policy. In that case, the death benefit could flow tax-free through the trust to your heirs. With an RCA, that death benefit would most likely face tax when flowed through to your heirs.

INDIVIDUAL PENSION PLAN (IPP)

An Individual Pension Plan, or IPP, is a defined benefit pension plan with just one member. The concept was allowed by Ottawa in 1991 so that key people in small companies could have the same high-quality pensions as executives in major corporations and government agencies. Since then, some corporate executives have been granted IPPs instead of more conventional arrangements in order to give them full control over their retirement planning. And some people well below the ranks of executives—such as teachers—have used IPPs to cash out their credits in conventional defined benefit pension plans on a tax-effective basis.

It's important to understand that an IPP is a Registered Pension Plan. While it's typically designed to be as generous as possible, it still faces the same payout limit described above—the annual pension is currently capped at $1,722.22 per year of service. So it's really a pension alternative, not a pension supplement. Also, the typical IPP will produce a maximum pension adjustment, so going this route pretty much means halting contributions to your own or your spouse's RRSP.

IPPs offer several advantages over RRSPs, the standard retirement funding vehicle for individuals. For example:

- Tax-deductible contribution limits are much higher than RRSP limits for those in their late 40s or older. These people—or, more accurately, their corporation—can put in whatever's required for the plan to be able to pay the promised benefits. Naturally, those benefits are made as generous as the rules allow. Funding levels can be particularly high for an entrepreneur who has built a business over many years and thereby qualifies for tons of past service credits. This, however, has been the subject of intense scrutiny by tax officials over the years. Professional advice is definitely a must.

- If your RRSP investments don't do well, tough luck. If your IPP investments don't do well, additional tax-deductible funding is allowed—indeed required—so the promised benefits can be paid.

- Suppose you're in a regular defined benefit pension plan that has generous early retirement provisions. If you leave that plan before retirement, tax rules often prevent you from transferring the full value of those credits to a locked-in RRSP or equivalent. A portion that represents the early retirement provisions gets taxed. You might, however, be able to avoid that by incorporating a business that then sponsors an IPP. That way, you could do a direct transfer from your old pension plan to your new one with no tax hit. This, however, is a tricky area that requires specialized professional guidance to avoid challenge. In 2000, tax officials and pension regulators expressed concern about the growing number of transfers by teachers and other members of generous public employee pension plans. The officials felt some of the transfer strategies were questionable, if not inappropriate. If you're challenged and lose, the Canada Customs and Revenue Agency can de-register the plan and tax its full value.

- An IPP is a Registered Pension Plan and therefore gets the same creditor-proofing as any other RPP.

But there are negatives as well as positives:

- You can't create an IPP on your own. It must be sponsored by an employer—and that employer must be willing to make a substantial financial commitment, since the company is legally responsible for all of the benefits promised. Arguably, this works best for the self-employed who've incorporated their businesses—those for whom the concept was devised.

- An IPP faces the same complex federal and provincial regulation as any other defined benefit pension plan. That means hefty fees for set-up and operation. In particular, the plan will need an actuarial valuation every three years. Set-up fees might run $5,000 or more. Ongoing fees might average $2,000 a year. Make sure the IPP really provides enough added tax deferral and flexibility to justify the cost and complexity. If you're an owner-manager, remember that your company's IPP contributions save tax at the company's marginal rate. That rate is probably well below the rate at which you'd save tax on your own RRSP contributions.

- As a pension plan, the IPP is much less flexible than an RRSP in how and when you receive retirement income. There's also no way to split retirement income with your mate as there is with spousal RRSP contributions.

- If the investments don't do well, your corporation might have to make unplanned contributions.

Don't expect your regular financial advisor to be well-versed in IPPs. There are many rules and they're quite complex. Your advisor or accountant might be able to refer you to an actuary or other pension specialist who is quite experienced in establishing these plans. But start early. Even if an off-the-shelf design meets your needs, it will likely take months to get the plan registered with federal and provincial authorities.

What Happens If You Change Jobs?

You stop earning pension credits when you leave your employer. Under most circumstances you then have the choice of leaving your pension in the plan or transferring its value to another plan that will also provide lifetime retirement income. Those "L-plans" are discussed in Chapter 16.

Your employer must provide details of your pension value and options in a timely manner. You're supposed to respond within 30 to 90 days, depending on the jurisdiction. Don't procrastinate; if you respond before the deadline, you're sure of getting the option you want.

The options—outlined below—are quite straightforward if you're now in a defined contribution plan. Assuming you're vested—also explained below—you can move your full account balance. That's because the money is yours; you're not part of a defined benefit pool that involves others, and your employer has made no guarantee about the level of your retirement income.

The options are less straightforward if you're now in a defined benefit plan. That's because you *are* in a pool that involves others, and your employer *has* made a guarantee about the level of your retirement income. For example, a transfer may not be allowed if you have enough age or service to start collecting a pension. You would then have to take a pension from that plan, either when you leave or at a later date.

VESTING

Under current rules, your pension must vest no later than the point at which you've completed two years of plan membership. What does this mean?

If you're in a defined contribution plan, vesting means you're entitled to the contributions made by your employer—in addition to your own contributions, plus investment earnings. If you belong to a defined benefit plan, vesting means you are entitled to eventually receive a pension—according to the plan formula—for the period you've been a member. In either case, if you leave before the vesting date, you're entitled only to a refund of your own contributions and their investment earnings. You do not benefit from any contributions your employer made.

Notice we said that "current" rules provide for two-year vesting. You might find that some of your credits won't vest until you're at least 45 years old and have 10 continuous years of employment. This "45 and 10" provision is a hangover from the old rules that applied in most of Canada until the mid-1980s. Around 1986, the provinces started to introduce the two-year rule, but only for benefits earned after that change. So, for example, Ontario has the 45-and-10 rule for benefits earned before 1987 and the two-year rule for service after that. Nova Scotia's 45-and-10 rule applies to benefits earned prior to 1988. In Quebec, it's 1990. Fortunately, many pension plans simply apply the more generous two-year rule to all service.

Commuting Means More Than Going to Work

When a defined benefit pension is "commuted," the benefits promised in the future are converted to a lump sum. That sum—called the "transfer value"— is the amount that must be invested today to fund the benefits when they're due. The actuary who does this must assume a rate of return between now and then. To keep things fair, this rate is set monthly by the Canadian Institute of Actuaries and generally reflects average yields on long-term government bonds. There are two rates—one for the first 15 years and a lower one for the period after that. The rates are posted on the institute's web site at www.actuaries.ca. If you're moving to a plan where you do the investing, ask what rates were used for your transfer value. If the assumption was, say, 7% for the next 15 years, your new plan must do at least that well to replace the pension promise you gave up.

This is not done for defined contribution plans. Your transfer value equals your account balance, no more and no less.

LOCKING-IN

So let's say you're vested and you're leaving the plan before retirement age. What happens to the money? There are several options, all of which are aimed at providing you with income through your whole retirement.

Option #1: Stay Put

You could simply leave your credits in your current plan and start receiving a pension when you reach the plan's retirement age. In effect, your membership is frozen until retirement. Suppose you've accumulated 10 years of defined benefit credit, your plan pays 1.5% of final average earnings for each year of service, and those earnings for you are $50,000. Your deferred pension would be 10 x 1.5% x $50,000 = $7,500.

Option #2: Transfer the Money to Your New Employer's Pension Plan

This option is available only if the new plan will accept your credits. That's normally not a problem if your new employer has a defined contribution plan, since the employer makes no guarantees about your level of retirement income.

If you transfer from one defined benefit plan to another, your new plan might recognize the service you had in your former plan. Transfers are often allowed by defined benefit plans for public employees because they tend to be quite similar, but are much less likely for private sector defined benefit plans. A DB transfer can be particularly valuable if the new plan will base your pension on your final average or best average earnings. That's because the value of your past pension credits will rise as your earnings increase. Let's use the same assumptions as in option #1 for the plan you're leaving. We'll further assume the new plan has the same payout structure and that you put in 12 years before retiring at final average earnings of $75,000. Your total pension membership thus spans 22 years. With a transfer at full credit, your pension would be based on 22 years of service and final average earnings of $75,000. That's 22 x 1.5% x $75,000 = $24,750. Without the transfer, option #1's deferred pension would be $7,500, and the pension from your new plan would be 12 x 1.5% x $75,000 = $13,500. So your total pension would be $21,000 a year, or $3,750 less than with a full-credit transfer. This is an expensive proposition for the new pension plan, so it is most commonly found where there is movement of staff between both employers. In that case, the plans usually have a reciprocal agreement that spells out how the pension credits from the old plan are valued under the new one. Even if there is no reciprocal agreement, there's no harm in asking if the new plan will accept your credits.

Option #3: Transfer the Money to an Insurance Company to Buy an Annuity

The annuity must guarantee income for life and can't start making payments to you until you reach the age when you would have been able to start a pension from the original plan. Currently, life insurance companies are the only financial organizations allowed to sell life annuities. From time to time, the chartered banks seek permission to offer them too. So far, they've been unsuccessful. If this option appeals to you, make sure you shop around. For various reasons, an insurer may not really want new annuity business. It'll still offer contracts, but at uncompetitive rates. Also make sure the insurer is rock solid and your monthly annuity payment is fully covered by the Canadian Life and Health Insurance Compensation

Corp., an industry-run fund commonly known as CompCorp, which protects contract holders in the event an insurer fails.

Option #4: Transfer the Money to a Special RRSP or RRIF

This is the most popular choice. Some jurisdictions still refer to these plans as locked-in RRSPs, but pension regulators have created names to more clearly distinguish them from regular RRSPs and RRIFs. While you're in pre-retirement mode, the money would go into a Locked-In Retirement Account (LIRA). Then, when you reach the earliest retirement age specified by the original pension plan, you can start making withdrawals by converting the LIRA to a Life Income Fund (LIF) or Locked-In Retirement Income Fund (LRIF). As with an RRSP, you must convert your LIRA to a LIF or LRIF by the end of the year in which you turn 69.

These plans are offered by virtually every financial organization that handles RRSPs and RRIFs. From an investment point of view, they're just like RRSPs and RRIFs. The key differences are the following:

- The money is locked in until the earliest retirement age set by the pension plan from which it came.

- Once withdrawals begin, there is a maximum limit on how much you can take out each year. This cap is aimed at ensuring that the plan provides lifetime retirement income as required for the original pension plan.

- At age 80, a LIF must generally be converted to a life annuity. Several jurisdictions have dropped that requirement, however, while others have adopted a Locked-In Retirement Fund that requires no annuitization.

The next chapter discusses these plans in more detail.

IS THERE ANY WAY JUST TO TAKE THE MONEY AND RUN?

Only in certain cases. The basic rule is that vested benefits must be locked in to provide lifetime retirement income—just like the pension plan the money came from. But most jurisdictions will let you cash in your pension if it's small. What does "small" mean? Typically, you qualify if the annual pension due is less that 2% of the average national wage—the YMPE—or, depending on the jurisdiction, if the transfer value of your credits is less than 4–20% of the YMPE. Some provinces also allow a cash-out if there is medical evidence that you have a shortened life expectancy.

Do you have credits from the old days when vesting occurred only at age 45 and 10 years of service? Your plan might allow you to cash out up to 25% of the pension earned during that time.

We mentioned above that you might not be allowed to transfer out your pension value if you've reached the age when you can start collecting a defined benefit pension. That's often 10 years before the normal retirement age. So, depending on your plan, it's likely 55, but might be 50. If you call the federal tax department or check the *Income Tax Act* yourself, you'll find that pension money can be transferred to a locked-in RRSP or RRIF even after retirement age. But that applies only if the plan allows such transfers. Many—probably most—don't. Pension legislation allows defined benefit plans to restrict transfers to protect them from cash flow problems. If you are approaching retirement age and have a long period of service, your credits could be very valuable. An annual pension of $30,000 can easily be worth $300,000 or more. If a significant number of employees with large pension values leave in a short period of time, there's a fear the cash drain might hurt the pension fund's investment performance. Consequently, plans are allowed to grant transfers only for departing employees who have not yet reached retirement age.

The "no transfer after early retirement age" rule does not apply to defined contribution plans. You're free to move your money because you are not part of a pool that involves others.

Some financial advisors urge people to leave defined benefit pension plans just before the cut-off age on the grounds that this is their last chance to transfer their funds to an RRSP. That can make sense for those who don't need retirement income and want to leave a large estate. For example, we know a couple who were about to retire as long-serving school principals. The husband's fully-indexed high-quality pension was more than enough for them, so the wife commuted her pension. Others should be very careful. A financial advisor might give you an impressive-looking analysis. Be aware that this advisor stands to earn a great deal in commissions when you transfer your pension money and have him or her invest it for you. Get a second opinion from a qualified advisor who will not benefit either way. There might even be fee-only financial planners or actuaries in your community who have done this many times.
Here are key points to check:

- Can the full transfer value really be rolled tax-free into a locked-in RRSP or similar plan? That may not be so if your pension plan has generous early retirement benefits. In the late '90s, many Ontario teachers looked into commuting and found that up to one-third of their transfer values would immediately be taxed. That hit means the remaining money must generate very high returns to produce the target income stream.

- Is the pension plan automatically indexed or does it have a strong record of *ad hoc* adjustments? Long-term indexing is expensive; make sure the commutation presentation deals with it the same way as the pension plan.

- Does the commutation presentation use unreasonably high investment returns— for example, long-term returns of 10% or more? Most actuaries would suggest you're doing very well if you average 4% over inflation—that's 6–7% overall.

Investment advisors might feel up to 6% over inflation is reasonable—that's about 8% overall. Ideally, see if you can get a Monte Carlo analysis that tests returns which vary from year to year, both up and down. Remember that your defined benefit pension immunizes you from market volatility.

- There are maximum withdrawal limits on the locked-in plan that will be the new home of your pension money. Make sure you can take out enough each year to meet your needs.

- Are you leaving early just to do the commutation? How much more pension would you earn simply by staying in the plan for a few years? There could be a big difference if you're in a final average plan.

Sometimes You Can't Do a Full Defined Benefit Transfer

Here are three situations in which tax or pension rules might prevent you from moving your full credits on a tax-sheltered basis:

- Suppose your current plan has generous early retirement benefits. The *Income Tax Act* requires your plan administrator to divide your transfer value into two amounts. First, there's a basic pension amount that can be transferred to a LIRA or similar vehicle. The second part reflects the generous early retirement subsidy. It must be taken as taxable cash. Of course, if you have unused RRSP room, you could put that money into your RRSP as a regular contribution—just like any other income—and thereby avoid the tax hit.

- If you leave a plan that has a large surplus, your transfer value might include your share of that excess. As with situation #1, this becomes a taxable payout unless you have enough unused RRSP room to keep the money sheltered.

- Pension legislation requires a plan administrator to restrict transfers for individuals if the plan's funding falls below a certain level. In that case, you would get a limited initial transfer and the balance with interest over the next five years.

JOB TRANSFERS OUT OF CANADA

More and more, Canadian companies and their employees are working all over the world. What happens to your pension?

We're assuming you'll come back to Canada. For example, some companies routinely send those on the executive track to spend a year here and a year there. Others move people with special skills to the projects that need them and then bring them back.

If you plan to return, make sure your pension is settled before you leave. Your employer needs tax department approval to keep making deductible contributions for you. That approval is difficult, if not impossible, to get once you've left.

Your personal tax status doesn't matter; you're free to become a non-resident for tax purposes. In this case, it's your employment status that matters to the Canada Customs and Revenue Agency. Are you really still working for the Canadian company and contributing to its business? There are no clear-cut standards; it's what tax officials call a "question of fact."

If your company can justify keeping you on the Canadian payroll, CCRA will let them continue making deductible contributions for you. So your pension plan membership continues. If the company can't persuade CCRA that you should remain on the Canadian payroll, your pension plan membership can continue only for five years while you're outside Canada. You'd then have to return for at least 12 months to keep it going. That five-year limit might not apply if the pension plan contains a long-term foreign service provision that was approved before 1993.

As you might expect, there's a whole lot more to the issue of foreign transfers. It's a complex area. The good news is that companies—especially big ones—will typically pay for the transferred worker to consult an advisor who specializes in this area. Our key message is that your boss might say "just pack and go; we'll take of your pension." Before you take out your suitcase, ask, "How and when?"

CHAPTER SIXTEEN

LIRAs, LIFs and LRIFs

So you thought that all retirement funding vehicles began with "R"—RPPs, RRSPs and RRIFs? Not quite. Welcome to the world of the "L-plans"—LIRAs, LIFs and LRIFs.

The L-plans are for lump sum transfers from Registered Pension Plans, usually when you change jobs (see the previous chapter). The L means the money is locked in and you face special limits on withdrawals.

WHY WERE L-PLANS CREATED?

There was a time when it was very unusual for lump sums—other than death benefits or refunds of contributions—to be transferred out of pension plans. There was a choice between a refund of your contributions—but not your employers'—and a deferred pension payable from normal retirement age. Opting for the deferred pension meant a mobile worker could end up at 65 with a whole bunch of small pensions from different employers. So most people settled for just taking their contributions.

Pension regulators were concerned that so many people were walking away from vested pensions. So they created the concept of locking-in. Once your pension was vested, you were stuck with a pension that would not be payable until you reached retirement age. That addressed the regulators' concerns. But employers didn't want to keep track of small amounts over many years and then have to find the former employees who were due payments starting at 65. Workers were unhappy because their money was locked in without any adjustment for inflation, which was then soaring. Generally, they wanted to transfer that money to RRSPs so they had investment control and would not have to go back to their former employers at retirement.

The regulators were sympathetic, but the main purpose of pension standards legislation was to encourage the provision of pension benefits. Legislators didn't like the idea that RRSPs could be cashed out before retirement and that RRIFs could be exhausted during retirement. Indeed, the rules in those days required RRIFs to be exhausted by age 90. The legislators were concerned that those who spent their retirement money too soon would create too much of a burden on federal and provincial low-income support programs. So the regulators developed the locked-in RRSP. Each plan holder got investment control. Meanwhile the regulators ensured the money would provide lifetime income because the money was locked in until retirement age and then could only be used for a life annuity. That annuity had to be purchased by the end of the year the plan holder turned 71, the maximum RRSP age at that time.

In 1990, Quebec pioneered a more flexible approach that later spread across the country. It introduced the Locked-In Retirement Account (LIRA) and the Life Income Fund (LIF). The LIRA was a somewhat more flexible version of the locked-in RRSP. The money was still locked in until retirement age, but you no longer had to buy a life annuity to draw income. As an alternative, you could move some or all of the money to a Life Income Fund. The LIF worked just like a RRIF in that you maintained investment control. But, unlike a RRIF, there was a limit on how much you could withdraw each year and at age 80 you were required to use the plan to buy a life annuity. (Some jurisdictions still use the term locked-in RRSP, but it's now synonymous with LIRA.)

L-Plan Rules: the Basics

- Can only accept transfers from an RPP, RRSP or another L-plan

- Spousal consent is not required for transfers

- Subject to pension standards rules for survivor benefits and marital breakdown

- Creditor-proof under pension legislation

- May be transferred before age 70 to an RPP or another L-plan, or be used to buy a life annuity

- May be converted to LIF/LRIF after 55 or pension plan's earliest retirement date

- Must be converted to LIF/LRIF or annuity by end of the year you turn 69

- May be commuted for shortened life expectancy

- At death, tax-free transfer to surviving spouse's RPP, L-plan or annuity

So the LIRA-LIF combination meant you could control the money from your previous pension plan until age 80, when you had to turn it over to a life insurance company. Many people still didn't like that because they lost control and had to accept a fixed income at a time when annuity rates might not be favourable. Also, if you die outside a life annuity's guarantee period, there's nothing for your heirs.

In 1993, Alberta's pension regulators created the Locked-In Retirement Fund (LRIF). As with a LIF, an LRIF caps how much you can take out each year to ensure the fund lasts as long as you do. Unlike a LIF, you can carry forward unused withdrawal entitlements and you never have to buy a life annuity. The plan can run until you die; then the balance goes to your heirs under the same tax rules that apply to RRSPs and RRIFs. LRIFs are now available in Newfoundland, Ontario, Manitoba, Saskatchewan, and Alberta. Several other provinces have adapted the LRIF idea by simply eliminating the requirement that a LIF be turned into a life annuity.

While all jurisdictions now allow L-plans, they vary a bit on the earliest age for withdrawals, how the maximum withdrawal limit is set and the degree to which you might be able to remove a lump sum.

Here's a summary of key rules across the country—as they stood in mid-2001. This is an area of great flux. For example, in late 2001 Saskatchewan's justice minister proposed that regular RRIFs—with unlimited withdrawals—to LIFs and LRIFs as an income option for locked in money regulated by the province. Your best bet is to determine which jurisdiction governed the pension plan from which your locked-in money came and then contact that regulatory body for the most current information. See Appendix D for how to contact pension regulators.

L-Plans: Who Allows What					
	Available Plans			**Earliest Age**	
Jurisdiction	**LIRA**	**LIF**	**LRIF**	**for Income**	**Lump Sum Withdrawal Allowed**
Federal	Yes	Yes		10 yrs before retirement age	If pension < 4% of YMPE Shortened life expectancy If you leave Canada
Alberta	Yes	Yes	Yes	10 yrs before retirement age	If plan value < 20% of YMPE If age 65 and plan value < 40% of YMPE If pension < 4% of YMPE Shortened life expectancy If you leave Canada
British Columbia	Yes	Yes	**	55	If plan value < 20% of YMPE If age 65 & plan value < 40% of YMPE If pension < 10% of YMPE Shortened life expectancy If you leave Canada

cont'd

Manitoba	Yes	Yes	Yes	No statutory age	If plan value at 65 < 40% of YMPE If pension < 4% of YMPE Shortened life expectancy
New Brunswick	Yes	Yes	*	No statutory age	If pension < 2% of YMPE One-time access to 17%–25% based on age Shortened life expectancy
Newfoundland	Yes	Yes	Yes	55	If plan value < 10% of YMPE If pension < 4% of YMPE Shortened life expectancy
Nova Scotia	Yes	Yes	*	10 yrs before retirement age	If pension < 2% of YMPE
Ontario	Yes	Yes	Yes	10 yrs before retirement age	If plan value < 40% of YMPE If pension < 2% of YMPE Shortened life expectancy Financial hardship
Prince Edward Island					If pension < 2% of YMPE
Quebec	Yes	Yes	*	No statutory age	If plan value < 20% of YMPE If 65 and plan value < 40% of YMPE Phased retirement option Shortened life expectancy Financial hardship
Saskatch-ewan	Yes	Yes	**	10 yrs before retirement age	If plan value < 4% of YMPE If pension < 2% of YMPE

* Quebec & New Brunswick LIFs no longer have to be annuitized. That's proposed in Nova Scotia and Saskatchewan.
** B.C. is developing an LRIF. Saskatchewan has proposed replacing LIF/LRIF with a regular RRIF.

WHICH L-PLAN RULES APPLY?

A LIRA, LIF or LRIF is governed by the rules for the jurisdiction that regulated the pension plan from which the money came. Suppose you worked for a chartered bank in Ontario, moved your pension money to a LIRA when you quit and are now retiring in Alberta. Will your LRIF fall under Ontario's rules or Alberta's? Neither! Pension plans for chartered bank employees are federally regulated, so your locked-in money falls under the federal rules. Unfortunately, those rules don't provide for an LRIF, only a LIF—at least at the time we wrote this.

> # If You Go Away
>
> The best time to check the rules that govern an L-plan is before you leave an RPP. That's because the person who releases your pension money must first document its status and any strings that will still be attached. Here are three key questions to ask your human resources officer or pension administrator:
>
> - Which pension regulator will oversee the L-plan to which I'm going to transfer my pension money?
> - What is the earliest date at which I can start withdrawals?
> - Under what circumstances could I get lump sum access?
>
> If you file the answers in a safe place, you can save yourself and your financial advisor a lot of trouble later on when the time comes to cash this cache.

CAN YOU CONSOLIDATE L-PLANS?

Picture this: you change jobs every two or three or four years. Will you be stuck with two or three or four LIRAs, each with a small value? Maybe, maybe not.

First, be aware that several jurisdictions let you cash out a LIRA if it's below a certain amount. That money could then be rolled tax-free into your regular RRSP. The cash-out limits vary widely. For example, Manitoba lets you cash out a LIRA if the balance is less than 4% of the YMPE, or about $1,600. Alberta, on the other hand, lets you cash out a LIRA that's below 20% of the YMPE (about $8,000).

What if the rules that govern your plans don't allow a cash-out, or perhaps your plans are too large? Consult the company that administers your LIRAs. As the trustee, they're responsible for administering the rules.

Suppose you have two LIRAs from pension plans governed by the same jurisdiction. If the plans have the same retirement ages, there should be no problem in combining the LIRAs. If the retirement ages differ, you'd have to accept the later one.

Combining LIRAs from pension plans in different jurisdictions would be more difficult, but not necessarily impossible. Again, you'd have to accept the lock-in rules that are more onerous.

BE CAREFUL ABOUT FEES

Many people now have LIRAs worth $5,000 or so. Investment account fees and commissions can really eat into that small a sum. Consider putting the full amount into an account with one mutual fund company if there's no annual administration fee. Or you might find that a compounding GIC or a stripped bond is the easiest, most secure way to match or beat the return assumed for the transfer value. Every financial institution offers GICs, and advisors who deal with life insurance companies can place deposits that run for more than the standard five-year GIC term. You'll need a self-directed plan to hold a stripped bond. Normally, those plans carry yearly administration fees of $100 or so, but some investment dealers waive the fee if the account holds only fixed-income securities.

Some people view small plans like this as play money. Don't. The money is very real and could prove handy in retirement.

WHAT ABOUT EARLY ACCESS?

Legislators and regulators are coming under increasing pressure to let people make lump sum withdrawals from LIFs and LRIFs. That's now widely allowed if there's evidence of a serious medical problem that will substantially reduce life expectancy.

Financial hardship is a trickier area because it's so subjective. Quebec, for example, simply allows limited access if your other income is below a certain level. That's available for all L-plan holders, though somewhat different rules apply to various age groups. New Brunswick gives LIF holders a one-time opportunity to take out as much as 25% based on their age. Ontario has taken the most interesting approach. In 2000 the government announced that any L-plan holder facing financial hardship could apply for lump sum access. But hardship was defined fairly narrowly and the application forms were made so long and complex that only the most desperate would make their way through them. Within a year several firms popped up and offered to fill out the forms, but they charged very steep fees. The Financial Services Commission of Ontario said those services were unnecessary; its staff would help people complete the forms with no charge at all.

Early access may not provide as much relief as people think. The withdrawal will be fully taxable as income and might affect eligibility for social benefits. Also, the withdrawn money is no longer creditor-proof, so creditors might pressure debt-laden L-plan holders to apply for hardship access if the governing jurisdiction allows it.

Be very careful if someone tells you they have a way to unlock your plan tax-free. In 2001 authorities across Canada reported that several promoters had taken advantage of unsuspecting L-plan holders. In one case, officials shut down a scheme in which L-plan money was transferred to a pension plan that was not properly set up—with the middleman taking as much as 30% of the transfer amount. Other schemes were based on a "loophole" that didn't exist. They required participants to borrow money by using their L-plans as collateral and then buy shares in near-worthless private companies. Those schemes ran afoul of both pension and tax laws. If a locked-in account is used as security for a loan or to buy shares in a company that is not a "qualified investment" under the *Income Tax Act*, the L-plan loses its status and its full value becomes taxable. Before you sign any papers, contact the pension regulator that governs the plan to see if the deal's legit.

What About Death and Disability?

Your Registered Pension Plan does more than support you in retirement. There are also provisions covering disability at any point before your retirement and death.

Let's first took at what happens after you die. Your named beneficiaries or estate will get a payment, but its amount and form will depend on whether you were still working or retired.

BENEFICIARY DESIGNATIONS

Certain benefits automatically go to your spouse unless you and your spouse agree otherwise. Those benefits are specified in the legislation that governs your plan. The aim is to protect a spouse who would otherwise be left with nothing.

Perhaps you have a spouse, but want your benefits to go to someone else. For example, you and your spouse might be separated but not divorced. Or, for estate planning reasons, you might want the money to go directly to your children or other dependents. Make sure you designate your intended recipient as beneficiary—to the extent that's allowed by the legislation which governs your plan.

The death benefits that are earmarked for your spouse or other designated beneficiary will go directly to that person without passing through your estate. That saves time and money since probate would not apply. It also protects that money from your creditors. Periodically check your pension beneficiary designations to make sure they're up to date.

Beneficiaries and the Tax Man

There are tax advantages if the beneficiary is a spouse, former spouse or a dependent child. But these advantages apply only if the death benefit is paid as a lump sum. A current or former spouse can transfer the benefit tax-free to an RRSP or RRIF. With a direct beneficiary designation, the pension administrator can make that payment directly to the person's plan. Otherwise, the money would have to follow a more cumbersome and time-consuming route through your estate; your province might also levy probate fees.

Dependent children and grandchildren get the same beneficiary's tax break as with an RRSP or RRIF. A minor gets the money tax-free, but only if it's used to buy an annuity that makes taxable payments until age 18. Those who are mentally or physically infirm can do a tax-free transfer to an RRSP and, until age 69, make taxable withdrawals only as required.

PRE-RETIREMENT DEATH

With retirement just a few years away, Abdul gets killed in a car crash. Does his family get any benefit from all of the pension contributions he's made? Yes.

Pension standards legislation requires that each plan provide a death benefit for the member's spouse. If there is no spouse, the payment is made to the member's designated beneficiary or to his or her estate. Your death benefit is detailed on your annual pension plan statement.

If you're in a defined contribution plan, your heirs or estate will likely receive your full account balance, even if the law sets a lower minimum payout.

If you're in a defined benefit plan, the benefit is typically 60% or 100% of the value of the pension earned to the date of death.

This wasn't always the case, and many Canadians have heard accounts of how Aunt Betty didn't get a cent from Uncle Joe's pension plan when he died early. Until the wave of pension reform in the 1980s, many plans simply returned the deceased's contributions with interest. In non-contributory plans—those where the employer pays the full cost—there were no member contributions to return. Some plans did pay pre-retirement death benefits to widows and orphans, but those payments were often modest.

Technically, today's legislation requires pre-retirement death benefits only for "post-reform" service—usually the time since major legislative changes were made in the mid- or late '80s. But it's common practice for plans to base death benefits on all earned pension.

DEATH DURING RETIREMENT

Silas finally retired after working—and making pension plan contributions—for 35 years. Two months later he suffered a heart attack and died. His pension stopped, leaving his family with nothing.

That doesn't seem fair, does it?

That happens less now than it used to, thanks to current safeguards. But it's important for you and your spouse to understand those safeguards. Otherwise, you might inadvertently defeat them.

Joint and Survivor Pensions

When you go to retire, pension legislation requires that you and your spouse be automatically offered a joint and survivor pension. That means payments would run until you both die. The survivor's pension payable to your spouse may be reduced, but typically must be at least 60% of the pension to which you were originally entitled. So if Silas was getting $1,000 a month, his widow would be due at least $600.

Got that? Now read this very carefully. You are not compelled to take the standard joint and survivor pension. If your spouse agrees in writing on the proper form, you could set the survivor's pension at less than 60% or even opt for a payout that covers only your life. Why would you do this? Depending on the plan, a 60% survivor's benefit could reduce your monthly pension by as much as 25% or so.

Alternatively, you might be willing to accept an even lower payout in order to leave your spouse with more than a 60% pension.

Was What Was Said What Was Heard?

Don't be offended if your pension administrator treats you like a child in explaining your pension options. The 1999 judgment in *Deraps v. Labourer's Pension Fund of Central and Eastern Canada* shocked the pension community. A couple chose a pension that would run only until the death of the retiring worker. Unfortunately, the new pensioner died soon after. The surviving spouse sued the plan administrator. The administrator had followed common practice in explaining the consequences of the couple's options, but the court ruled that administrators must also ensure that explanation is *understood*.

So you and your spouse have several options: the standard survivor's benefit set by pension legislation, a benefit below that level—perhaps zero—and, if the plan offers it, a benefit above that level. That decision involves a tradeoff—the higher the survivor's income, the lower your retirement income.

So how do the two of you decide?

First, determine the extent to which your spouse needs survivor's income. If your pension is the family's only sizeable financial asset, you face a difficult balancing act. Go for the highest survivor benefit you can while still ensuring that the pension you receive while alive is enough to support the two of you.

Then again, you may find that your spouse can rely on other assets and therefore needs little or nothing in continuing pension income from you. For example, you might have adequate life insurance, a large RRSP or other investments. If so, consider now whether your spouse will be able to prudently manage that money. If he or she lacks the ability or interest, why not line up professional assistance before it's needed?

Perhaps you both work and are both in line for adequate pensions. The issues then become whether there's a significant difference between the two payouts and which is most important: maximizing retirement income or deferring tax.

If there's a significant difference between the two plans, consider coordinating the survivor benefits so you each wind up with about the same income if the other dies first. That means the spouse with the higher pension would opt for a higher survivor benefit.

To maximize retirement income, you could each waive the survivor's entitlement altogether and take a life-only pension. You would each receive a full pension while alive. After the first death, the survivor would then live on his or her own pension—which means the household income might be half what it was before.

To defer tax, consider the opposite approach. You could each opt for a 100% survivor's benefit. That would substantially reduce the taxable income while both of you are alive, shifting that payout to the survivor after the first death—hopefully many years away.

This need not be an all-or-nothing proposition. In a middle-of-the-road strategy, you could each select a 50% or 75% survivor pension.

Be careful if you have different retirement dates. These decisions are irrevocable. That means the spouse who retires first will make a one-time choice based on assumptions that might go awry. For example, the second spouse might lose his or her job, suffer a big drop in pay or be forced into early retirement by health concerns. His or her pension may then be much less than the first spouse assumed.

Don't make this decision in a vacuum. Each spouse should ask his or her pension plan administrator for a list of the available options and the dollars-and-cents impact of adding or reducing survivor coverage, if that's allowed. Then play with the numbers to see what works best.

Guaranteed Payments

Pensions are frequently offered with a guaranteed number of payments—for example, five years. That means the plan is obligated to make 60 monthly payments on your behalf. Let's go back to Silas. He received two payments while alive. His spouse would then be entitled to the 58 payments still guaranteed. If there is no spouse, former spouse or eligible dependent, tax rules require the present value of those payments to be calculated and paid as a lump sum—taxable, of course. What if Silas had died right after receiving his sixtieth monthly payment? In that case, the guarantee would have run out and there would be nothing for his spouse.

Pension plans normally offer a choice of guarantee periods, though tax rules cap the longest at 15 years. Plans also normally let you and your spouse choose the level of continuing pension. As you might expect, there's a cost to choosing a longer guarantee and/or higher survivor's pension. This cost is paid by taking a lower monthly pension from day one.

Jim is 60 and his spouse, Mary, is 57. He's about to retire with an annual pension of $30,000 that ceases on his death. Because he has a spouse, he knows that he must convert to a joint and survivor pension with 60% continuing to Mary after his death unless they both sign a waiver. James asks the plan administrator how much this and other options would cost.

Option	Pension
Life only pension—ends at Jim's death	$30,000
Guarantee 60 monthly payments (5 years)	29,718
Guarantee 120 monthly payments (10 years)	28,937
Guarantee 180 monthly payments (15 years)	27,787
50% joint & survivor pension	26,798
60% joint & survivor pension	26,238
66.67% joint & survivor pension	25,877
75% joint & survivor pension	25,440
100% joint & survivor pension	24,213

Suppose that Jim and Mary agree that he'll take a single-life pension with a 10-year guarantee. He'll receive $28,937 a year for as long as he lives. If he dies within 10 years, Mary will get the value of the payments left in the guarantee. If Jim dies after 10 years, Mary gets nothing.

What if they choose the 60% joint and survivor option? That's the basic requirement in most jurisdictions. Jim would receive $26,238 each year. When he dies, Mary would receive $15,743—that's $26,238 x 60%—for as long as she lives.

Obviously, your pension selection is a very important decision. Make sure to discuss it fully with your spouse. Do you have a financial advisor or insurance agent? Ask him or her to review your pension options in the context of your overall financial plan. Your family might already be well provided for without a survivor's pension. Then again, a survivor's pension might be crucial even if it means living on less in retirement.

Cash Refund Plans

Your plan might use a different approach that's simpler but perhaps less effective in providing security for your loved ones. Suppose the pension contributions that Silas made during his career totalled $75,000 and he received $2,000 in benefits during his two months as a retiree. Under a cash refund provision, the pension plan would pay his beneficiaries or estate $73,000—the difference between what he put into the plan and what he got from it. The plan might also pay interest on that amount.

WHAT ABOUT PRE-RETIREMENT DISABILITY?

Many defined benefit RPPs provide special benefits if you become disabled before retirement. These may take the form of a disability pension paid from the plan, or you might continue to earn pension credits even though you are not actually working. The latter approach is usually taken if you are entitled to receive group insurance benefits while disabled. At normal retirement age the insurance benefits will cease and a retirement pension will start. Tax rules normally restrict pension benefits to those that can be shown to relate to actual periods of employment. An exception is made for disabled employees.

Let's look first at the situation where the plan pays a disability pension. You will already have earned a certain amount of pension to be paid starting on your normal retirement date—see your annual pension statement. If you're disabled, the plan is allowed—if its terms provide—to start paying you that pension starting immediately without any reduction.

Eric is in a defined benefit plan and accrues a monthly pension of $45 for each year of service. With 20 years so far, he has earned a pension of $900 monthly. He's now 55. He could take early retirement, but his pension would be reduced by 6% for each year to the normal retirement age of 65. So, his pension would be 40% of the full amount, or $360 monthly. Eric suffers a crippling accident. The plan may pay him the full $900 pension starting immediately. It may also calculate the additional amount of pension that he would have earned if he had remained employed until age 65 and add that to his pension. This would increase his pension by $45 x 10, or $450, for a total of $1,350 monthly. The additional credit for those future years is not allowed to increase the pension beyond the YMPE. But that's not an issue since Eric's total annual pension is $16,200 ($1,350 x 12) and the YMPE is about $40,000. Tax rules also permit Eric's pension to be inflation-indexed.

If Eric were in a defined contribution plan, all he would have at the start of his disability would be the value of his account without any immediate enhancements. If he receives payments from the company insurance program, he's still considered an employee and would not be able to transfer his pension money to a locked-in RRSP or other personal account. Rather, the DC plan would likely provide for continuing employer contributions that accumulate until retirement age. These contributions could be based on Eric's full earnings before he became disabled.

What Happens If Your Marriage Ends?

Every province now has legislation that includes pension benefits in the assets to be shared on marriage breakdown. So, these assets must be dealt with on separation or divorce. But the two of you can't simply decide to split everything down the middle and scribble that on a piece of paper. The pension plan administrator will insist on getting the proper documents specified by your provincial legislation or a court order.

Anyone who has been through it will tell you there's absolutely nothing simple or easy about divorce. The issues surrounding pension benefits are, frankly, too complex to do full justice here; it would take a book. (There is a book. The Ontario Law Reform Commission wrote it. It's called the *Report on Pensions as Family Property*. If you really want the full story, get a copy. If you're willing to settle for an overview, read on.)

There are four methods for dealing with your pension:

- **Compensation:** You keep the pension and let your ex have another asset of equal value. This is neat and tidy, but your pension might be so valuable that it's difficult to find an asset of equal value.

- **Direct payment:** You keep the pension and send your ex a cheque every month after you retire. Would your ex go for that? Can pigs fly?

- **Transfer:** You agree to split the pension and have the plan transfer the share for your ex to his or her RRSP. That's a pretty good solution, but the legislation that governs your plan might not allow it until you change jobs, retire or die. See the table below.

- **Benefit split:** You agree to split the pension and when you retire, the plan pays part of the pension to you and part to your ex. That might be what's required by the legislation that governs your plan. Of course, your ex then has to stay in touch with the plan.

There might be more than one ex. Suppose you separate from your legally married spouse and don't actually divorce. Meanwhile, you move into a common-law relationship. Unless there's an airtight separation agreement, your original spouse has a claim since there was no divorce and your common-law partner might qualify as a spouse based on the legislation governing your plan—see Appendix C. In Ontario, for example, pension law grants a common-law partner no right to a claim, but a court order for support could override that.

So what's the value to be split? That's easy if you're in a defined contribution plan. The lawyers can see precisely how much went into the plan, when it went in and how much that money grew. That's not easy at all if you're in a defined benefit plan.

There are two ways to value a DB pension. The "pro rata" method divides the total value at separation based on how long the marriage ran in relation to the total period in which credits were earned. If the law requires a 50-50 split and you were married for 80% of your pension service, your spouse would get 80% of 50%. The "value-added" method subtracts the value of the pension earned before the marriage and then applies the split.

In its 1999 judgment in *Best v. Best*, the Supreme Court of Canada favoured the pro rata method as being more fair. But the court left the door open to other methods if they can be shown to be appropriate.

Your Ex Might Have to Wait for the Pension Money	
Jurisdiction	**When Your Ex Gets the Money**
Federal	Immediate transfer after separation/divorce
Alberta	DB plan: when you cease accruing benefits
	DC plan: immediate transfer after separation/divorce
British Columbia	DB plan: when you become eligible to retire, die or leave plan
	DC plan: immediate transfer after separation/divorce
Manitoba	Immediate transfer after separation/divorce
New Brunswick	Immediate transfer after separation/divorce
Newfoundland	Immediate transfer after separation/divorce
Nova Scotia	DB plan: when you become eligible to retire
	DC plan: immediate transfer after separation/divorce
Ontario	No transfer until you retire, die or leave plan.
Prince Edward Island	No transfer until you retire, die or leave plan
Quebec	Immediate transfer after separation/divorce
Saskatchewan	Immediate transfer after separation/divorce

Can Your Employer Change the Plan?

Yes, but what you've earned so far is protected.

Your employer is allowed to change your pension plan with two provisos. First, the plan text must allow for amendments—and they generally do. Second, the amendment must not reduce any benefits you've already earned. (There is an exception to this rule for multi-employer plans; see Chapter 6.)

While benefits earned so far are safe, an amendment can reduce those earned in the future. For example, a flat benefit plan that provides a pension of $40 a month for each year of service might be reduced to $30 a month for those years after the amendment takes effect. Or the accrual rate for a final average plan might be reduced from 2% to 1%—but only for those credits earned after the change is made; retroactive reductions are not allowed.

Every amendment must be registered with the plan's regulator. The plan can implement that change once the registration application is made, but would then have to undo everything if the regulator rejects the request. Regulators won't register an "adverse amendment" unless plan members are notified and given 45 days to comment. An adverse amendment is one that reduces future benefits or affects the rights and obligations of plan members. If the amendment is accepted, the plan must notify its members, the affected former members and any relevant unions.

CONVERSIONS

In recent years employers have shown considerable interest in converting defined benefit plans to defined contribution structures. The impetus may come from younger employees who do not feel the DB structure meets their needs, or from employers who wish to make their pension costs more predictable by shifting the investment risk to their employees.

There are basically two ways to structure a conversion. A "prospective" conversion would freeze the benefits already earned under the DB plan and switch to DC credits for service going forward. A "retrospective" conversion would give you the option of going DC all the way. Your DB credits earned so far would be converted to an amount that becomes the opening balance for your DC account. There are strict rules on how this balance is to be calculated, and you must be given detailed information on your rights and options at the time of the conversion. You can't be forced to accept a retrospective conversion. If you don't go along, your DB credits would be kept intact.

WINDING UP

Sometimes a defined benefit plan is shut down and its assets distributed. That's called a "wind-up." The employer might instigate the wind-up or it might be ordered by the pension regulator if the employer goes bankrupt or fails to make the contributions required by law. As we mentioned in Chapter 11, some jurisdictions have the concept of a "partial wind-up," usually triggered by a plant closing or other large-scale terminations. Under a partial wind-up, the plan is effectively divided into two parts. The part covering the terminated employees is wound up. The part covering ongoing employees remains unchanged.

When a plan is wound up, the assets must be distributed. Usually the money is transferred to some form of locked-in RRSP, such as a Locked-In Retirement Account (LIRA), or used to buy an annuity. The plan's surplus, if any, must also be disposed of.

Each member must be given notice of the wind-up and a statement detailing his or her entitlements and options. The members are also entitled to see the special actuarial report that details the plan's financial position and the proposed method of dealing with any surplus or deficit.

At wind-up, you have the right to full vesting of the benefits you've earned so far—even if you haven't reached the normal vesting date. You also have the right to transfer the value of your benefits no matter what the normal plan rules say. But—aside from benefits for current, and perhaps new, pensioners—no money can leave the plan until the regulator approves the wind-up.

What if there's not enough to go around? Current retirees get first claim. Next come those employees now eligible for pensions. Remaining money is then divided among the rest. Yes, there is a risk that you might not get the benefits you were promised. That's why you should keep an eye on your plan's health through your annual statement, as discussed in Chapter 9, and ask questions if there has been a substantial deterioration. The Ontario government maintains a fund, financed by pension sponsors, that's earmarked to cover shortfalls on wind-ups.

Ontario and Nova Scotia have special benefit provisions that kick in on plan wind-up. These are known as "grow-in" rights. A member whose combination of age and years of employment adds up to 55 or more is entitled to these rights, which can be very valuable if the plan has early retirement subsidies.

Basically, the grow-in rule assumes the employee would have stayed on long enough to qualify for an unreduced pension. Take Peter, who is now 50 and has 10 years of service. Due to a wind-up, Peter is leaving the plan whether he wants to or not. Normally, a 50-year-old who leaves his plan early has the right to a pension starting at 65, but one who stays until 60 can then retire on a full pension without actuarial reduction. The grow-in rules assume Peter would have stayed on. So, at wind-up, his earned pension is enhanced to make it payable at age 60 instead of 65. In his case, this increases the value by about 30% and he has the right to transfer that amount out of the plan.

WHAT IF YOUR EMPLOYER IS SOLD?

That depends on how the pension plan is structured. If the plan covers all employees, the new employer would have to set up a new pension plan and transfer in assets from the old plan. Does the new plan have to be as good as your current one? No, but as we noted at the start of this chapter, the benefits you've earned so far are safe. Any negative change would apply only to the benefits you earn in the future.

Some companies have a separate pension plan for each facility or division. In that case, the new owner could simply assume responsibility for the plan and continue it as before, but with a new name.

The new owner must get regulatory permission to transfer assets from your current plan to a new one. Based on complex rules, the regulator will see if the benefits of plan members are protected by examining a report that details what's going to happen to the fund's assets and liabilities.

WHAT IF YOUR EMPLOYER FAILS?

See the section above on winding up a pension plan.

Canada's International Benefits Agreements

Many Canadians spend part of their careers working in other countries. You might have emigrated to Canada. You might have been raised here, but decide to work elsewhere for a few years. Or you might decide to leave Canada and settle elsewhere.

This is a list of the social security agreements Canada had with other countries in July, 2001. While the terms might vary, the idea is the same: the two countries have agreed to recognize each other's retirement and disability plan credits in determining whether a mobile worker is eligible for benefits. That way, you don't lose out if you move before accumulating enough credit to qualify for at least a minimum payout. These agreements are particularly beneficial if someone dies or becomes disabled within a few years of changing countries.

The terms and status of each agreement are available through HRDC's web site at www.hrdc-drhc.gc.ca. Go to the Income Security Programs section and click on International Benefits. You can also phone HRDC's International Operations section directly at 1-613-957-1954 or through the general information line at 1-800-277-9914.

If you are due foreign credits for either Old Age Security or C/QPP, provide ample time for officials to process the claim. You can apply for OAS or C/QPP up to 12 months before the date when benefits would start.

* indicates agreement with Quebec relating to QPP
† indicates agreement not yet in force as of July, 2001

Antigua and Barbuda	Korea
Argentina †	Luxembourg *
Australia	Malta *
Austria *	Mexico
Barbados *	Morocco †
Belgium	Netherlands
Chile	New Zealand
Croatia	Norway *
Cyprus *	Philippines *
Czech Republic †	Poland †
Denmark *	Portugal *
Dominica *	St. Kitts and Nevis
Finland *	Saint Lucia *
France *	Saint Vincent and the Grenadines
Germany *	Slovakia †
Greece *	Slovenia
Grenada	Spain
Guernsey	Sweden *
Hungary †	Switzerland *
Iceland	Trinidad and Tobago
Ireland *	Turkey †
Israel †	United Kingdom
Italy *	United States *
Jamaica*	Uruguay †
Jersey	

Highlights: Minimum Pension Standards

FEDERAL	
Eligibility:	
• Full-time	2 years' continuous employment
• Part-time	In each of past 2 years earned at least 35% of YMPE
Vesting	2 years' membership. Pre-1987 credits: age 45+10 years' continuous service/membership
Benefits locked-in	At vesting
Transfer on termination	Commuted value of vested benefits may be transferred to another RPP, a LI-RRSP/LIF or used to buy an annuity. Transfer need not be offered if within 10 years of normal retirement age
Access to locked-in pension	See Chapter 16 table for lump sum access
Normal retirement	Age-related as defined in plan
Early retirement	10 years before normal retirement age
Delayed retirement	Pension credits must continue to accrue unless member receives pension
Employer DB plan contributions	Employer must fund at least 50% of cost of post-1986 vested pension. Excess employee contributions earn interest and may be transferred to RPP, LI-RRSP, LIF, annuity or taken as additional pension if allowed by plan. Waived if deferred pension is indexed by at least 75% of CPI less 1%
Interest on required contributions	DB: Rate earned by fund or average 5-year chartered bank deposit rate DC: Rate earned by fund

cont'd

FEDERAL cont'd	
Government benefit integration	No restrictions
Gender-specific rules	Unisex rules required for member contributions & benefits for post-1986 service
Definition of spouse	See Appendix C
Marriage breakdown	Pension is subject to asset splitting. Immediate settlement allowed after divorce or separation
Death benefit: • Member dies before retirement	DB: Spouse due commuted value of pension earned after 1986, paid in cash or as pension. Spouse due 60% pension if member was eligible for early retirement at time of death. If no spouse, commuted value paid to beneficiary or estate. Payout may be reduced by value of group life insurance benefit. DC: Spouse due full account balance
• Member dies during retirement	Unless waived, spouse due at least 60% of pension commencing after 1987. Actuarial adjustment allowed
• Remarriage affect benefit	No
Member input into plan administration	Employer must create an advisory committee if plan has 50 members and requested by a majority of members

ALBERTA	
Eligibility:	
• Full-time	2 years' continuous employment having earned at least 35% of YMPE in each of 2 consecutive calendar years immediately prior to membership
• Part-time	As above
Vesting	After 2 years continuous membership for post-1999 credits, 5 years for 1987-99 credits and for pre-1987 credits, age 45 + 10 years service
Benefits locked-in	At vesting
Transfer on termination	Commuted value of vested benefits may be transferred to another RPP, or a LIRA or used to buy an annuity (if plan permits). Transfer need not be offered if termination occurs less than 10 yrs prior to normal retirement age
Access to locked-in pension	See Chapter 16 table for lump sum access
Normal retirement	Age-related as defined in plan
Early retirement	Within 10 years of normal retirement age
Delayed retirement	Pension credits may continue to accrue unless member receives pension
Employer DB plan contributions	Employer must fund at least 50% of cost of post-1986 vested pension. Excess employee contributions earn interest and are refunded as cash or as additional pension if allowed by plan or transferred to RPP, RRSP or RRIF
Interest on required contributions	DB: Rate earned by fund or average 5-year chartered bank desposit rate DC: Rate earned by fund
Government benefit integration	C/QPP reduction allowed. OAS reduction allowed only for pre-1987 credits
Gender-specific rules	None
Definition of spouse	See Appendix C
Marriage breakdown	Pension is subject to asset splitting. DB settlement occurs when member leaves plan or reaches normal retirement age. Immediate DC settlement allowed after divorce or separation
Death benefit:	
• Member dies before retirement	Spouse due full value of pension earned post-1999, 60% if earned 1986-1999, paid in cash or as pension. DC: 60% of vested employer contributions pre-2000 & 100% of those post-1999. If no spouse, beneficiary or estate due member contributions with interest plus 100% of post-1999 employer contributions
• Member dies during retirement	Unless waived, spouse due at least 60% of pension for post-1986 service. Actuarial adjustment allowed
• Remarriage affect benefit	No
Member input into plan administration	Not mandated

BRITISH COLUMBIA	
Eligibility: • Full-time	2 years' continuous employment having earned at least 35% of YMPE in each of 2 calendar years immediately prior to membership
• Part-time	As above. Separate but comparable plan permitted for part-time employees
Vesting	2 years' continuous membership
Benefits locked-in	At vesting (for post-1992 credits only)
Transfer on termination	Commuted value of vested benefits may be transferred to another RPP, an LI-RRSP/LIF or used to buy an annuity. Transfer need not be offered if termination occurs after age 55
Access to locked-in pension	See Chapter 16 table for lump sum access
Normal retirement	Age-related as defined in plan
Early retirement	After age 55
Delayed retirement	Pension credits may continue to accrue unless member receives a pension
Employer DB plan contributions	Employer must fund at least 50% of cost of post-1992 pension. Excess employee contributions earn interest and are refunded as cash, transferred to RPP, RRSP or RRIF, purchase deferred annuity or (if allowed by plan) taken as additional pension
Interest on required contributions	DB: Rate earned by fund or average 5-year chartered bank deposit rate DC: Rate earned by fund
Government benefit integration	C/QPP reduction allowed. OAS reduction allowed only for pre-1993 credits
Gender-specific rules	Unisex rules required for eligibility, member contributions & benefits
Definition of spouse	See Appendix C
Marriage breakdown	Pension is subject to asset splitting. DB Settlement occurs when member leaves plan or becomes eligible to retire. Immediate DC settlement allowed after divorce or separation
Death benefit: • Member dies before retirement	Spouse due at least 60% of commuted value of pension earned after 1992, paid in cash or as pension. DC plan: 60% of employer account value. If no spouse, commuted value paid to beneficiary or estate
• Member dies during retirement	Unless waived, spouse due at least 60% of pension for post-1992 service. Actuarial adjustment allowed
• Remarriage affect benefit	No
Member input into plan administration	Employer must create an advisory committee if requested by a majority of members

MANITOBA	
Eligibility:	
• Full-time	After 2 years' continuous service
• Part-time	In each of past 2 years earned at least 35% of YMPE or worked 700 hours
Vesting	After 2 years' membership. For pre-1986 credits: age 45 + 10 years service
Benefits locked-in	At vesting
Transfer on termination	Commuted value of vested benefits may be transferred to another RPP, a LIRA/LIF/LRIF or used to buy an annuity. Transfer need not be offered if pension is payable at time of termination
Access to locked-in pension	See Chapter 16 table for lump sum access
Normal retirement	Age-related as defined in plan
Early retirement	10 years before normal retirement age
Delayed retirement	Pension credits must continue to accrue unless member receives a pension
Employer DB plan contributions	Employer must fund at least 50% of cost of vested pension. Excess employee contributions earn interest and are refunded as cash or as additional pension at member's option
Interest on required contributions	DB: Rate earned by fund or average 5-year chartered bank deposit rate DC: Rate earned by fund
Government benefit integration	C/QPP reduction allowed. OAS reduction allowed only for pre-1987 credits
Gender-specific rules	Unisex rules required for eligibility contributions & benefits covering post-1986 service
Definition of spouse	See Appendix C
Marriage breakdown	Pension is subject to asset splitting. Immediate settlement allowed after divorce or separation
Death benefit:	
• Member dies before retirement	Spouse due full commuted value of pension earned after 1986, paid in cash or as pension. If no spouse, commuted value paid to beneficiary or estate.
• Member dies during retirement	Unless waived, spouse due at least 60% of pension for post-1986 service. Actuarial adjustment allowed
• Remarriage affect benefit	No
Member input into plan administration	Employer must create an advisory committee if requested by a majority of members

NEW BRUNSWICK	
Eligibility: • Full-time • Part-time	 After 2 years' continuous service In each of past 2 years earned at least 35% of YMPE
Vesting	After 2 years' membership
Benefits locked-in	At vesting
Transfer on termination	Commuted value of vested benefits may be transferred to another RPP, a LIRA or LIF or used to buy an annuity. Transfer need not be offered if less than 10 years from normal retirement age
Access to locked-in pension	See Chapter 16 table for lump sum access
Normal retirement	No later than 1 year after 65th birthday
Early retirement	10 years before normal retirement age
Delayed retirement	Pension credits may continue to accrue unless member receives pension
Employer DB plan contributions	Employer must fund at least 50% of cost of post-1992 vested pension unless plan specifies otherwise. Excess employee contributions earn interest and are refunded as cash or as additional pension if allowed by plan
Interest on required contributions	DB: Rate earned by fund or average 5-year chartered bank deposit rate DC: Rate earned by fund
Government benefit integration	C/QPP reduction allowed. OAS reduction allowed only for pre-1992 credits
Gender-specific rules	Unisex rules required for eligibility contributions & benefits covering post-1991 service
Definition of spouse	See Appendix C
Marriage breakdown	Pension is subject to asset splitting. Immediate settlement allowed after divorce or separation
Death benefit: • Member dies before retirement • Member dies during retirement • Remarriage affect benefit	 Spouse due at least 60% of commuted value of pension, paid in cash or as pension. If no spouse, commuted value paid to beneficiary or estate. Payout may be reduced by value of group life insurance benefit. Unless waived, spouse due at least 60% of pension for post–1986 service. Actuarial adjustment allowed No
Member input into plan administration	Employer must create an advisory committee if requested by a majority of members

NEWFOUNDLAND	
Eligibility:	
• Full-time	After 2 years' continuous service
• Part-time	In each of past 2 years earned at least 35% of YMPE
Vesting	After 2 years' membership. For pre-1997 credits: age 45 + 10 years service
Benefits locked-in	At vesting
Transfer on termination	Commuted value of vested benefits may be transferred to another RPP, a LIRA/LIF/LRIF or used to buy an annuity. Transfer need not be offered if pension is payable at time of termination
Access to locked-in pension	See Chapter 16 table for lump sum access
Normal retirement	No later than 66th birthday
Early retirement	After age 55
Delayed retirement	Pension may not be paid before active membership ceases
Employer DB plan contributions	Employer must fund at least 50% of cost of vested pension accrued after 1996. Excess employee contributions earn interest and are refunded as cash or as additional pension or transferred to another RPP/RRSP/RRIF
Interest on required contributions	DB: Rate earned by fund or long-term Canada bond rate DC: Rate earned by fund
Integration with government benefits	C/QPP reduction allowed. OAS reduction allowed only for pre-1997 credits
Gender-specific rules	None
Definition of spouse	See Appendix C
Marriage breakdown	Pension is subject to asset splitting. Immediate settlement allowed after divorce or separation
Death benefit:	
• Member dies before retirement	Spouse due full commuted value of pension, paid in cash or as pension. If no spouse, commuted value paid to beneficiary or estate
• Member dies during retirement	Unless waived, spouse due at least 60% of pension for post-1986 service. Actuarial adjustment allowed
• Remarriage affect benefit	No
Member input into plan administration	Not mandated

NOVA SCOTIA	
Eligibility: • Full-time • Part-time	 After 2 years' continuous employment In each of past 2 years earned at least 35% of YMPE
Vesting	After 2 years' membership. For 1987-97 credits: age 45 + 10 years service
Benefits locked-in	At vesting
Transfer on termination	Commuted value of vested benefits may be transferred to another RPP, an LI-RRSP/LIF (if less than 10 yrs from normal retirement age) or used to buy an annuity.
Access to locked-in pension	See Chapter 16 table for lump sum access
Normal retirement	No later than 1 year after 65th birthday
Early retirement	10 years before normal retirement age
Delayed retirement	Pension credits may continue to accrue unless member receives pension
Employer DB plan contributions	Employer must fund at least 50% of cost of 1988 and later vested pension. Excess employee contributions earn interest and are refunded as cash, paid as member directs or taken as additional pension if allowed by plan
Interest on required contributions	DB: Rate earned by fund or average 5-year chartered bank deposit rate DC: Rate earned by fund
Government benefit integration	C/QPP reduction allowed. OAS reduction allowed only for pre-1988 credits
Gender-specific rules	Unisex rules required for eligibility, member contributions & benefits covering post-1987 service
Definition of spouse	See Appendix C
Marriage breakdown	Pension is subject to asset splitting. DB settlement occurs when member becomes eligible to retire. Immediate DC settlement allowed after divorce or separation
Death benefit: • Member dies before retirement • Member dies during retirement • Remarriage affect benefit	 Spouse due at least 60% of commuted value of pension earned after 1987. If no spouse, member's contributions with interest paid to beneficiary or estate. Payout may be reduced by value of group life insurance benefit. Unless waived, spouse due at least 60% of pension. Actuarial adjustment allowed No
Member input into plan administration	Not mandated

ONTARIO	
Eligibility:	
• Full-time	2 years' continuous employment
• Part-time	In each of past 2 years earned at least 35% of YMPE or worked 700 hours
Vesting	2 years' membership. Pre-1987 credits: age 45 +10 years' continuous service/membership
Benefits locked-in	At vesting
Transfer on termination	Commuted value of vested benefits may be transferred to another RPP, a LIRA/LIF/LRIF or used to buy an annuity. Transfer need not be offered if pension is payable at time of termination
Access to locked-in pension	See Chapter 16 table for lump sum access
Normal retirement	No later than age 66
Early retirement	10 years before normal retirement age
Delayed retirement	Pension credits may continue to accrue unless member receives pension
Employer DB plan contributions	Employer must fund at least 50% of cost of post-1986 vested pension. Excess employee contributions earn interest and are refunded as cash or as additional pension if allowed by plan
Interest on required contributions	DB: Rate earned by fund or average 5-year chartered bank deposit rate DC: Rate earned by fund
Government benefit integration	C/QPP reduction allowed. OAS reduction allowed only for pre-1987 credits
Gender-specific rules	Unisex rules required for eligibility, contributions & benefits covering post-1986 service
Definition of spouse	See Appendix C
Marriage breakdown	Pension is subject to asset splitting. Settlement occurs when member leaves plan or reaches normal retirement age
Death benefit:	
• Member dies before retirement	Spouse due full commuted value of pension earned after 1986, paid in cash or as pension. If no spouse, commuted value paid to beneficiary or estate. Payout may be reduced by value of group life insurance benefit.
• Member dies during retirement	Unless waived, spouse due at least 60% of pension. Actuarial adjustment allowed
• Remarriage affect benefit	No
Member input into plan administration	Employer must create an advisory committee if requested by a majority of members

PRINCE EDWARD ISLAND (Legislation passed in 1990, but not yet in force)	
Eligibility: • Full-time • Part-time	 After 2 years' continuous service In each of past 2 years earned at least 35% of YMPE or worked 700 hours
Vesting	Pending legislation sets 3 years' membership plus 5 years of continuous service after law becomes operative
Benefits locked-in	At vesting
Transfer on termination	Commuted value of vested benefits may be transferred to another RPP, prescribed retirement savings arrangement or used to buy an annuity. Transfer need not be offered if within 10 years of normal retirement age
Access to locked-in pension	See Chapter 16 table for lump sum access
Normal retirement	No later than 1 year after 65th birthday
Early retirement	After age 55
Delayed retirement	Pension credits may continue to accrue unless member receives pension
Employer DB plan contributions	Employer must fund at least 50% of cost of vested pension earned after operative date of legislation. Excess employee contributions earn interest and must be used to provide additional pension. Waived if deferred pension indexed by at least 75% of CPI less 1%
Interest on required contributions	To be prescribed
Integration with government benefits	C/QPP reduction allowed. No OAS reduction allowed once legislation takes effect
Gender-specific rules	Unisex rules required for eligibility contributions & benefits covering service after legislation becomes operative
Definition of spouse	See Appendix C
Marriage breakdown	Pension is subject to asset splitting. Settlement occurs when member leaves plan or reaches normal retirement age
Death benefit: • Member dies before retirement	 Spouse due at least 60% of commuted value of pension earned after operative date of legislation, paid in cash or as pension. If no spouse, member contributions with interest paid to beneficiary or estate
• Member dies during retirement	Unless waived, spouse due at least 60% of pension for post-1986 service. Actuarial adjustment allowed
• Remarriage affect benefit	No
Member input into plan administration	Employer must create an advisory committee if requested by a majority of members

QUEBEC	
Eligibility: • Full-time • Part-time	 After 2 years' continuous employment In each of past 2 years earned at least 35% of YMPE or worked 700 hours
Vesting	After 2 years' membership. For pre-1990 credits: age 45 + 10 years service
Benefits locked-in	At vesting
Transfer on termination	Commuted value of vested benefits may be transferred to another RPP, an LI-RRSP/LIF or used to buy an annuity. Transfer need not be offered if within 10 years of normal retirement age or eligible for unreduced pension
Access to locked-in pension	See Chapter 16 table for lump sum access
Normal retirement	No later than first day of month following 65th birthday
Early retirement	10 years before normal retirement age. Phased-in retirement permitted if reduced work hours agreed with employer
Delayed retirement	Continuation of membership not required. Under certain circumstances pension may be paid during delay period. Value of pension to be increased if deferred
Employer DB plan contributions	Employer must fund at least 50% of cost of post-1989 vested pension. Excess employee contributions earn interest and may be transferred to LIRA/LIF, used to purchase annuity, or taken as additional pension
Interest on required contributions	DB: Rate earned by fund or average 5-year chartered bank deposit rate DC: Rate earned by fund
Government benefit integration	C/QPP reduction allowed. OAS reduction allowed only for pre-1990 credits
Gender-specific rules	Unisex rules required for eligibility, member contributions & benefits covering post-1989 service
Definition of spouse	See Appendix C
Marriage breakdown	Spouse entitled to benefits under court order applying Civil Code or agreement between unmarried partners applying pension legislation. Immediate settlement allowed after divorce or separation
Death benefit: • Member dies before retirement • Member dies during retirement • Remarriage affect benefit	 Spouse due full commuted value of pension earned after 1989, paid in cash or transfer to RRSP, RRIF or RPP. If no spouse, commuted value paid to beneficiary or estate Unless waived, spouse due at least 60% of pension. Actuarial adjustment allowed No
Member input into plan administration	Plan must be administered by committee including member and third-party representation. Annual meeting required at which members may elect representation

SASKATCHEWAN	
Eligibility: • Full-time • Part-time	 2 years' continuous service In each of past 2 years earned at least 35% of YMPE or worked 700 hours
Vesting	2 years' continuous service. Pre-1994 credits: age + service/membership = 45
Benefits locked-in	At vesting
Transfer on termination	Commuted value of vested benefits may be transferred to another RPP, a LIRA (LIF/LRIF if 55 or reached early retirement age under plan) or used to buy an annuity. Transfer need not be offered within 10 years of normal retirement age
Access to locked-in pension	See Chapter 16 table for lump sum access
Normal retirement	Age-related as determined by plan
Early retirement	10 years before normal retirement age
Delayed retirement	Pension credits may continue to accrue unless member receives pension
Employer DB plan contributions	Employer must fund at least 50% of cost of post-1968 pension. Excess employee contributions earn interest and are used to provide additional pension or transferred to an RPP, RRSP or RRIF.
Interest on required contributions	DB: Rate earned by fund or average 5-year chartered bank deposit rate DC: Rate earned by fund
Government benefit integration	C/QPP reduction allowed. OAS reduction allowed on a limited basis
Gender-specific rules	Unisex rules required for eligibility, member contributions & benefits covering post-1986 service
Definition of spouse	Common law partner qualifies after 1 year
Marriage breakdown	Pension is subject to asset splitting. Immediate settlement allowed after divorce or separation
Death benefit: • Member dies before retirement	 Spouse due full commuted value of pension earned after 1993, paid in cash or as pension. Minimum of 60% of pension if member reached early retirement age. If no spouse, commuted value paid to beneficiary or estate
• Member dies during retirement	Unless waived, spouse due at least 60% of pension for post-1986 service. Actuarial adjustment allowed
• Remarriage affect benefit	No
Member input into plan administration	Employer must create an advisory committee if plan has 50 members and requested by a majority of members

Who's a Spouse for Pension Purposes?

That question can be trickier than you think—much trickier. We've homed in on the most important points that apply to most people. For simplicity, we decided there are two "standard" cases: couples who are legally married, and couples who are not legally married but live together in a conjugal relationship.

There are other scenarios. For example, there are rules for "voidable" marriages and those that are annulled. The lawyers who wrote the rules for some jurisdictions envisioned that some people might go through "a form of marriage—whatever that's supposed to mean." If you're not legally married or "living together" as widely understood, definitely consult a lawyer or your pension plan administrator.

LEGALLY MARRIED

The most clear-cut case is when you and your partner are legally married and living together. Your spouse is then considered your spouse for pension purposes. What happens if you separate, but don't divorce? Half the jurisdictions continue to treat your partner as your spouse. Here are those that don't:

- **Federal:** Your estranged spouse loses status if you have a common-law spouse
- **Alberta:** Your spouse loses status after three years of separation
- **British Columbia:** Your spouse loses status after two years of separation
- **Newfoundland:** Your spouse loses status if the two of you are not cohabiting
- **Ontario:** Your spouse loses status if the two of you are not cohabiting

What if your marriage is not working and you're going to seek an annulment? Don't ask! At least, don't ask us—ask a lawyer or your pension plan administrator. The rules vary among jurisdictions and are too complex to summarize. Good luck!

The same goes if you and your partner went through "a form of marriage" that was outside the norm.

LIVING TOGETHER

Does your conjugal partner have any rights under your pension plan? Maybe. The key determinant is how long you've been together.

Minimum Time Together for Spousal Status	
Federal	1 year
Alberta	3 years
British Columbia	2 years
Manitoba	1 year if you can legally marry—3 years if you can't
New Brunswick	3 years (including preceding year) if one member dependent on the other for support. No time limit if parents of child in relationship of some permanence
Newfoundland	1 year if you can legally marry—3 years if you can't
Nova Scotia	3 years & still together
Ontario	3 years together, or parents of a child in a relationship of some permanence
Prince Edward Island	3 years & still together
Quebec	3 years or 1 year if parents of a child
Saskatchewan	1 year & still together

Does it matter if you're a same-sex couple? The British Columbia, Ontario, Quebec and federal rules provide the same coverage for same-sex couples as for heterosexual couples. If you live elsewhere, check with a lawyer or your pension plan administrator; this is a rapidly changing legal area.

Retirement-Related Links

Here's how to contact pension regulators and securities regulators, plus some handy web sites as well as all of the other contacts mentioned in the book. That's except for the provincial departments that pay low-income supplements; they're at the end of Chapter 3.

Jurisdiction	Pension Regulator	Web Site & Telephone
	National association: Canadian Association of Pension Supervisory Authorities	www.capsa-acor.org
Federal	Office of the Superintendent of Financial Institutions	www.osfi-bsif.gc.ca 1-800-385-8647
Alberta	Alberta Finance	www.treas.gov.ab.ca/business/pensions 780-427-8322
British Columbia	Pension Standards Branch	www.labour.gov.bc.ca/psb 604-775-1266
Manitoba	Manitoba Pension Commission	www.gov.mb.ca/labour/pen 204-945-2740
New Brunswick	Superintendent of Financial Institutions	www.gnb.ca (Click to Training & Employment—Branch descriptions) 506-453-2055
Newfoundland	Insurance & Pensions Division	www.gov.nf.ca/gsl/cca/ip/about.stm 709-729-2594
Nova Scotia	Pension Regulation Division	www.gov.ns.ca/enla/pensions 902-424-8915

cont'd

Jurisdiction	Pension Regulator	Web Site & Telephone
Ontario	Financial Services Commission	www.fsco.gov.on.ca 1-800-668-0128
Prince Edward Island	No regulator: Pension Benefits Act not yet proclaimed into law	
Quebec	Régie des rentes du Quebéc	www.rrq.gouv.qc.ca 1-800-463-5185
Saskatchewan	Pension Benefits Branch	www.saskjustice.gov.sk.ca 306-787-7650

Jurisdiction	Securities Tegulator	Web Site & Telephone
	Continental association: North American Securities Administrators Association	www.nasaa.org
Alberta	Securities Commission	www.albertasecurities.com 780-427-5201
British Columbia	Securities Commission	www.bcsc.bc.ca 604-899-6500
Manitoba	Securities Commission	www.msc.gov.mb.ca 204-945-2548
New Brunswick	Justice Department	www.gov.nb.ca/justice 506-658-3060
Newfoundland	Securities Commission	www.gov.nf.ca/gsl/cca/s/default.stm 709-729-3699
Nova Scotia	Securities Commission	www.gov.ns.ca/nssc 902-424-7768
Ontario	Securities Commission	www.osc.gov.on.ca 1-877-785-1555
Prince Edward Island	Attorney General	www.gov.pe.ca 902-368-4550
Quebec	Securities Commission	www.cvmq.com 1-800-361-5072
Saskatchewan	Securities Commission	www.ssc.gov.sk.ca 306-787-7650

OTHER ORGANIZATIONS MENTIONED IN BOOK

Organization	Web Site	Telephone
Canada Pension Plan	www.hrdc-drhc.gc.ca	1-800-277-9914
Canada Customs & Revenue Agency	www.ccra-adrc.gc.ca	1-800-267-3395
Canadian Institute of Actuaries	www.actuaries.ca	613-236-8196
CompCorp (insurance consumer plan)	www.compcorp.ca	1-800-268-8099
Old Age Security	www.hrdc-drhc.gc.ca	1-800-277-9914
Quebec Pension Plan	www.rrq.gouv.gc.ca	1-800-463-5185
RRIFmetic (software)	www.fimetrics.com	1-800-663-4088
Retireweb (software)	www.retireweb.com	
Seniors Policies & Programs Database	www.sppd.gc.ca	

MORE USEFUL PENSION-RELATED WEB SITES

Organization	What They Do	Web Site
Association of Canadian Pension Management	Represents pension sponsors	www.acpm.com
Canadian Pension & Benefits Institute	Pension & benefits industry education	www.cpbi-icra.ca
Benefits Canada	Pension & benefits industry magazine	www.benefitscanada.com
Statistics Canada	Federal statistical agency	www.statcan.ca

WEB SITES ABOUT FINANCIAL PLANNING

Organization	What They Do	Web Site
Canadian Association of Insurance and Financial Advisors	Voluntary associations for financial advisors— promote education and ethics	www.caifa.com
Canadian Association of Financial Planners		www.cafp.org
Financial Planners Standards Council		www.cfp-ca.org
Investment Executive	Industry news services for financial advisors	www.investmentexecutive.com
Advisor's Edge		www.advisor.ca
Bylo Selhi	Consumer advocates who promote low-cost investing	www.bylo.org
Norman Rothery		www.stingyinvestor.com
The Boomer Inc.	Discussion forum often has lively threads on Canadian retirement funding	www.theboomer.com

The Actuarial Report:
Keeping a DB Plan Healthy

Members of a defined benefit pension plan are promised a certain sum in retirement to be paid from a pool that covers all plan members.

How do you make sure that promise can be kept? That's the job of the actuarial valuation which must be done at least every three years. It's like a periodic medical exam. The idea is to make sure the plan stays healthy enough to do its job.

Let's peek over her shoulder as actuary Mary Paul does a valuation of the ABC Pension Plan. Mary uses the "unit credit" or "projected unit credit" approach. It's the most common valuation method and the one most readily accepted by pension regulators. There are, however, other acceptable methods.

What to Look For in an Actuarial Report

- Start with the actuarial balance sheet and remember the distinction between amounts already in the fund and those that are promised as future contributions.

- Does the actuarial opinion indicate that contributions should be increased?

- Look for a summary of the data the actuary used to make her calculations. This will show the numbers of active employees, retired employees, survivors, etc., and their average ages.

- Does the actuary's summary of the plan's benefits agree with the one you got from your employer? Check the dates; the plan may have been amended since your booklet was printed.

- Look at the actuarial assumptions. Note that they're meant to be conservative and long-term.

First, Mary collects data on all current members. This includes current employees and retirees who are now on pension. In addition, there are former employees who are entitled to a pension at retirement age, as well as disabled workers. Mary also collects data on beneficiaries of former members who are due a survivor benefit. She does not concern herself at this point with employees who might become members in the future.

Mary starts with the retired employees. She must know what benefits they now get and whether those benefits will change in the future. She must also know their ages and gender. Using mortality tables based on past experience for this plan or for pension plan members in general, she forecasts how many will die each year. If the pensions are indexed she makes allowance for this in her calculations. The idea is to predict the pension amounts that will be paid out each year to this group until the last one dies. Mary also projects payments to their survivors.

Using a suitable interest rate assumption, she then discounts all of those payments back to the date of the actuarial valuation. This tells her how much has to be set aside today so the capital plus investment earnings can fund the benefits promised to current pensioners, their survivors and beneficiaries. This capital sum is called the "retired members' actuarial liability." Mary does a similar calculation for the people who are now receiving survivor/beneficiary benefits and also for disabled and terminated members who still have benefits under the plan.

Of course these calculations depend on Mary's assumptions for mortality, interest rates and inflation.

Assumption	Impact If Mary Is	
	Too High	Too Low
Inflation	Over-estimate total pensions due	Under-estimate total pensions due
Mortality	Under-estimate capital to be set aside now	Over-estimate capital to be set aside now
Interest rates		

Mary deals with these risks by using a discount rate that is slightly lower than her best estimate, an inflation rate slightly higher than her best estimate and a mortality table that expects plan members to live a little longer than her best estimate. The actuarial liability in Mary's report is therefore not her best estimate but a conservative one.

She does this to reduce the risk that a deficit will turn up in the next valuation. Deficits are bad news, because they mean higher contributions and perhaps a delay in planned improvements. If the plan does better than her conservative assumptions suggest, there will be a surplus. A surplus is good news; it can be used to decrease contributions or increase benefits.

Mary next moves to the active employees. She must predict how many will leave each year, how much benefit they will be entitled to and for how long it will be paid. That means projecting the numbers and timing of retirements, terminations, disabilities and deaths while employed. Again she uses tables of factors that are based on past experience. The ABC Pension Plan is a final average plan, so Mary must know the current earnings of the employees, their ages and the number of years of service credits they've earned so far.

Using this information, she prepares a cash flow schedule for future benefits, allowing for salary increases, and then discounts it back to the capital sum needed now to pay the benefits. If this number also includes the future credits the members are expected to earn, it represents the total cost of all future benefits for current active members. This would be a very substantial sum of money for a typical pension plan—too much for the employer and employees to fund at once. So Mary splits the liability into two portions. The first portion—called the "actuarial liability for active members"—covers service prior to the valuation. The second portion—called the "current service cost"—covers the liability for benefits earned in the year following the valuation. This approach allows the benefits to be funded as they are earned by the active members.

Funding for active members' benefits earned after the valuation date are covered by the current service contribution. Under this approach the benefits for active members are funded over their working lifetime and—if the assumptions work out—are fully funded by the time they reach retirement.

Now, the big question. Are the plan's total assets enough to cover the total liabilities? If so, the plan is "fully funded." The ABC plan's actuarial report has a table that looks like this. The actuarial liabilities total $19,000,000, compared with $20 million in assets. So there's a $1 million surplus.

Actuarial Balance Sheet—Year 1			
Actuarial Liabilities		**Assets**	
Active members	$11,000,000	Pension fund	$20,000,000
Disabled members	2,000,000		
Terminated members*	1,000,000		
Retired members	4,000,000		
Survivors & beneficiaries	1,000,000		
Surplus/(deficit)	**1,000,000**		
Total	**$20,000000**	**Total**	**$20,000000**
* with vested pensions that have not yet started payment			

The plan is thus fully funded; benefits for service prior to the valuation are taken care of. The employer (and perhaps employees) need only contribute enough during the coming year to cover the current service cost.

If Mary's assumptions prove too conservative, there will be a surplus at the next valuation. If it turns out that her assumptions were not conservative enough, there will be a deficit or "experience deficiency." Let's look at the valuation balance sheet one year later.

Actuarial Balance Sheet—Year 2			
Actuarial Liabilities		**Assets**	
Active members	$12,000,000	Pension fund	$20,000,000
Disabled members	2,050,000		
Terminated members*	1,050,000		
Retired members	4,500,000		
Survivors & beneficiaries	1,100,000		
Surplus/(deficit)	**(700,000)**		
Total	**$20,000,000**	**Total**	**$20,000,000**
* with vested pensions that have not yet started payment			

The active members have added a year of service and are one year closer to retirement or termination. So their liability has increased. Some have already moved into one of the other groups by retiring, terminating their employment, dying or becoming disabled. So the liabilities for those groups have increased a little. The plan received the current service contributions that Mary calculated—$1 million—but the market did not do well and the fund's rate of return was very poor. The fund wound up where it had been the previous year, at $20 million.

This time the assets are less than the liabilities, so we have a deficit. This shortfall must be funded by making special payments in addition to the current service contributions.

The deficit we just discussed was due to adverse experience. But there's another reason why a pension plan might have a deficit. Say ABC Inc. agrees to boost the retirement benefit. Previously the plan paid 1% of final average salary for each year of service. Now, it will pay 1.5%. Consider what this means for Rhonda, a member with 25 years of credit, five years until retirement at the 30-year mark and projected final average earnings of $60,000 a year.

	Earnings	x	Accrual Rate	x	Years of Credit	=	Pension
New formula:	$60,000	x	1.5%	x	30	=	$27,000
Old formula:	$60,000	x	1%	x	30	=	$18,000
Pension increase							$9,000

This seemingly small change—0.5%—means Rhonda's pension will be 50% higher. So the actuarial liability for her and the required current service contributions will increase by 50%. Increased current service contributions over her remaining five years will cover the rest.

This benefit change takes place at the beginning of the second year. So, going back to our second balance sheet, the liabilities increase by $6 million—$12,000,000 x 50%—with no other changes. This liability is called a "past service liability."

Actuarial Balance Sheet—Year 2 Revised			
Actuarial Liabilities		**Assets**	
Active members	$18,000,000	Pension fund	$20,000,000
Disabled members	2,050,000	Present value	
Terminated members*	1,050,000	of past service	
Retired members	4,500,000	payments	6,000,000
Survivors & beneficiaries	1,100,000	Present value of	
Surplus/(deficit)	**0**	experience deficiency	700,000
Total	**$26,700,000**	**Total**	**$26,700,000**
* with vested pensions that have not yet started payment			

First, the liability for active members has increased by $6 million because the past benefits were increased. Second, there is a new item: present value of past service payments. This is the value of the instalments required to pay off the past service liability. Why is this shown as an asset? Because the employer is required by law to make all of those payments. The third change is the asset in respect of the instalments required to make up the experience deficiency. The result is that the balance sheet shows no surplus or deficit—but the plan would be "fully funded" only if the past service improvement and experience deficiency were paid for immediately.

The general approach is that these unfunded liabilities may be paid off in instalments over up to 15 years. That's if the plan is solvent—meaning that if it had to, it could go out today and buy annuities covering the benefits now due to active members. If it can't do that, there's a "solvency deficiency" and some or all of the instalment payments must be speeded up. Depending on the jurisdiction, the period for payment may then be as short as three years.

Accrual rate   The annual rate by which an employee earns a pension. A 1% accrual rate means the employee has earned a pension equal to 1% of that year's pensionable earnings.

Actuary   A person with specialized skills in financial forecasting. The actuary forecasts the future cash flows under the pension plan and determines the contributions required to match those cash flows.

Administrator   Person or body designated as being ultimately responsible for the management of a pension plan in accordance with the *Income Tax Act* and the pension standards legislation.

Annuity   An insurance contract under which payments are made at monthly intervals, usually throughout the lifetime of the beneficiary.

Beneficiary   The person who will receive the survivor benefits when a pension plan member dies. Under pension standards legislation, this is automatically his or her spouse unless that spouse signs a waiver.

Bridge   A pension payable for a limited period of time, usually from early retirement date to normal retirement date.

CCRA   Canada Customs and Revenue Agency, formerly known as Revenue Canada.

Commuted value   The lump sum payment that has the same value as the future payments under a pension.

C/QPP   Canada or Quebec Pension Plan.

Deferred pension   Pension that starts at a later date, usually to a terminating plan member who has not yet reached retirement age.

Defined benefit plan   Plan under which the pension is determined by a formula, usually based on earnings and years of participation.

Defined contribution plan   Plan under which pension depends on the amount of contributions accumulated with investment income.

Fiduciary   A person authorized to exercise rights and powers for the benefit of another person or other persons. A fiduciary cannot benefit personally from the exercise of this responsibility.

Guaranteed annuity   Annuity under which payments are guaranteed to continue for a minimum number of months.

GIC   Guaranteed Investment Certificate, a deposit for which a financial institution normally sets an interest rate for one to five years.

G-RRSP   Group Registered Retirement Savings Plan.

Indexing   Increases to monthly pension amounts based on the annual increase in the cost of living, usually based on the Consumer Price Index maintained by Statistics Canada.

Integration   The method by which a defined benefit pension is adjusted to factor in benefits from the Canada/Quebec Pension Plan.

Joint and survivor annuity   Annuity under which monthly payments are made while both partners are alive and continue, perhaps at a reduced level, after the first death until the second dies.

LIF   Life Income Fund.

LIRA   Locked-in Retirement Account.

LRIF   Locked-in Retirement Income Fund.

LI-RRSP   Locked-in Registered Retirement Savings Plan.

Locking-in   Rules that restrict access to money transferred from a pension plan to a personal account in order to ensure the funds provide lifetime income.

OAS   Old Age Security, the basic government retirement plan.

PA   Pension adjustment. The deemed value of pension credits earned in the prior year. Reduces personal RRSP deduction room.

PAR   Pension adjustment reversal. Granted when a person leaves a pension plan before retirement. Increases RRSP room by the difference between the total PAs reported and the pension transfer value.

PSPA   Past service pension adjustment. Reduces RRSP room to keep retroactive pension improvement within the overall tax shelter limit.

Pay as you go (PAYGO)   Promised benefits are not pre-funded, but rather paid from current revenue.

RPP   Registered Pension Plan.

RRIF   Registered Retirement Income Fund.

RRSP   Registered Retirement Savings Plan.

Reciprocal agreement   Agreement between two or more pension plans setting out the rules for transferring money and/or credits between the plans for individual members.

Retiring allowance   Defined under the *Income Tax Act* as a payment made either on or after retirement in recognition of long service, or in respect of loss of office or employment. To certain limits it may be transferred tax-free to an RRSP.

Spouse   A conjugal partner who meets the jurisdiction's requirements for legal marriage, heterosexual common-law relationship or homosexual common-law relationship.

Vesting   The point at which an employee becomes entitled to a pension provided by employer contributions.

Wind-up   The process by which a defined benefit pension plan is shut down.

YMPE   Year's Maximum Pensionable Earnings. A measure of the average national wage as determined by Statistics Canada and reported each fall by the Canada Customs and Revenue Agency. The YMPE forms the base for C/QPP benefits and most pension plans.

Accumulation factors, 105
Actuarial reduction, 3, 115, 132
Actuarial report, 111
Adverse amendment, 178
Alberta Seniors Benefit, 28
Annual information return, 111
Annual pension statement, 112–117
Annuity, 65, 153
Approved downsizing, 141
Audit, pension fund, 128

Beneficiary designation, 113
Best v Best, 172
Bismarck, Otto von, 19
Black, Conrad, 61
Bridge benefit, 140–141
British Columbia Seniors Supplement, 28

Canada/Quebec Pension Plan, *see also* CPP
    and QPP, 12, 22, 24, 31–46
        assignments, 39
        basic exemption, 40
        benefits, 31, 32
        break-even age, 36
        calculation of benefits, 34–35
        child-rearing dropouts, 35
        common-law couples, 38
        contributions, 2, 40
        contributory period, 34
        cost of benefits, 40
        covered earnings, 40
        credit splitting, 38
        credit-splitting for same sex couples, 39
        death benefits, 32
        disability benefits, 32, 33
        disability definition, 33
        disability dropouts, 35

        dropouts, 35
        early retirement, 35, 36
        employee/employer contribution rate,
            40
        employer contributions, deductible, 40
        federal/provincial agreement, 44
        expectation, 37
        future of, 39
        general dropouts, 35
        income, 11
        income tax credit on contributions, 40
        indexation, 31
        late retirement, 36
        marriage breakdown, 38
        maximum benefit, 31
        PAYGO funding, 42–43
        pension sharing, 39
        pension splitting, 38
        pensionable earnings, 34
        pessimism, price of, 45, 46
        retirement benefit, 32
        remarriage, 34
        retirement pension, 33, 36
        savings to replace C/QPP
            and OAS, 45–46
        substantially gainful employment, 33
        survivor benefits, 32, 33
        wage indexing, 42
Caisse de depot et placement du Quebec 41
Canada Customs and Revenue Agency
    (CCRA), 11, 21, 60, 77, 80, 110, 137
        Netfile, 81
        Telefile, 81
        website, 33
Canada Pension Plan (CPP), 12, 13, 16, 17,
    31–46
        17th actuarial report, 43

annual statement, 33

benefits for common-law couples, 33

chief actuary, 41

contributions, 4, 41

contributory period for disability
payments, 33

contributory period for survivor
payments, 33

credits from former partners, 34

disability benefit, 172

drop-out provisions, 35

indexation, 31

internal rate of return, 44

maximum pension, 31

retirement benefit, 34

return on contributions, 43

social security agreements, 34

Canadian Economic Statistics, Report on, 93

Canadian Institute of Actuaries (CIA), 48, 93

Capital gains, 22, 83

CCRA, see Canada Customs and Revenue
Agency

Chretien, Jean, 77

and Seniors' Benefit, 23

Clawback, see Old Age Security

Common-law couples—
statutory declaration, 26

CompCorp, 87, 136, 137, 153–154

Consumer Price Index (CPI), 21, 93

Continuous employment, 119

Conversions, plan, 133–134

CPP, see Canada Pension Plan

Creditor-proofing, 64, 148

Custodian, 126

Deferred annuity, 89, 137

Deferred Profit Sharing Plans (DPSP), 12, 14,
16, 51, 60, 69–70

withdrawals, 11

Defined Benefit (DB) plan, 6, 48, 51, 122–3,
137–142

accrual rate, 140

career average earnings, 62, 138

contributory, 61

final average earnings, 62, 138

flat benefit, 62, 138

flexible plan, 64

integration, 61, 139–140

maximum funding, 57

maximum pension accrual, 48, 55

multi-employer plan, 63

transfers limited, 156

Defined benefit pension, 50

Defined Contribution (DC) plan, 6, 48, 51,
65, 121

Defined contribution pension, 60

Deraps v Labourers' Pension Fund, 167

Discount factors, 104

Dodge, David, 54

Dominion Stores, 61

Downsizing programs, 141

DPSP, see Deferred Profit Sharing Plans

Early retirement, 131

penalty, 131

30 and out, 133

age, 155

Employer-sponsored plans, 3, 7, 8, 12, 51

Employment insurance (EI), 4, 11, 40

Factor of 9, 51–52

Federal-provincial regulation, 52, 142

Flexible pension plan, see Registered Pension
Plan

Fiduciary, 125

Final average plan, see Registered Pension
Plan

Finance Department, 48, 57, 110

Financial statements, Pension Plan, 111

Flat benefit plan, see Registered Pension Plan

Funded ratio, 116

Funding factors, 8, 102

Generation Xers and CPP, 31

Gross Replacement Ratio, 92

Group RRSP, see RRSP—group

Grow-in, 174–175
Growth Factors, 103
G-RRSP, *see* RRSP, group
GST, *see* Goods and Sales Tax
Guaranteed Income Certificate (GIC), 89
Guaranteed Income Supplement (GIS), 13,
    14, 16, 17, 23–25, 27

Harris, Walter, 77
Hellyer, Paul and mandatory RRSPs, 41
House of Commons, Canada,
    and state pensions, 19
    finance committee, 54
Human Resource Development Canada
    (HRDC), 17, 20, 22, 172
        website, 18, 26, 33
        OAS application forms, 25
        Income Security Program, 17, 18, 177
Hybrid plans, 60, 142

Income replacement ratio, 3, 4–6
Income Security Program, *see* HRDC
Income Tax Act, 110, 132, 155, 156
Individual Pension Plan (IPP), 147–149
Inflation factors, 8, 29, 103
Internet
    calculators, 6
    worksheets, 1
Investment manager, 126
Investment return, average annual, 8, 29, 46
Investor Economics Inc, 15

Joint and survivor pensions, 167

Lalonde, Marc, 50
Lennon, John, 4
Liberals
    1963 election campaign, 40
    and CPP, 40
    and OAS, 19
Life annuity—purchase, 135
Life expectancy, 1, 3, 6–7
Life Income Fund (LIF), 154, 159–164

Locked-in Retirement Account (LIRA), 72,
    154, 159–164, 174
Locked-in Retirement Income Fund (LRIF),
    154, 159–164
Locking-in, 152
Low-income allowances, 27
Low-income government benefits, 12, 33
        qualifying, 26
Low-income supplements (and see OAS), 11,
    13, 24, 26
L-plans, 151, 159–164
Lump sum value, 29

Management expense ratio (MER), 77
Mandatory pension contributions, 6
Manitoba—55 Plus, 28
Manufacturer's Sales Tax, 19
Manulife Financial, 85
Martin, Paul, 21, 54
        and Seniors Benefit, 23
Members of Parliament
    and retirement savings legislation, 54
Money purchase, *see* Defined Contribution
Monsanto, 130
Monte Carlo simulation, 84
Mortgages, 5
    reverse, 15, 22
Mulroney, Brian
        and OAS benefits, 22, 23
        and CPP benefits, 32
        and OAS clawback, 44
Multi-employer plans, 63, 173
Mutual funds, 6, 71, 84

Netfile, *see* Canada Customs and Revenue
    Agency
Newfoundland Seniors Benefit, 28
Normal retirement, 113, 131
Nunavut Senior Supplement, 28
NWT Seniors Supplementary Benefit, 28

Old Age Pension Tax, 19, 44
Old Age Pensions Act, 19

Old Age Security (OAS), 12, 13, 16, 17–30, 33
  application form, 25
  application kit, 26
  background, 19
  clawback, 12, 13, 22, 36
  clawback defined, 21
  clawback indexed for inflation, 23
  common-law partners, 24
  eligibility for full pension, 18, 20
  expectation, 23, 27
  income, 11
  income questionnaire, 26
  income-based benefit reduction, 26
  income test, 26
  indexation, 18
  low-income supplements, 23–28
  maximum benefits, 18
  non-residents, 22
  overview, 8
  pessimism, price of, 29
Ontario Guaranteed Annual Income System (GAINS), 28
Ontario Law Reform Commission, 171

PA, *see* Pension Adjustment,
PAR, *see* Pension Adjustment Reversal
Partial plan wind-up, 130
Past Service Pension Adjustment (PSPA), 54–55
Past service pension credits
Pay as you go (PAYGO), 40, 41, 44
Pearson, Lester B
  and contributory public pensions, 40, 41
Pension
  contributions, 3, 4
  income, 11
Pension Adjustment (PA), 50–51, 64
  calculations, 50, 79
  formula, 50
  offset, 50
Pension Adjustment Reversal (PAR), 53–54
Pension Benefits Standards Act (PBSA), 109

Pension booklet, 110
Pension Plan, *see also* Registered Pension Plan (RPP)
Pension, securities and insurance regulators, 65
Pensionable earnings, 49, 62
Phased retirement, 131, 133
Plan administrator, 66, 126
Postponed retirement, 131
Pregnancy and parental leave, 141
Pre-retirement income, 4, 5
Provincial low-income supplements, 16, 28
Provincial pension regulators, 110
PSPA, *see* Past Service Pension Adjustment

Quebec Pension Plan (QPP) *see also* CPP and C/QPP, 12, 16, 17, 31–46
  partition, 38
  phased retirement, 37
  website, 33

Reciprocal agreement, 139
Registered Pension Plan (RPP), 1, 16, 48
  1976 maximum limit, 56
  accrual rate, 49
  amendment, 111, 173–176
  beneficiary designation, 113
  career average earnings, 60
  combination plan, 73–74, 60, 142
  covered population, 14
  defined benefit, 60
  defined contribution, 60
  final average earnings, 60
  flat benefit, 60
  flexible plan, 60
  full-time employment, 119
  hybrid plan, 73–74
  part-time employment, 119
  plan text, 111
  registration number, 112, 113
Registered Retirement Income Fund (RRIF), 15, 36, 154
  and indexation, 17

withdrawals, 11

Registered Retirement Savings Plan (RRSP),
   3, 12, 15, 16, 17, 36, 60
   $2,000 over-contribution, 80
   and indexation, 17
   asset-splitting, 82
   contributions, 4
   contribution limit, 3, 49, 50, 51
   contribution room, 68
   group, 12, 14, 16, 51, 66–67
   group, key questions, 66
   Home Buyers' Plan, 82
   mandatory, 41, 43
   mandatory contributions, 41
   season, 47
   spousal contribution holding period, 83
   spousal contributions, 22, 82
   tax-sheltered, 5, 48
   unused contribution room, 55
   withdrawals, 11, 55
Replacement ratio, 4, 5
   target, 5, 8, 115
Report on Pensions as Family Property, 171
Retirement Compensation Arrangement
   (RCA), 145
   tax, 146
Retirement income
   determining, 8
   sources, 16
   target, 7
Retirement income, target, 13
Retirement savings system, Canada, 1, 47, 50
Reverse mortgage, *see* mortgages
Royalty trust, 22
RPP, *see* Registered Pension Plans
RRIF, *see* Registered Retirement Income Fund
RRIFmetic, 92

Saint John Shipbuilding Ltd., 66
Saskatchewan Income Plan, 28
Savings factors, 29
Secular trust, 147

Seniors' Benefit, 23
Seniors' Policies and Programs Database, 28
Severance, 83
Shortened life expectancy, 161–162
SIP and G, *see* Statement of Investment Poli-
   cies and Goals
SIP and P, *see* Statement of Investment Poli-
   cies and Procedures
Social security agreements, 20, 177
Solvency ratio, 116
Special solvency payments, 116
Spouse's Allowance (SPA), 24–26
St. Laurent, Louis, 14, 19, 77
Statement of Investment Policies and Goals
   (SIP and G), 111, 127
Statement of Investment Policies and Proce-
   dures (SIP and P), 111, 127
Statistics Canada (StatsCan), 5, 7, 15, 119
Supplementary Employee Retirement Plan
   (SERP), 16, 56, 143–147
Supreme Court of Canada, 130, 172
Surplus ownership, 65, 128–129
Survivors' Allowance, 24–26

Target replacement ratio, *see* Replacement
   ratio
Target retirement income, *see* Retirement
   income
Tax-assisted retirement savings, integration
   of, 49
Telefile, *see* Canada Customs and Revenue
   Agency
Trustee, 126

Uniform Law Conference of Canada, 64
Unused RRSP room, *see* RRSP

Vesting, 113, 152

Wilson, Michael, 21, 54
Winding-up, 174
Woodward v Stelco, 146

Year's Maximum Pensionable Earnings
    (YMPE), 119
        definition, 34
Yukon Income Supplement, 28